Sati

Sakuntala Narasimhan

SATI

A Study of Widow Burning in India

VIKING

VIKING

Penguin Books (India) Limited, 72–B Himalaya House, 23 Kasturba Gandhi Marg, New Delhi 110 001, India
Penguin Books Ltd., Harmondsworth, Middlesex, England
Penguin Books USA Inc., 375 Hudson Street, New York, New York 10014, U.S.A.
Penguin Books Australia Ltd., Ringwood, Victoria, Australia
Penguin Books Canada Ltd., 2801 John Street, Markham, Ontario, Canada L3R 1 B4
Penguin Books (N.Z.) Ltd., 182–190 Wairau Road, Auckland 10, New Zealand

First published in Viking by Penguin Books India Ltd. 1990
Copyright © Sakuntala Narasimhan 1990

Typeset in Times Roman by Tulika Print Communications Services, New Delhi
Made and printed in India by Ananda Offset Private Ltd., Calcutta

To

Shobhana and Mohan

A Note by the Author

The word sati (now in common parlance) refers to the burning of a widow on the funeral pyre of her husband in a rite that is seen as a manifestation of extreme loyalty and virtue. However, in the original Sanskrit meaning, the word 'sati' means a virtuous or a chaste woman. Over the last three centuries the phrase 'committing sati' has been commonly used to describe a widow's immolation. A woman who perishes thus is said to have 'become a sati'. The next step is usually the deification of the widow who has died.

In order to distinguish between the rite of immolation and the woman who immolates herself, English chronicles often used 'Suttee' for the former and 'sati' for the latter (the former spelling is rarely used today). This book uses the contemporary spelling of sati, with references to the woman or the rite becoming apparent in context.

Contents

Contents

Acknowledgements

During the months that I spent gathering material for this book, a number of scholars, journalists, officials and women known and unknown readily responded to my queries and extended help in various ways. In particular, I would like to mention and thank Tarkateertha Laxmanshastri Joshi, N.T. Srinivasa Iyengar of Bangalore, Rev. John Correia Afonso, Mohan Mukerji IAS (retd.), my former colleague at the *Times* group R. Gopalakrishna (RGK), Vithal C. Nadkarni and Saleem Peeradina. The hints and pointers that they provided enabled me to tap rich veins of material on the subject.

Veteran journalist M.V. Kamath gave unstintingly of his time and advice while I was working on the book; he has truly been 'friend, philosopher and guide'. A special word of thanks is due to Rajam Thirumalai for all the help that she has extended over the years.

The staff of the Asiatic Library in Bombay patiently unearthed dusty *tomes* a century-and-a-half (or more) old for my reference. G.S. Koppikar of the railways and Vijayalakshmi Koppikar of the tourist department assisted me with my travel itinerary for gathering the material. Sunita Bapna and Sudha extended gracious hospitality in Jaipur and Sara Mitter's help was invaluable in securing the cover transparency from the *Bibliotheque Nationale*, Paris. I thank them all.

I am especially thankful to the *Deccan Herald*, and in particular to its editor-in-chief, K.N. Hari Kumar, for their support. The report I filed for this newspaper after the Roop Kanwar sati incident of 1987 became the starting point for this book.

I am grateful to David Davidar of Penguin Books India for suggesting that I do this book and for encouraging me during the year that it took me to deliver the manuscript. The assistance I received from K.P. Menon of the UNI and the *India magazine* in locating some of the photographs for this book is gratefully acknowledged. I extend my thanks to Gopal Sunger, who lent me some excellent pictures on the Deorala sati incident of '87.

One final note: The spellings of Indian place names, particularly in the early days of the Raj, were extremely idiosyncratic and wildly inconsistent. I have, however, retained some of these spellings where I've reproduced direct quotes or extracts. In all other cases, I've standardized the spellings of proper nouns.

Bombay, 1990   *Sakuntala Narasimhan*

1

Introduction

Along the western boundary of India, bordering Pakistan, lies the state of Rajasthan, largely arid and partly desert but colourful nevertheless with its fabulous palaces and forts built by the Rajput rulers in the years before the native princely states became part of independent India. The state capital, Jaipur, is a major tourist attraction and is known as the Pink City because of the extensive use of pink stone in its architecture.

A ninety minute drive into the Sikar district north of Jaipur brings one to Deorala. This is the village where eighteen-year-old Roop Kanwar burned to death on the pyre of her husband Maal Singh, on 4 September 1987. As villages go, Deorala seems prosperous, almost a small town, with pucca brick and cement houses, tractors, a large high school, medical stores and a dispensary. The fields all round look lush green after the monsoon rains in August, and none of the customary manifestations of destitution or distress that one would expect in a village are in evidence. Peacocks trailing magnificent plumes run hither and thither; their occasional raucous cries break into the quiet that pervades the place.

The villagers readily point the way to what they call the 'temple' and suddenly, in a clearing in the middle of the village, one comes upon the *sati sthal* (the site of sati) where the pyre was lit for Maal Singh and his wife Roop Kanwar.

In the centre is a brick platform fenced off all round with bamboo. The saffron canopy raised for the thirteenth day *chunari* (glorification) ceremony on 16 September 1987 hangs in weatherbeaten shreds; underneath, in the middle of the cordoned off area, stands the puppet-like shape of a faded, red cloth wrapped round a *trishul* (the trident venerated as a symbol of Shiva). Some thirty or forty men and women are gathered at the site, and as the hour of noon approaches, preparations begin for the daily puja while half-a-dozen policemen sit idly to one side, watching the proceedings.

The *sthal* draws, on an average, over one hundred visitors per day and five times as many on special days like *ekadashi* (the eleventh day of the lunar cycle, considered important for religious observances).

Rajasthani women in traditional, colourful attire stand around in awed silence or prostrate themselves before the platform, seeking the benediction of the *sati mata* (Mother Sati), the girl who is believed to have become deified through her fiery immolation on the pyre of her husband.

On one side of the clearing stand two small structures commemorating satis. Inside each are two pairs of footprints in marble, with a bunch of incense sticks placed before them. The larger of the two edifices has in addition the imprint of a palm on the wall outside, the customary imprint that a woman leaves after staining her palm with bridal-red dye or henna just before mounting the pyre. Inside the room that is referred to as the temple, there is a portrait of Roop Kanwar sitting amidst flames with her husband's head on her lap; an inscription underneath records for posterity the time, date and other details of the immolation.

Roop Kanwar and her twenty-four-year-old husband had been married for less than eight months when he died on the morning of 4 September 1987 reportedly of gastroenteritis. Dressed in bridal finery, she walked at the head of the funeral procession to the centre of the village where, in the presence of a crowd that is said to have been 4,000 strong, she ascended the pyre and was reduced to ashes along with the body of her husband.

According to a report compiled by the fact-finding team that was sent to Deorala by the Women and Media group of Bombay, the police arrived in the village in the afternoon after having been alerted to the immolation by a message from a revenue official who saw the burning pyre. The First Information Report (FIR) filed by the head constable recorded that there were some 200 onlookers at the cremation at that time. However, no arrests were made although sati had been illegal since 1829 when Lord Bentinck, the then governor-general of British India, passed a law to abolish the custom. Ironically, Jaipur was the first among the Rajput states in this region to prohibit sati in 1846. As news of the event spread, a group of women activists tried to meet the chief minister of the state to demand action against those involved in the event, but the state government took the stand that the matter was a purely religious one and it was not their place to interfere. After the press broke the story about the incident, Roop Kanwar's brother-in-law, fifteen-year-old Pushpendra Singh who had lighted the pyre, was arrested on 9 September. By then, Roop Kanwar had, in the eyes of the people of the region, already become exalted and deified as the *sati mata*.

Visitors in their thousands began to pour into the village to seek the "blessings" of the girl who had become a devi. Reasoning that only a woman endowed with divine strength would have chosen an end through fire, they converged on the *chabutra* (funeral platform) with offerings of coconut and incense. "She has blessed the family for seven generations before and after", said members of her family. "We believe that this was an act of God", insisted a paternal uncle of the deceased Maal Singh, adding that his son (Maal Singh's cousin) who was studying medicine, also believed that there was "something spiritual about what happened" "She has brought honour to the family", her parents and brother added.

The chief minister issued a condemnation of the incident nine days later. When a group of women activists sought his intervention in stopping plans that were afoot for glorifying the event through a *chunari* ceremony on the thirteenth day, and did not receive a response, they filed a writ petition in the high court seeking a ban on the ceremony. Following this, an order was issued by the court on 14 September directing the state government to prevent the glorification function. The same day a few hundred women representing eleven different organizations led a protest march to the secretariat in the state capital.

Despite a court order forbidding people from assembling for the event, and despite the fact that the state government had stopped all public transport buses going to Deorala, around 2,50,000 to 3,00,000 persons "stretching to a three kilometer-long stream of people" (according to one eye-witness) turned up at the *sati sthal*, travelling on foot or by camel cart or whatever transport was available. Private buses were, according to one description, overloaded with thirty to forty people sitting on top or hanging on to the sides; taxi rates were doubled for the day; even so every vehicle had an extra load of passengers perched on its roof. Over 800 wayside shops sprang up and did brisk business in souvenirs, snacks, toys, coconuts and incense, along with a photo collage showing a smiling Roop Kanwar with her dead husband's head on her lap while flames enveloped the couple. These were priced at anything up to twenty rupees and some 30,000 copies are reported to have been sold.

The *chunari* ceremony itself was advanced by two hours in order to pre-empt any attempt by the police to stop the event. The flames of the funeral pyre that had been kept alive for the occasion were ritualistically extinguished with milk and Ganga water. A festive *chunari* (a piece of cloth worn as a veil by women) embroidered in gold and reportedly costing over 4,000 rupees was set aflame after Roop Kanwar's brothers had taken the cloth round in a procession and draped it over a *trishul* to resemble the form of a woman.

With cries of *Sati mata ki jai* (Victory to the Sati goddess) and other slogans filling the air, the religious fervour was "palpable, as all-pervasive as the sand in the air", as one eye-witness account records it. Among those present at the ritual were politicians and VIPs, including the state Janata Party president, the state chief of the Yuva Janata (the youth wing of the party) and at least four members of the legislative assembly.

Two weeks after the sati incident, on the eve of the visit to the state by a union minister, the state government finally swung into action and transferred the district magistrate and the superintendent of police. It also arrested Roop Kanwar's father-in-law, the priest who had officiated at the ceremony, and two others, but subsequently they were all let out on bail. The family itself had acquired not ignominy but instant celebrity status. The father-in-law was seen "blessing" visitors who came for the *chunari* ceremony, and the natal family hosted a feast for 1,001 Brahmins to commemorate the daughter's deification as *sati mata*.

On 18 September 1987, the *Jansatta*, one of the *Indian Express* group of papers with a large circulation, carried an editorial comment that said, "One in a million widows resolves to become a sati, and it is only natural that her self-sacrifice should become the centre of people's devotion and worship. Therefore this cannot be called a question of the civil rights of women or discrimination between the sexes. . . ."

This editorial created a furore, with angry groups of women demonstrators picketing the office of the paper, and added to the gathering division of opinion on the issue.

On 1 October 1987, the government promulgated the Rajasthan Sati (Prevention) Ordinance which made the glorification of sati through the observance of public rituals, processions and the creation of commemorative trusts or funds, a criminal offence. Under this ordinance, any action aiding or abetting the practice of sati became punishable with the death-sentence.

One of the religious heads of the Hindu community, Swami Niranjan Dev Teerth (also known as the Shankaracharya of Puri) called the ordinance "a great insult to democracy", insisting that widow immolation was enjoined by the scriptures and that the government had no right to forbid a religious practice that he claimed was part of the Hindu dharma (others objected on legal and constitutional grounds). Article 25 of the Indian constitution guarantees freedom of religion. Legal enactments forbidding a practice that was claimed to be part of Hindu religious observances amounted to an infringement of democratic rights, these petitioners held and they went to court challenging the constitutional validity of the ordinance (one of these petitions was from a former officer of the Indian Administrative Service—IAS).

On the other side, among those protesting the atrocity of burning a woman alive, was Swami Agnivesh, a human rights activist-monk of the Arya Samaj reformist sect, who insisted that sati had no scriptural sanction, and that prohibiting the glorification of the custom did not in any way amount to an infringement of one's right to religion, freedom of expression, assembly or worship, as the pro-sati faction claimed.

The Sati Dharma Raksha Samiti, an organization of orthodox Rajputs set up to oppose the ban on sati and to "uphold and protect" Hindu traditions (which in its opinion included the practice of widow immolation) had to drop the word Sati from its name following the ordinance, but that did not prevent it from organizing a show of strength that took even the organizers by surprise. At a six-hour rally in Jaipur in mid–October (1987), some 70,000 Rajasthanis were reported to have turned up, carrying saffron banners and chanting *"Dharam ki raksha kaun karega, hum karenge, hum karenge"* (Who will safeguard our religion? We will, we will) and *"Jab tak chand suraj rahega, tab tak* Roop Kanwar *ka naam rahega"* (As long as the moon and sun survive, Roop Kanwar's name will remain alive too). At the end of the rally, the participants took a mass pledge to convene even bigger rallies and "to leave their houses in darkness on Divali" unless the government released the detenus and revoked the ordinance.

Even among those who saw the burning of a woman alive as abhorrent and condemned it, there were some who betrayed a susceptibility to the mystification that had come to be associated with the rite, when they described sati as signifying a display of "tremendous courage by women who cared more for their cherished ideal of wifely devotion than for their lives"; for this reason, they claimed, the women became worthy of admiration and veneration.

The Vishwa Hindu Parishad, a Hindu revivalist organization, said it was opposed to sati and its encouragement in any form; however, its president declared "sati under spiritual influence could not be prevented by society".

Amidst all the action for and against sati, however, puja was performed twice a day at the *sati sthal* in the village. This, despite the fact that Section 144 of the Criminal Procedure Code (prohibiting an assemblage of more than four persons) promulgated in September 1987 was still in force with the Rajasthan Armed Constabulary maintaining a round-the-clock vigil.

Swami Agnivesh who was leading the anti-sati movement, challenged the Shankaracharya of Puri, who had been vociferously defending sati, to a *shastrarth* (public debate) on the subject, but on his way to the meeting with the Shankaracharya, Agnivesh and his supporters were arrested on grounds of threatening the peace, and the debate could not take place.

In the months that followed the Deorala sati incident, the media thrashed the issue threadbare; at seminars, symposia, public meetings and scholars' get-togethers, the issues were further discussed and dissected to analyze the implications of the reactions that Roop Kanwar's death had effected. In the process, a number of questions were raised:

- Do the Hindu scriptures sanction, condone or enjoin the custom of widow burning? In other words, is there religious approval for sati?
- Or is the practice part of the larger issue of women's oppression, where a socio-economic nexus emphasizes the worthlessness and expendability of women's lives?
- And why did this particular case generate protests, debates and discussions on such a scale, when other recent cases similar to Roop Kanwar's did not, even when they got reported in the papers as small news items?

A year before the infamous Roop Kanwar incident took place, a twenty-five-year-old woman had burned on the pyre of her husband at Umaria village in the state of Madhya Pradesh in central India. In 1984, just twenty kilometres away, another sati incident had taken place. In Kusuma village of Banda district, a woman named Dasiya was reported to have burned to death with her deceased husband in 1983 and a *chabutra* (memorial structure) was raised to mark the spot and the event. In Pagnara village that same year, a woman named Gayatri immolated herself when the village elders reportedly refused to allow the cremation of her husband unless she agreed to become a sati. The police, along with thousands of onlookers, watched while she burned to death; photographic evidence of this event is said to exist but although the sub-divisional magistrate and the station officer were transferred, the case was apparently hushed up by the local political leaders who were "friendly with the woman's in-laws".

The Illustrated Weekly of India which has a nationwide readership, published a graphic photo-essay in 1980 on a sati immolation that had taken place some months earlier. In 1979, a woman named Javitri burned to death on her husband's pyre in Jari village; within a year, a two-storeyed temple with a marble samadhi was raised and a transport company owner confessed a few months later that he had made at least a million rupees by bringing visitors to the cremation spot. When twenty-four-year-old Gayatri became a sati in the Bundelkhand region in

1983, criminal charges were registered by the police, but her in-laws and the villagers who glorified the event are today richer by more than five lakh rupees. According to the Women and Media Committee of Bombay, there has been on an average one sati incident every year in Sikar district alone.

And yet, none of these other sati incidents caused sentiments of horror, anger and disgust, or invited media attention and controversy, on the same scale as the Deorala incident of Roop Kanwar. Was there, then, perhaps something in its timing and the socio-political mood prevalent at the time of the incident, that resulted in the spotlights being focussed on the immolation in a manner different from the media attention that the other immolations got?

Was it, perhaps, one more manifestation of the rising trend of fundamentalism in several areas in the recent times?

Not far from Deorala, in the same Shekhawati region of the state of Rajasthan, is the town of Jhunjhunu where an imposing sati temple has been built for Dadi Narayani Devi who is said to have jumped into the pyre of her husband Tandhan Das. She was a seventeen-year-old girl of the Bania caste. The legend is that the nawab coveted the white mare that her betrothed rode on, and in the confrontation that ensued Tandhan Das was killed, leaving his faithful servant as the only survivor apart from Dadi Narayani Devi and the mare. When the servant asked her whether he should take her back to her father's or to her father-in-law's, she is said to have replied that she would become a sati and that wherever the horse stopped while carrying the ashes of the couple, a temple to their memory should be raised.

This incident is nearly 700 years old but the temple erected to her memory is very recent. This temple is reported to have assets estimated at seventy-seven lakh rupees and an annual income of around twenty lakh rupees. The day of its yearly fair used to be a state holiday, with some four lakh people turning up to worship at the shrine; even the government would put up stalls at this annual event. The temple complex, spread over thirty acres, boasts no less than 350 rooms for the use of visitors. The state governor who signed the ordinance banning the glorification of sati on 1 October 1987 following the Roop Kanwar immolation, was himself the chief guest at this fair the year before.

In 1988 the fair which was to have taken place on 10 September did not take place because of the prohibitory statute; the trustees of the temple, however, obtained a supreme court order permitting worship inside the temple complex while banning the fair outside the precincts. An estimated 10,000 devotees turned up that year, so in effect, sati was glorified in spite of the absence of the customary fair. The trustees of the temple had even contemplated changing the name of the temple from Rani Sati to Rani Shakti temple, if the supreme court forbade worship under the prevention of glorification act.

Emboldened by the continuation of worship as usual at the Jhunjhunu temple, the Dharma Raksha Samiti organized a week-long religious discourse of the *Gita* to coincide with the first anniversary of Roop Kanwar's immolation. Unsure of how the police would react to the anniversary observances, the group bought time by deciding to observe 22 September (and not 4 September) as the anniversary (also as the custom is to observe such anniversaries according to the Indian calendar, the 22nd *was* the date of the anniversary by the lunar calendar).

The religious discourse at Deorala was unobjectionable, but during the proceedings Roop Kanwar's portrait was displayed and slogans glorifying her were raised, notwithstanding the presence of the collector and the superintendent of police. The procession taken out on the occasion was reported to be 4,000 strong, with women making up half that number.

In the face of such defiance, the authorities decided on tactics of retreat; police pickets which had been strengthened a fortnight earlier in anticipation of the anniversary observances were relaxed the night before the procession. On the other hand, a Reuters photographer at the site had his camera seized; the reason given was that Section 144 was in force. The priest who gave the discourse called Deorala "sacred ground", clearly implying, without mentioning her name, that Roop Kanwar's immolation had sanctified the village. Although this amounted to glorifying sati in spirit, no arrests were made.

All these incidents went to show that in spite of the law, the police contingent, and the nationwide furore over sati, the pro-sati groups were succeeding in their attempts to whip up communal and reactionary sentiments in favour of widow burning. And that raises a few questions:

- Why were people so intent on going to such devious lengths to circumvent the law and scuttle the government's moves to prohibit the glorification of sati?
- Why hasn't the money (estimated as seventy-five lakh rupees) collected to commemorate Roop Kanwar's sati been confiscated years after the event, although the law clearly provides for such confiscation?
- Why is it that a former union law minister agreed to plead the case of the Rani Sati temple at Jhunjhunu in the supreme court for the continuation of the annual fair?
- And more specifically, with reference to the Roop Kanwar incident: why didn't the family—her father-in-law who is a

graduate twice over and a schoolteacher, and her brothers-in-law who were all exposed to the modern Indian milieu—dissuade her from immolation even if she, in a state of distress at her bereavement, took such a decision?

- Again, did she walk to the cremation ground after a "voluntary" decision to burn herself, as the family (and even the Shankaracharya of Puri) claimed?

- How can people claim, as they have done, that the girl's gesture of flailing her arms when the flames caught, was one of benediction to the gathering witnessing her immolation, rather than a gesture of agony?

- Why was it that the Shankaracharya of Puri who made provocative pronouncements accusing the government of being "anti-Hindu" in condemning widow immolation, was not arrested, while Swami Agnivesh was arrested reportedly for "threatening the peace" when he set out for the public debate with the Shankaracharya on the scriptural stand on sati?

- Agnivesh and the Shankaracharya represent in essence two polarized responses that typify the larger confrontation between regressive-fundamentalist trends on the one hand, and rational-progressive forces on the other. How effective are legal enactments in a confrontation like this? Has the ordinance passed in the aftermath of the Deorala incident made for any changes in the attitudes of the people towards widow burning? And in general, how much do laws added to the statute books, particularly those pertaining to women's issues, contribute to day-to-day changes in lifestyles?

- There are some who believe that the media blew the Deorala episode out of all proportion. Police officials, politicians and some religious leaders are among those who subscribe to this theory. There are others who feel that widow burning deserves to be ignored as 'inconsequential' because the number of immolations is minuscule compared to the size of the population. Yet others, particularly womens' groups, see it as one more "frightening indicator of a deep-seated social malaise". How much validity is there in these theories?

- And what is it about the burning alive of a widow on the pyre of her deceased husband that adds layers of mystique to an event that ought to be seen for the gruesome rite it is, perpetrated and praised in the name of religion?

- Do the pro- and anti-sati groups represent, as some see it, a 'tradition vs. modernization', 'illiterate vs. educated' and 'rural vs. urban' divide, or is this a specious correlation?
- Was it political expediency or fundamentalism at work, or a combination of several socio-economic-political factors (including an attitude of denigration towards women) that resulted in the sacrifice of a life under the banner of "custom" and tradition?

The chapters that follow try to look for answers to some of these questions, from the religious, social, cultural, legal and political points of view. Some of these questions can be answered but the others will never be resolved for the answers were reduced to ashes with an eighteen-year-old bride of less than eight months' standing.

2

Heaven in the Hereafter

All the actions of a woman should be the same as that of her husband. If her husband is happy, she should be happy, if he is sad she should be sad, and if he is dead she should also die. Such a wife is called *pativrata*.

—*Shuddhitattva*

She who follows her husband in death dwells in heaven for as many years as there are hairs on the human body—that is, thirty-five million years. . . .

—*Parasara samhita*

Sati has now come to mean widow burning, but the original sense in which it was used was different; it meant a virtuous or a pious woman. The word sati is derived from *sat* meaning truth, and a sati was a woman who was "true to her ideals". Since Indian tradition holds chastity, purity and loyalty to the husband (*pativrata*) as the highest ideals for women, there appears to be an inexorable logic behind a decision to give up one's life on the death of the husband as proof of chastity or the ultimate expression of a wife's "fidelity".

The original Sati of mythology was not a widow and did not immolate herself on her husband's pyre. She was the daughter of Daksha, son of Brahma, the creator of the universe. Sati was married to Shiva, another of the Trinity which includes Brahma and Vishnu. Once, when Daksha wished to perform a grand sacrificial ceremony, he invited everyone except his son-in-law whom he wanted to humiliate. Sati felt so outraged at this insult to her husband that she invoked a yogic fire and was reduced to ashes, with a prayer that she should be reborn as Parvati and become Shiva's consort again.

This giving up of her body voluntarily in a fiery immolation was construed in time as a 'divine example of wifely devotion'. In the modern interpretation, this has been twisted round into a belief which holds that if a woman gives up her body by burning, like the original Sati, she deserves to be venerated and honoured.

There are several examples of women who did not immolate themselves but nonetheless came to be known as sati. Women like Savitri,
Arundhati and Anasuya of Indian mythology were all exalted as
pativratas or paragons of connubial dedication. None of them
"committed sati" in the sense in which the word is used now. Savitri,
for instance, argued with Yama (the God of Death), when he came to
carry off her husband Satyavan, and cleverly restored him to life.
Stemming from such resolute wifely strength is the phrase "Sati
Savitri" used commonly all over the country as an epithet when referring to a devoted wife. Gandhi's wife Kasturba is referred to fondly as
Sati Kasturba, although she did not immolate herself.

In Balara, Rajasthan, there is a sati temple dedicated to a woman
called Balaji; she is revered as a woman of great piety although she did
not die on her husband's pyre. Another woman who tried to become a
sati in 1985 but was persuaded by the police not to burn is now worshipped as a 'living sati' by the people of the area.

Despite the religious and the historical roots of the concept, sati in
popular usage has now come to mean a woman who burns herself along
with the body of her deceased husband.

Do the Hindu scriptures sanction, or suggest sati in the sense of
immolation of a widow on the death of her husband?

To begin with, it must be pointed out that there is no single,
supreme, religious textual authority in Hinduism the way there is in
other religions. The Hindu scriptures include a very large, heterogeneous corpus of texts codified and evolved over a period of some four
thousand years, beginning in the second millennium BC and stretching
into the second millennium AD. These canonical works, along with
commentaries and digests that were added from time to time over the
centuries, recorded in careful detail the precepts and codes of the time,
and became the rules that governed all aspects of religious, social and
familïal observances. However, because of the extraordinary time span
that they are spread over, the large number of authors who contributed
to this body of scriptures, and the changes that were inevitable in the
ethos of a community over centuries, one often comes across
contradictory edicts. As a result of this, scriptural sanction is claimed
for a variety of diametrically opposed opinions.

The earliest scriptures are the Vedas, the Brahmanas and the
Upanishads, which are dated between 4,000 BC and 1,000 BC. The period
of the *Grihyasutras* followed (800–400 BC) and this was followed by the
period marked by texts like Kautilya's *Arthashastra* (fourth century BC)
and Manu's *Manusmriti*, around the beginning of the Christian era.
(Manu is placed variously between 200 BC and AD 200).

The Puranas bring us into the first few centuries AD, while the *Agnipurana* and some of the later *smritis* take us into the closing centuries of the first millennium. Some of the major commentaries—Medhatithi's on Manu, for instance—are believed to have been added around this period, and these were taken as the main source of Hindu law in the pre-British period.

Then followed the period of the digests on Hindu law like *Dayabhaga* and *Mitakshara*. Interpretative texts and digests like *Nirnayasindhu* and *Dharmasindhu* were additions of the post-medieval period (as late as the seventeenth–eighteenth centuries).

All these sacred laws governed and moulded Hindu life through the ages. Some of the *Grihyasutras* are believed to be later interpolations; Manu's text, likewise, is believed to include additions by later writers, and it is possible to find, even within the work purportedly by one author, edicts that seem grossly at variance with each other.

The dates of these various texts can be deduced only with a margin of error of several centuries each way. As a result, different sets of codes, often contradictory, overlap. In fact, there is no unanimity about the chronology of these different works. When identical quotations are found in some of the texts, it is not always clear who is quoting from whom.

The main Vedic texts are four—the *Rig-Veda, Atharva-Veda, Sama-Veda* and the *Yajur-Veda*. The *Rig-Veda* is said to predate the rest, with some of its hymns believed to have been composed even earlier than 4,000 BC.[1] The Brahmanas are a set of works by different authors and are included within the Vedas.

The body of the scriptural texts is divided into *sruti* and *smriti*, with the former ranking higher than the latter. *Sruti* are considered divine revelations (literally, 'that which was heard'), for instance, the Vedas and the Brahmanas; the *smritis* are, in contrast, attributed to human creativity (literally, 'that from memory') and include the *vedangas, sutras*; the two epics *Mahabharata* and *Ramayana*; the Puranas; and texts like *Manusmriti* and *Parasarasmriti*. The *smriti* edicts are considered dynamic, subject to changes in interpretation in keeping with the altered ethos of each time; they describe codes of conduct for man in everyday matters whereas *sruti* pronouncements are invariant and not subject to change.

There is no reference to sati in the Brahmana literature up to AD 700. In the Vedic texts, although funeral procedures are described in detail, widow immolation does not find a mention. It should, therefore, be possible to deduce that the custom was unknown in the Vedic period.

However, a verse in the *Rig-Veda* is often quoted to show that widows were, in fact, required to ascend the pyre at the funeral of the husbands:

Imā nāriravidhavāh sapatneerānjanena sarpishā samvishantu
Anashravoanameevah suratnā ārohantu janayo yonimagre

The original injunction in this verse was for "the women to advance to the altar first" (*agre*: to come forward). By changing the last syllable in the verse to *agne* ("let the woman go into the womb of the fire"—*agni:* fire) the hymn can be cited as a mandate for widow burning. But this is believed to be an interpretation based on a fraudulent substitution of the consonant; scholars contend that even when the last word is changed to *agne* it is only a forced construction that can detect in this stanza a reference to widow immolation. Whether this alteration of the text was a careless slip during transcription or a deliberate tampering by unscrupulous priests (as Max Mueller believed) it is impossible to say. The accepted view among pundits is that the hymn described the funeral procedure in which "the widow lay down beside the dead man and a bow was placed in his hand, to be removed subsequently and the woman called on to return to the land of the living".[2] This procedure of "lying down beside the dead man" is also subject to controversial interpretations, with some claiming that it was only a symbolic description, not an actual deed; others infer from this rite that the practice of immolation was known long before the Vedic period and that subsequently the custom was stopped and reduced to a ritualistic lying down next to the corpse.

Often passages in the *Atharva-Veda* are cited as evidence of the prevalence of formalities resembling sati. In the *Rig-Veda*, the widow was first made to lie down by the side of the husband's body and then get up on being directed to "lead a prosperous life enjoying the bliss of children and wealth".[3] The *Atharva-Veda* also clearly mentions widow remarriage, and it has been pointed out that widow burning could not have been decreed since the two are contradictory.

Among the four Vedas the *Atharva-Veda* is believed to be the most recent; Manu does not refer to it as a Veda. Also, the *Atharva-Veda* is not used in religious ceremonies, while the other three Vedic texts are. For this reason, too, the pronouncements of this text are taken to be of less importance.

Ambiguity together with metaphoric, cryptic construction that marks the ancient Sanskrit texts makes for difficulty in decoding the true intent of some of the passages and edicts. However, the unanimous view of authoritative interpreters of the scriptures is that none of the *sruti* texts refer to widow immolations.

The *Baudhayana Grihyasutra* lists rules governing a widow's conduct, which implies that widows lived on and were not required to end their lives on the pyre of the husband—"A widow should eschew for a year honey, meat, liquor and salt, and sleep only on the floor".[4]

That widows continued to live on after the death of the husband is borne out by other texts which spell out guidelines that a widow was to follow in her lifestyle. Apasthamba (dated between 800 and 400 BC) for instance, does not allow the widow of a sonless male to succeed as heir to property.[5] He also disapproves of the custom known as niyoga which was then prevalent. (Niyoga was the practice of a woman marrying, or cohabiting with, her brother-in-law or other near kin for the sake of producing a son to offer oblations to the dead man if he had no sons of his own to undertake this important rite). Apasthamba in fact prescribes the 'prajapatya' penance for women who, after resolving to burn, turn back at the last moment. The *Dharmasutra* of Gautama (prior to 600 BC) declared, on the other hand, that a widow could inherit the property of her husband. Gautama's tract is, along with Apasthamba's, and the *Baudhayana* text, considered the most important among the *Dharmasutras*. Although Apasthamba, Harita and Gautama are sometimes quoted as authors of verses on sati, these passages are not found in their *Dharmasutras* where they have elaborated on the duties of widows in great detail. Also, these works mention widows' inheritance rights. The inference is that these verses referring to sati immolations were later interpolations.

Thus, along with the *srutis*, the principal *smritis* are also silent on sati.

In the *Mahabharata* (which is dated around 900 BC, although one opinion holds that it belongs to a period prior to 3,100 BC)[6], Madri chooses immolation on the death of her husband Pandu. The story is that Pandu's other wife Kunti wanted to burn herself but was dissuaded by Madri. Although this incident of Madri's immolation is quoted often, one opinion holds that she did not in fact die in this fashion; this inference is based on a difference of opinion about whether or not the description in the epic refers to 'two bodies'. The Sanskrit word *shareera* is construed as bones in one interpretation and as body in another. There is, however, no mention of immolation by the widows of the Kauravas who were slain in battle.

On the death of Vasudeva, four of his wives are said to have mounted the pyre; on Krishna's death, five women became satis, but the wives of Abhimanyu, Ghatotkacha and Drona did not burn themselves. According to the account given in the *Vishnupurana* (AD 300–600), eight queens ascended the pyre at Krishna's death while Satyabhama chose not death but ascetism and life as a recluse.[7]

There is one passage from the *Mahabharata* claiming the support of the *Rig-Veda* which seems to eulogize sati:

> Though the husband died unhappy by the disobedience of his wife, if from motives of love, disgust of the world, fear of living unprotected, or sorrow, she commits herself to the flames, she is entitled to veneration, and the obsequies as for suicide are forbidden; the Rig Veda expressly declares that the loyal wife who burns herself shall not be deemed a suicide. . . .[8]

However, no such passage can be traced in the *Rig-Veda*. And it is well-known that the *Mahabharata* text as we know it, contains much that is of equivocal authenticity and uncertain dates. Additions were made to the text at different points of time over the centuries as a result of which original portions and later additions are not distinguishable from each other. Portions have been lost and rediscovered, versions changed with each succeeding commentary, and with the date of the epic itself subject to controversy (ranging over more than two millennia) no conclusive deductions can be made on the question of sati. One other argument put forward in connection with the *Mahabharata* is that Vyasa who is said to have composed the original story, was "a great advocate of female sacrifice".

Like the *Mahabharata*, the *Ramayana* too has different versions. One view holds that sati is not mentioned in the epic, while another infers, from the mention of a woman entering the fire on the death of her husband in a story narrated to Ravana, that sati was known at that time. Another opinion believes that Kausalya, mother of Rama, contemplated burning herself on the death of Dasaratha but kept herself alive in order to be able to see Rama again after his return from exile.[9] In the popular version of the story, none of the wives of Dasaratha burn as satis.

Manusmriti does not mention sati at all; Manu suggests that a widow "may if she chooses, emaciate her body by subsisting on flowers, roots and fruit", and declares that if she stayed virtuous and celibate, she would go to heaven even if she were sonless. Manu is considered the foremost law-giver in the Hindu tradition and his work formed the base for the law codes of later times.

If the practice of widow immolation had been prevalent in his time then, he would have surely made mention of it.

Kautilya's *Arthashastra*, another important text of the pre-Christian era, recognized both niyoga and widow remarriage; he forbade suicide of any kind overtly and suggested stringent punishment for those who attempted or condoned it.[10]

The son of a remarried widow, known as *punarbhu,* is mentioned by some writers like Narada and Parasara, and from this it is possible to infer that "even in times long after Kautilya, sati was not a general practice".[11]

The evidence available shows that till around 500 BC the custom of sati was not prevalent even among the Kshatriyas who practised widow burning much before the other classes took to it in imitation.

The fifth century BC saw the rise of Buddhism and this had a bearing on the mores of the times through an increased emphasis on asceticism and a simultaneous denigration of women as "temptation incarnate". The *Jataka Tales,* for instance, portray the demoralizing influence of women. The arrival of invaders and the consequent social unrest and perversion of tradition added to this trend.

Yajnavalkyasmriti (between first and third century AD) mentions a widow as the first heir of a sonless man; there is no mention of widow immolation. From the time of the Gupta period, however, stray references become available—*Vishnusmriti* mentions sati though "not as a religious duty". After the death of the husband, a woman had to "preserve her chastity or ascend the funeral pile". Likewise, Brahaspati declares, "the wife is half of the man's body; a virtuous wife, whether she burns herself on her husband's funeral fire or lives after him, tends to the spiritual benefit of her husband".[12]

Sati is not recommended but merely mentioned; and immolation is one of the two options, the other being a life of celibacy.

Narada and Vishnu, who belong roughly to the same period, mention widow immolation but Narada adds a qualifying clause—a widow should not immolate herself if she has young children or if she is pregnant. Although he mentions immolation, he does not consider it the most desirable among the alternative courses he lists.

Commentators on the original texts distinguish between *naimittika* and *kamya,* guidelines that are incumbent on the one hand, and optional on the other. *Brahmacharya* or celibacy was the preferred course; immolation was the *anukalpa* or a secondary alternative. Those who did not choose either of these could remarry. Interestingly, not only a widow but also a woman whose husband had disappeared for a long time or had become a recluse, joined a monastic order or was impotent, could marry a second time.[13]

Vishnusmriti mentions celibacy and immolation as the two courses open to a widow. The *Vedavyasasmriti* (written around sixth century AD) likewise mentions both alternatives, but reverses the order, enjoining immolation as superior to life as a recluse.

What we see as we proceed chronologically from the earliest known sources to the medieval period is a steady shift in the attitude to women down the ages—to begin with, they were allowed remarriage; later, celibacy was enjoined; later still, celibacy and immolation were mentioned as alternatives; next, immolation became the more meritorious alternative; and finally, as we come to the last of the additions to the corpus of scriptural texts, we find an outright glorification of widow burning, as in the case of the *Nirnayasindhu.*

It is in this light that we find Angirasa (around AD 700) decreeing—and Sankha, another writer, echoing the view—that "for all women, there is no other duty except falling into the funeral pyre when the husband dies".[14]

"Even if the husband had committed the sin of killing a Brahmin, the wife, who burns herself clasping his body on the pyre, purifies him of the sin. Through this act of immolation she commands the same honours as the legendary Arundhati and will be praised in Heaven. And as long as a woman does not burn herself on the death of her husband, she is never free from rebirth as a woman".[15]

However, Brahmin women were forbidden to reach for this salvation; only women of other castes were entitled to this. A Brahmin woman who broke this rule became guilty of suicide and "would therefore lead neither herself nor her husband to heaven".[16]

Parasarasmriti, another major text of this period, offers three different points of view and is an interesting example of how amendments to the text over a period of time in keeping with the changing attitudes, were made for confusion and contradiction. Of the three different opinions offered, one approves of remarriage, as in Narada's text (even while the husband is alive, if the circumstances merit it); the second resembles Manu's edict in decreeing a life of chastity for the widow in order to attain heaven. (This verse is believed to have been added at a later stage). The third view, presumed to be yet another later addition, is the much-quoted verse: "She who follows her husband will abide in heaven for three-and-a-half crore years" (as many as the number of hairs on a human body). Also, "Just as a snake catcher draws out a snake from a hole, similarly a woman who burns herself draws her husband out (from hell or wherever he may be) to enjoy heavenly bliss with him".

These three different statements span the changing attitudes towards women. The early years of the sixth to seventh centuries were marked by political and social uncertainties and with invasions and strife arose the threat of rape and abduction. Women began to be secluded "to protect them" and as an extension of this reasoning, immolation came to be looked upon as a solution, to be enjoined as "superior" to a life threatened with "impurity". This is the period that saw an increase of child marriages: inter-caste marriage was forbidden. It was, a "period of cultural decline, with certain elements of Hinduism not found in earlier centuries surfacing".[17] Sati in the sense of the burning of widows was one of the aberrations.

Harita reflected the pervading attitudes of the times in his unambiguous pronouncement: "She who dies when he dies, is a good and loyal wife".[18] He also added for good measure, "that a woman who follows her husband in death purifies three families—that of her mother, father and husband".

The most explicit authority for widow burning is said to be found in the *Taittiriya samhita*, quoted in the *Narayaniya Upanishad*.

> O Agni (fire), I will observe the vow of following my husband. Do thou enable me to accomplish it. . . . to gain the heavenly mansion I enter into thee—inspire me with courage and take me to my lord. . . .

(If she is firm in her resolve, she enters the fire; if not, she returns home).

This passage is offered in conjunction with the supportive verse: "The loyal wife who burns herself shall not be deemed a suicide", from the *Brahmapurana*,

Rigveda vādāt sādhwi stree na bhavedātmaghātinee

to assert that the Vedas sanctioned *sahamarana* (meaning dying together; it refers to the burning of a widow on a pyre along with the husband's body; it is also known as *sahagamana*, meaning to go together. When she immolated herself separately, after her husband's cremation—because she could not ascend the pyre with him for some reason, when the husband died away from home, for instance—clutching some possession of his, usually his sandals, turban or similar artifact, it was known as *anugamana* or *anumarana*).

Even this passage from the *Taittiriya samhita* cannot be considered unequivocal proof of the prevalence of the sati rite because often the same verse with slight variations in wording, and therefore with different import and application, occurs in different contexts within the same Veda. Apart from the problem of authenticity and interpolations, the meanings of some of the passages acquire shades of differing emphasis in translation; this is further compounded by the fact that often the exact connotation of a particular usage is not clear. (One example is "a widow is not a widow because her soul is wedded to her husband".)

Commenting on the quotations from the *Narayaniya Upanishad*, the Sanskrit scholar, H.H. Wilson adds the caveat that the Upanishads are "of varying dates and not unequivocal". In addition, the particular *anuvaka* (section) in which the reference to sati is said to occur is not available. He also concludes that since at least one commentator has called it a supplementary section, the passage in question cannot be a part of the original *aranyaka*.[19]

To begin with, Brahmin women were forbidden to burn themselves as sati. Why, it is not clear, if immolation promised salvation and eternal bliss in heaven. Since Brahmins were the ones who interpreted the sacred texts, it would have been logical to ensure that their own women had access to such a privilege—and thereby assured the ascent to heaven of the husbands too. Two explanations are commonly put forth for this—one is that chicanery and motives of selfishness induced the Brahmins to exempt their own women from a fiery death; the other is that immolations originated not as a religious rite for salvation but as a political device among the nobility and warrior classes, to ensure that the "purity" of their women was not violated by the invading armies. Sati, therefore, in all likelihood began as a Kshatriya practice and gradually spread to the other castes. (One other explanation offered is that the Brahmins, by virtue of their lifelong study and recitation of the sacred verses, acquired so much merit that they did not need their women to burn themselves in order to "pull them out towards heaven"). However, some of the texts soon began to extol the virtues of immolation for Brahmin widows too:

> A Brahmin woman should enter the fire clasping the dead body of the husband. If she lives (does not become a sati) she being *thyaktakesha* (having shaved off her hair?) should emaciate her body through penance.[20]

We also have the anomaly of the *Mitakshara*, a commentary on Yajnavalkya's text, declaring that "the duty of *anvarohana* (immolation) was common to all women of all castes from Brahmans to Chandala—provided they were not pregnant or having young children", when Yajnavalkya himself discussed a widow's status as the first heir to the property of a man.

A practice that was 'not common' until around the fifth or sixth century AD thus slowly gained a social foothold, abetted by the approval of those whose interpretations of the scriptures carried weight.

A number of references on immolation become available from this time on, both in scriptural texts and in secular Sanskrit classics and literature. In the celebrated play *Mritchakatika*, Charudatta's wife wishes to burn herself even before receiving news of her husband's death. The poet Bana of the seventh century, author of *Kadambari* and *Harshacharita*, mentions queen Yashomati's decision to commit herself to the fire even before the husband was dead. This was not sati in the sense of widow burning. But the idea of immolation rather than living on as a widow made it, in essence, no different. However, Bana condemned the practice; describing it as an act of foolishness, he said the act brought "no good whatsoever to the deceased and does not result in bringing religious merit".

The tantric sects, which venerate the female, did not approve of sati; in their view, a woman committing sati went "straight to hell".

The period from ninth to tenth century saw a coexistence of both views; writers like Medhatithi (a prominent commentator on *Manusmriti*) reflected on this dichotomy when they declared that sati was "not obligatory" but could be condoned as "a transgression caused by distress".

*

The Puranas are a set of eighteen texts, the earliest of which is placed around the sixth century AD and the latest as recent as the sixteenth century. References to sati are available in some of these, particularly the later ones:

> Tell the faithful wife of the greatest duty of women; she is loyal and pure who burns herself with her husband's corpse. Should the husband die on a journey, holding his sandals to her breast let her pass into the flames.[21]
>
> When the widow consigns herself to the same pile with the corpse of the deceased, whoever performs *kriya* (rites) for her husband shall perform it for her.[22]

The procedure to be followed by the woman in burning herself is also spelt out in detail:

> Having first bathed, the widow dresses in two clean garments and holding some *kusa* grass, sips water from the palm of her hand. Bearing *kusa* and *tila* (sesame) in her hand, she looks towards the east or north while the Brahmana utters the mystic word OM. Bowing to Narayana, she next declares: 'On this month, so named in such a *paksha* (lunar cycle), on such a *thithi* (date), I (naming herself) that I may meet Arundhati and reside in *swarga* (heaven), that the years of my stay may be numerous as the hairs on the human body, that I may enjoy with my husband the felicity of heaven and sanctify my paternal and maternal progenitors and the ancestry of my husband's family, that lauded by the *apsaras* (celestial nymphs), I may be happy with my lord, through the reigns of fourteen Indras, that expiation be made for my husband's offences whether he has killed a Brahmana, broken the ties of gratitude or murdered his friend; thus I ascend my husband's burning pile. I call on you, ye guardians of the eight regions of the world, Sun and Moon, Air, Fire, Ether, Earth and

Water! My own soul! Yama! Day, Night and Twilight! And thou, conscience, bear witness. I follow my husband's corpse on the funeral pile.

(With this *sankalpa* (resolve) she circumambulates the pyre thrice and
ascends it).

If, after the *sankalpa,* she decides not to go ahead with the
immolation, she becomes subject to the penalty of defilement, but may
be purified by observing the 'prajapatya' fast.[23] However, those who
quote the *sankalpa* as evidence of scriptural support often conveniently
overlook this.

The *Garudapurana* praises the immolation of a wife on her husband's
pyre and refers to the miraculous power of a *pativrata*; it states that "a
Brahmana woman should not burn herself apart from her husband's
body (or after he is cremated) but that Kshatriyas and other women may
do so while pregnant women and those having young children should
not do so". A woman does not become free from the liability to be born
again and again as a woman, it declares, until she becomes a sati.[24]

The *Vishnupurana* includes a number of anecdotes referring to
immolations by women on the death of the husband. One of these is
the legend of King Satadhanu and his wife Saivya, described as a
woman of great virtue. While the couple was observing a purificatory
fast, a heretic passed by and the king spoke to him. The wife on the
other hand looked away. Because of this audacious offence, the king was
reborn as a dog although his wife had ascended the funeral pyre with
him. His wife reborn as a princess had knowledge of her earlier life and
recognized her husband; she married him and reminded him of his earlier
incarnation. In his subsequent birth, the king was born as a jackal; once
again the virtuous wife recognized him; he starved to death in order to
be rid of that life and was reborn again, this time as a wolf. After being
born next as a vulture, a crow and a peacock, he was finally born as a
human, whereupon she married him and lived happily with him till he
died in a battle. She then "cheerfully" ascended the pyre once again with
his body, and the two of them went to heaven.

Exaggeration and far-fetchedness are often part of mythological legends but since texts like these are cited as authoritative pronouncements
on religious edicts, one cannot help but wonder: If the wife was a
virtuous woman and had ascended the pyre with her husband the first
time, and if such a supreme sacrifice was capable of pulling a man from
hell and taking him to heaven, why was he reborn as a dog and a variety
of other animals and birds before he could assume the human form
again?

Another story in this Purana refers to prince Bahu who was killed in
battle. His wife wished to burn herself on the funeral pyre but was for-

bidden to do so by a sage who told her that the child she was carrying was destined to be a great emperor. This child grew up to become King Sagara.

Vishnupurana also includes a description of the funeral of Krishna. Rukmini, it says, led a retinue of eight queens who embraced the body of Hari (Krishna) and entered the fire. Balarama's wife, Revati likewise, burned herself with her husband's body. Hearing of these events, Ugrasena, Krishna's maternal grandfather and Vasudeva, along with Devaki and Rohini, committed themselves to the flames too. (Balarama was Vasudeva's and Rohini's son). In this instance, the wives, father and mother all chose a fiery death. But all these anomalies in the Puranas could be, as we've seen, be the result of accretions to the original text: As Wilson says:

> In their present condition (the Puranas) must be received with caution as authorities for the mythological religion of the Hindus at any remote period. They preserve no doubt many ancient notions and traditions, but these have been so much mixed up with foreign matter, intended to favour the popularity of particular forms of worship or articles of faith that they cannot be unreservedly recognised as genuine representations of what we have reason to believe the Puranas originally were.[25]

The same *Vishnupurana* decrees in another chapter that compassion should be the overriding principle and that the householder should "abstain from virtuous or religious acts if they involve misery, or are censured by the world".[26] It is obviously difficult to reconcile to this injunction with the sanction of sati immolation.

The *Padmapurana* (AD 1100) praises the act of immolation by a widow but only in the case of Kshatriya women; anyone helping a Brahmin woman to ascend the pyre would be "committing a grave sin of murdering a Brahmana". It is thus clear that there is no unequivocal pattern in edicts—some later ones prohibit, some enjoin and some earlier ones mention both views. Each author took a stance that he personally identified with.

In spite of the texts forbidding sati immolations by Brahmin women, by the end of the first millennium they too were burning themselves, supposedly in a bid "not to be considered wanting or in any way less courageous than the other castes". The prohibitory injunction was interpreted to mean that only *anumarana* was forbidden for Brahmin women and that *sahamarana* was sanctioned.

Madhvacharya, a religious leader and philosopher of the medieval years (thirteenth century) praised self-immolation and held it up as the ideal for widows. Although he conceded that the *sruti* texts did not enjoin immolation and that whatever guidelines the *srutis* gave took precedence over all other texts, yet this rule, he claimed, did not apply in the matter of sati which he called "an exception allowed for women desirous of honour".[27]

Clearly, it was (and is) possible to revert to the Vedas when such a reversion suits one's purpose, and also possible to declare exceptions to the rule to seek justification for something not sanctioned in the texts!

Deification of women who became satis is said to have intensified during the centuries of the second half of this millennium. The *Nirnayasindhu* and *Dharmasindhu*, which belong to this period (sixteenth–seventeenth century) are the latest works on the *Dharmashastras*. This was a period of political and social turbulence, with an attendant clash of cultures following the Mughal rule. The *Nirnayasindhu* and *Dharmasindhu* approve of sati immolation and these are the texts that the Shankaracharya of Puri quoted in support of his pro-sati stand. "If a woman is so deeply in love with her husband that after his death she does not want to live for a minute, she should burn herself on his pyre", he said adding that that was what the *Nirnayasindhu*, *Dharmasindhu*, Angirasa and *Sakhasmriti* laid down.[28] The modern-day equivalent of the ancient law-makers then described how a woman should become a sati:

> She should go near her husband's pyre, with flowers, fruit etc. In her *aanchal* (the end portion of a sari), give the symbols of her fortunate marital status to other fortunate women and then placing a pearl in her mouth, should pray to Agni the fire god, and enter the flames. At the moment of her entering the fire, Brahmins should chant mantras, to the effect that this woman who is entering the flames should be awarded with entry into heaven via her husband's pyre.[29]

A pregnant or a menstruating woman, he conceded, should not burn herself. Neither should a woman with small children. He added "Should a menstruating woman desire to become a sati, she should immolate herself five days later along with her husband's footwear. If such a woman feels that she cannot possibly wait four days before immolating herself, she should grind ten kilos of rice grain with a grinder in an earthenware container. This will purify her blood. Then she should donate 30, 20 or 10 cows—30 if it is the first day, 20 if it is the second, 10 on the third—bathe five times in mud and that very day immolate herself".[30]

The same texts that he cited also "allowed the wife to perform rites after death, with Vedic mantras".[31] What the Shankaracharya didn't see (or chose to ignore) was the contradiction—on the one hand, the wife was authorized to perform funeral rites for the husband, yet she was not supposed to live after the death of the husband!

Given the heterogeneous nature of the collection of edicts that make up the Hindu scriptures, the question of precedence and of distinction between the older and more authoritative texts and the relatively later ones is vital for deciding religious guidelines; and yet, asked how old the *Dharmasindhu* (from which he was quoting) was, the Shankaracharya's answer was that it was "ageless".

The Shankaracharya of Kanchi, another pontifical head of the same sect, however, came out with a condemnation of sati saying that it was not an integral part of Hindu dharma now, though it found mention in some of the Shastras. (The scriptural texts themselves describe certain edicts as *kalivarjya* or inappropriate for modern times). In the Kerala region of South India, the great philosopher-seer-teacher Adi Shankara laid down "sixty-four *acharas*" (observances) among which is also the prohibition of sati. This Adi Shankara (literally, the first Shankara) who lived in the eighth century, established seats of religious learning in different parts of the country, and those chosen to head these institutions or 'mutts' are ascetics who come to be known as Shankaracharyas (*acharya* is a teacher or a revered and learned person). Oddly enough, it is one of these spiritual heirs of Adi Shankara who is now in the forefront of the pro-sati movement, claiming that widow immolation is a part of Hindu dharma. There is no logical explanation of how a religious descendant of the original Shankara who forbade sati burnings can take a stance in favour of sati.

This has incidentally, but quite relevantly, raised the question of who in a fragmented society like the present Indian one, has the authority to draw up edicts. "The Shankaracharyas of the different mutts, although revered for traditional reasons, do not enjoy any undisputed ecclesiastical authority".[32]

Like Adi Shankara, Madhvacharya too passed on a religious tradition that is propagated by eight mutts. The head of one of these, the Pejawar mutt, declared in the context of the recent immolation of Roop Kanwar, that "all Hindu leaders should oppose the revival of sati. It has no religious sanction".[33]

Another head of the same sect, the swami of the Admar mutt, likewise declared that the practice of sati has no religious sanction. And yet, Madhvacharya whose spiritual heirs these pontiffs are, had taken a stance in favour of sati—another instance of contradictory postures confounding the question of a religious base for the custom of immolation.

What the Shastras say is important for two reasons—one is that the faction that seeks to glorify sati in the twentieth century includes a religious head—the Shankaracharya of Puri; it is therefore important that the scriptural position on sati is resolved. The other is that, those who have challenged the introduction of statutes seeking to penalize abetment and glorification of sati allege that such enactments are a violation of Article 25 of the Indian constitution which guarantees freedom of religion.

Do the scriptures enjoin or endorse sati, or do they condemn it?

Because of the diversity of the edicts that have come down through a few thousand years, it is possible to assert with equal vehemence that the scriptures do, and do not, sanction widow burning. But in looking to the scriptures for guidelines, the assumption is that practice falls in line with what the textual proclamations enjoin; this ignores the possibility of textual references being reinterpreted with a view to validate social practices that are sought to be imposed for one reason or the other. This reverse process sets in a vicious circle, with textual ambiguities being reinforced to support custom and practice. The question is not whether there is support in the books for sati, but how authoritative these references are and how much weight they command.

Transgressions were allowed in extenuating circumstances, and at times these went on to become the norm. This is why certain commentators could take the stand that though the *sruti* texts forbade suicide, self-destruction by a widow would not count as suicide.

The Shankaracharya of Puri who insisted that scriptural sanction exists for the practice of widow burning also said that a woman as compared to a man is "quite degraded" and "it is to curb her and put her on the right path that we have these tenets."[34] Widow remarriage is not mentioned in the Vedas, he insisted—which is patently wrong.

"In my family, the widow enjoys a position no one else in the house does", he said in one interview.[35] On the other hand he also said that according to the Hindu Shastras and Vedas, the only choice before the widow was "to suffer throughout her life or to commit sati". A related point: as an ascetic of the rank of Shankaracharya, he should have, in fact, no "family" for he is supposed to have renounced all kinship ties before taking up his religious duties as the Shankaracharya. Seen in the light of remarks like these, and taken in conjunction with the fact that he ridicules the concept of equality between the male and the female as "shameful", one cannot escape the conclusion that this pontiff comes through as less than deserving of respect, much less a following.

Swami Agnivesh who challenged the arguments of the Shankaracharya of Puri, makes a distinction between spurious and authentic texts—"It is the four Vedas alone, the *samhitas*, that have authority. All the rest, the Upanishads, the *smritis*. . . are acceptable only so far as they conform to the Vedas. Where they clash, the Vedas will prevail and the others will be rejected as *ultra vires*. . . the other scriptures have to derive their authority from the Vedas and if something is in contravention of the Vedas, it cannot stand."[36]

One interesting argument that has been advanced is that the *Gita*, considered the supreme ethical edict, forbids action based on the expectation of future rewards, and hence immolation in the expectation of felicity in an afterlife, can only be immoral.

The essence of Vedic edicts is that one's worth and status are determined by one's action and attitudes, and not by the accidents of birth. When the subjugation of women began, these ideas were misinterpreted and distorted. Some of the edicts in the later scriptures are themselves based on changing attitudes towards women through the centuries. And these attitudes in turn are part of the larger canvas of how women have been perceived in relation to society at different periods in history.

The rite of sati seen as part of this wider canvas of women's status in society shows how immolations take their place as an extension of the elaborate grid of pressures brought to bear on women, right from childhood on to turn what is in fact murder, into a mystical act.

3

But Hell on Earth

Rani Devi, a Jat woman, said that Roop Kanwar's act of sati was good only because if she had been alive, her life as a Rajput widow would have been hell. She could not have remarried, she could not have worn jewellery or good clothes, she could not have eaten good food, she would have had to stay indoors for the rest of her life. She could not even have gone to the well to draw water. She would have been treated with contempt, as an inauspicious person all her life. As such she would not have been allowed to participate in any happy occasion, ceremonies or rituals of the family. Therefore it was better for her to have chosen death....
—Vishal Mangalwadi, *The Indian Express,* 19 September 1987

In almost all cultures and ages, over extended periods in time, disdain for the female has marked social attitudes in general. Most laws, religious practices and secular customs have mirrored this outlook that condemns women to a lowly status; so it has been in the Indian context too. If there exists, in the last quarter of the twentieth century, a sizeable faction in favour of sati immolation necessitating the enactment of a prohibitory law, one of the reasons is that the approval of the notion of a woman ceasing to exist on the death of her husband is part of this wider canvas of social attitudes towards women and the trivialization of their lives.

References are available in plenty from the time of the earliest of the ancient texts, to illustrate how women were denigrated and held worthy of only contempt. "A man with a hundred tongues would die before finishing the task of lecturing upon the vices and defects of women, even if he were to do nothing else throughout a long life of a hundred years", says the *Mahabharata*, to which the *Anusasanaparva* adds that "women combine the wickedness of a razor's edge, poison, snake and fire". And the same thread of disparagement and censure runs through the *Ramayana* which lists (in the *Aranyakanda*) "falsehood, thoughtless action, trickery, folly, great greed, impurity and cruelty" as the "natural faults of women".[1]

"Women, *shudra* (the lowest of the four castes), dog and crow embody untruth, sin and darkness", declares the *Satapatha Brahmana*, adding for good measure that women are "lascivious, fickle-minded and falsehood incarnate"; women, it declares, also "have the hearts of Hyaenas".

A wife's presence alongside the husband was essential for carrying out certain religious rituals; and yet, even Adi Shankara declared that if a woman happened merely to overhear recitations of Vedic mantras by chance, hot molten glass should be poured into her ears.

'Women and Shudras' was a common bracketing in many works of the early literature; penance and pilgrimage were forbidden to both by the sage Atri; *achamana* (ritual sipping of water as a purificatory gesture) was decreed only once for both, while all Dvijatis (the twice-born category which includes the top three—Brahmins, Kshatriyas and Vaishyas—of the four caste divisions) were to sip water thrice. Dvijatis were to bathe to the accompaniment of Vedic mantras, but women and Shudras were to bathe silently. Also, the *Baudhayanasutra* prescribes the same penance for killing a Shudra or a woman (while the penalty for killing a Brahmin male is harsher).

If women had a lower status, when they menstruated, they fell even lower in society's esteem and came to be clubbed with either outcastes or dogs—"If a Brahmana hears the voice of a *chandala* or a woman in her course, he should at once leave eating; if he eats even one morsel after hearing their voice he has to observe a fast for one day".[2] Likewise, Manu, the law-giver decreed that, "One should never eat food touched by menstruating women or by a dog".

This pollution and condemnation pursued her even after death—the *Vishnu Dharmasutra*, for instance, decrees that if a menstruating woman dies, her corpse should be bathed after three days and then cremated.[3]

Morally and intellectually, women were held to be inferior and weak. They were not permitted to study the Vedas; marriage and motherhood (begetting sons, in particular) were the only goals. And marriage meant self-effacement in the services of the husband. For the ideal woman, the *pativrata*, there could be no existence apart from that of the husband:

> If her husband is happy, she should be happy; if he is sad, she should be sad, and if he is dead, she should also die. Such a wife is called *pativrata*.

A girl's upbringing was patterned entirely around this concept of *pativrata*, right from birth; this was the indoctrination she received, through societal rituals, religious observances and familial attitudes and responses, all this reinforced by tales from mythology and folklore.

The *Ramayana*, for instance, says that a wife obtains the highest heaven by serving her husband:

Car and steed and gilded palace, vain are these to woman's life,
Dearer is her husband's shadow to the loved and loving wife!
For my mother often taught me and my father often spake,
That her home the wedded woman doth beside her husband make,
As the shadow to the substance, to her lord is faithful wife,
And she parts not from her consort till she parts with fleeting life![4]

The *Mahabharata, Matsyapurana*, Kalidasa's plays and Manu's edicts are among the numerous sources echoing the same sentiments. "Though destitute of virtue or seeking pleasure (elsewhere) or devoid of good qualities, (yet) a husband must be constantly worshipped as a god by a faithful wife".[5]

While men had various practices prescribed for ensuring their place in heaven, there were none for women because all that a woman needed to merit ascent to heaven was devotion to her husband; a life spent in the service of the *patidev* (the husband-who-is-god) could not be improved upon—the performance of domestic duties was "equal to worshipping fire, and attendance on the husband equalled the highest religious merit".

Treatise after treatise, in Sanskrit and in other languages, eulogizes the wife who relegates herself to the background and puts herself last, in matters large and small.

No Vedic mantras were to be recited at *sanskaras* (ceremonial rites) for women except at marriage when they were "gifted away" to the groom. (The marriage ritual itself is known, to this day, as *kanyadan*, or the gifting away of a virgin).

The husband had "natural proprietary rights" over the wife. Harishchandra, in the famous story of that name, for instance, sold his wife, and Draupadi's husband staked her at the gambling table in the *Mahabharata*. Interestingly, although Draupadi questioned her husband's right to put her up as a stake, her point was not that he had no right to do so as a husband, but that having staked himself and lost in an earlier game, he no longer had any claims to possessions.[6]

Manu, describing the procedure at the *annaprasana* ceremony (the initiation of a child to solid food) says:

> The father should prepare food of goat's flesh or fish or boiled rice, and give it to the child... The mother is to eat the remnants of the food thus prepared. . . .

Manu's pronouncements on the duties of women are of particular interest because his treatise, the *Manusmriti* heavily influenced the edicts and laws drawn up in subsequent centuries. Much of the inspiration for the social norms governing conjugal rights and privileges as they evolved over the last 2,000 years can be traced back to Manu.

"A wife's marital duty", he declares, "does not come to an end even if the husband were to sell or abandon her". The husband had the right to discard the wife at any moment if she proved disagreeable to him, but even if he were vicious, self-willed, degenerate and a moral wreck, the wife was to worship him as god. If a self-respecting wife found it impossible to live with a man who had married a second time and left his house, she was to be compel'.ed to stay with him.[7]

"Stealing grain or cattle, having intercourse with a woman who drinks liquor, or slaying a woman, are all *minor* offences", he declares (italics mine), for which the punishment was "loss of caste".

Remarriage for a widower was not only allowed but insisted upon—after describing the funeral procedure to be adopted by the wife. Manu informs the bereaved husband that he should marry again "in order to be able to continue to perform religious rites" (for which a wife's presence was essential). A widow, however, should "never think of remarriage" because she should aspire for *mukti* (salvation) rather than *swarga*.

Ironically, Manu has said elsewhere that "the family where women are not happy would come to grief" and that "where women are revered, there the gods rejoice". One possible explanation for the contradictions in his edicts is that there were subsequent interpolations added to certain portions of his treatise by later writers who slipped in codes that they thought were appropriate for the changing mores of the time, and which they knew would find ready and unquestioned acceptance as a part of *Manusmriti*. Even so, the fact remains that persons in authority, in charge of interpreting the texts, felt strongly enough to express anti-woman sentiments and to introduce these into an authoritative manual.

It is also possible that with each subsequent change in the social ethos, interpretations of what Manu actually meant also kept changing, to suit (and perhaps to justify) the mores current at that time. One of his famous pronouncements can be cited as an example—"In childhood, a woman (should be) under the charge of her father, in youth under the husband and in old age, her son". This can be interpreted in two ways—one interpretation would be that the father, husband and son had an obligation to protect her, and the other could mean that a woman was to be controlled by a male at all times because she did not merit independence at any stage in her life.

In addition, it is also possible that Manu's edicts merely reflect the persistent dichotomy that has marked Indian society's attitudes towards women—on the one hand, women are worshipped as Devi and Shakti incarnate—the Supreme Being manifest as feminine power—and on the other they are treated with that curious mix of contempt-hatred that marks all male response to something that one cannot do without but is loathe to acknowledge as indispensable.

To cite one example—Yajnavalkya declares that a widow is the first heir to a man's property; at the same time he also forbids one to eat food served by a widow. Oppression, if not in economic terms, was nonetheless very much manifest in psychological terms.

The examples of women like Visvavara, Maitreyi and Gargi who were revered as eminent philosophers and scholars, are often mentioned to claim that women in ancient India had an exalted place in society. Ghosha composed hymns that have been incorporated into the Vedas, but then it is necessary to remember that what we refer to as the ancient period actually stretches over a few millennia, different spans of which perhaps saw different attitudes to women in society. The consensus is that from the tenth century BC onwards, the position of women did deteriorate steadily. A number of social and political developments intensified this trend in the last few centuries before the dawn of the Christian era, till women became indubitably second-class citizens by the time of the first millennium AD.

It is also possible that just as bride burning cases and crimes against women continued to be registered even while the country was led by a woman prime minister, the eminent women mentioned in the ancient chronicles were perhaps exceptions to the actual situation of the average women of those times. In addition, the idealization of women in the abstract and in religious rites could, and did often, exist side by side with social practices that denigrated women. In part, this idealization itself sprang from the awesome capacity for selflessness and unstinted sacrifice that made her lot subservient to begin with.

Further, as we've seen, whatever the prevailing ethos, the apotheosis of traditional Hindu womanhood was the concept of *pativrata* which called for total subordination in the service of the supreme deity in the form of her husband. There was no corresponding concept of conjugal loyalty spelt out for husbands.

If a *pativrata*'s pleasure lay in acquiescing in her husband's every wish, how was she to respond when he ill-treated her? The answer was that she should look upon even the ill-treatment as an opportunity given to her to purge herself of her sins, if not of this life then those of a previous birth; the husband was therefore doing a meritorious deed, since he was providing her with an opportunity to atone for her misdeeds.[8]

"A woman's power springs from her total submission to her husband in which again it finds its perfect fulfilment". The way to become a goddess, in other words, was to become a slave.

If loyalty, chastity and devotion in a woman assumed such an over-riding emphasis, it followed that her existence lost its rationale once the husband was dead.

Among the primitive warrior tribes, it was thought necessary to despatch a man's favourite belongings along with him when he died, so that he could continue to enjoy their use in the other world. Hence along with his horses and swords and other artifacts, his woman was also "sent". But then in that case, should not women on their death have their husbands sent along too, to the next world? Apparently, the argument did not hold bothways, since "man wielded supreme power in society... and was not prepared to sanction a custom adverse to his own interest and comfort".[9]

*

The paramountcy of a woman's chastity was one of the excuses given for the continuation of customs like sati that sought to invalidate a woman's continued existence after the death of the husband. As Rammohun Roy remarked in his famous tract urging the British to abolish sati, "If there was no concremation, widows may go astray; if they burn, this fear is removed. Their family and relations are freed from apprehension".[10]

An unmarried girl was (and still is) considered a responsibility and a burden on the parents, to be carefully protected and handed over to the groom, in chaste and pure condition. Threats to, or violation of, her chastity were—and are—the greatest calamity that could befall a woman and her family. Seen in this light, sati becomes by extension, "proof of devotion beyond the grave" and also "the ultimate chastity belt".

This primacy of chastity in the Indian tradition seems to have had a parallel in traditional Chinese society during the Ch'ing dynasty. "Chastity as in India was given such importance that the social pressures to remain chaste or to commit suicide out of loyalty to their deceased husbands were particularly intense, and applied even to young girls whose betrothed had died before their marriage could be consummated".[11]

If a husband went away abroad without making provision for the wife's maintenance, she was required to sustain herself through "crafts like spinning *which are unblamable*"[12] (italics mine). Never mind even if the husband had defaulted on his obligations, the woman had to make sure that she was blameless and unblemished!

A woman, once given in marriage to a man, if again given to another, was called *punarbhu* (living again) "One should not eat at her place", declared Angirasa.[13] The issue was thus not just faithfulness or monogamy, but a one-time use of the woman.

This outlook has continued down the ages, and it was on this score that, religious leaders like Pandit Ghanashyamji of Bombay opposed the move to legalize widow remarriage during the nineteenth century. He said,". . . the thing called woman is the crowning piece of all objects of enjoyment in this world, and being subject to the special powers of the husband, is not like a house and capable of being enjoyed by her husband's relations. How much more incapable must she then be of being fit for remarriage and enjoyment by a stranger. Like a dining leaf used previously by another person, she is unfit to be enjoyed by another person".[14] Reinforcing this emphasis on possession and "exclusive sexual enjoyment" for the male were a whole lot of fables and mythological stories. Even Sita, in the *Ramayana*, had to prove that she was still chaste, even after her abduction by Ravana. Revered as an all-time ideal in everything that is praiseworthy in a woman, she nonetheless had to undergo a trial by fire, before Rama would accept her back as his wife.

> For she dwelt in Ravana's dwelling—rumour clouds a woman's fame—
> . . . Dearer than a dark suspicion to a woman were her death!
> . . . A woman pleadeth vainly when suspicion clouds her name,
> Lakshman, if thou lov'st thy sister, light for me the funeral flame,
> When the shadow of dishonour darkens o'er a woman's life,
> Death alone is friend and refuge of a true and trustful wife,
> When a righteous lord and husband turns his cold averted eyes
> Funeral flame dispels suspicion, honour lives when woman dies!
> Fearless in her faith and valour Sita stepped upon the pyre!
> . . . Sita vanished in the red fire of the newly lighted pyre!
> Rishis and the great Gandharvas, Gods who know each secret deed,
> Witnessed Sita's high devotion and woman's lofty creed. . . . [15]

One who was chaste could work miracles, and the power of a "good" woman over even the gods and demons is a popular theme in many classic legends. The character of Savitri in mythology is cited repeatedly in this context. She chose Satyavan as her husband, knowing that he was destined to die in a year. With the help of extraordinary powers conferred on her by her devotion and chastity, she saw Yama when he arrived to take away Satyavan on the day he was to die. In response to her urgings, Yama agreed to grant her a boon, as long as she did not ask for Satyavan's life. She chose motherhood and Yama, having given his word, had to grant her wish. She then pointed out that as a chaste woman she could not become a mother if her husband were not alive. Yama had to concede defeat and restore her husband to life. She became

Sati Savitri, the "virtuous" Savitri whose exceptional devotion vanquished even the force of death.

The story of Sukanya, a princess who was married to a blind sage, is another example. Attracted by her beauty, the celestial twins known as Ashwins appeared before her in human form one day and asked her to marry one of them. She refused. The twins then challenged her to identify her husband after they had turned him into a young man exactly like themselves; if she failed to identify him correctly, she was to accede to their request and accept their advances. Sukanya's devotion to her husband was such that she received divine inspiration in identifying her husband correctly from the three identical figures before her. She not only retained her chastity but also restored her husband's sight and youth in the process.

Another famous legend is that of Kannagi whose husband Kovalan fell in love with the courtesan Madhavi. Kannagi, devoted wife that she was, gave him one of her silver anklets to sell after he had exhausted all his money in the company of his mistress. The king's minions arrested Kovalan when he tried to sell the anklet, thinking that he had stolen it from the royal household, and had him beheaded. Enraged at this injustice, Kannagi produced the other anklet of the pair before the king, and reduced the city of Madurai to ashes with the power of her chastity and devotion.

The message is that she was a wronged woman not so much because her husband was unfaithful to her as because she had been unjustly widowed (never mind that while he was alive, the husband spent all his time and money on the courtesan—in fact this only served to heighten the wife's steadfast loyalty).

The story of Kannagi is nearly two thousand years old. In 1975, (which was observed as the International Women's Year) the Sixty-fourth Law Commission debating the question of whether a man patronizing a prostitute should be punished, declared that a professional prostitute, being a social outcaste, could be periodically punished without disturbing the usual course of society; but the man was however "something more than a partner in an immoral act; he discharges important social and business relations, is a father or a brother responsible for the maintenance of others, has commercial or industrial duties to meet. He cannot be imprisoned without damaging society" [16]

So, while a woman could be punished even if she was driven to this means of earning her livelihood and even if putting her in prison meant depriving her children of their source of livelihood, the man who went to her for his pleasure could not be held guilty or contemptible. She, being an unchaste woman, deserved punishment, but he, even if he was equally unchaste and a partner in her act, did not. Morality was not so much the issue as whether the immoral person had "important social and business relations"; her being a mother or a sister did not merit the same consideration as his being a father or a brother.

This emphasis on, and mythologizing of, chastity and purity in a woman leads on naturally to the mythopoeia of widow burning a "moving ritual that symbolises the reaffirmation of the purity, self-sacrifice and power and dignity of women".[17]

Chastity, along with devotion and extreme humility, has made up the core of Indian cultural attitudes in relation to women all through the ages. Thus, even in immolating herself as an expression of devotion, a woman is required to "clutch her husband's *sandals*" (italics mine) and mount the pyre. Reducing herself to the lowliest of his possessions would, apparently, show the great purity of a woman.

"There was something magnificent in her self-effacement that India associates with her womanhood", observes a biography of Kasturba Gandhi. This kind of surreptitious but strong seduction of the state of self-negation as the exalted ideal lies at the root of most of the aberrations that prevent one half of the Indian society from leading productive and fulfilling lives.

The Status of Widows

If a woman's salvation lay in the service of her husband, it followed that she lost her *raison d'etre* the moment her husband died. Widowhood therefore, came to be seen as the worst calamity that could ever befall a woman; it became the ultimate degradation because it practically invalidated her continued existence. If a woman who became widowed continued to exist, it was a miserable existence at best, with social, economic and religious injunctions against her.

The death of a loved one is painful whatever the circumstances, but apart from the pain of loss, widows in Indian culture have had to bear an additional burden of social opprobrium of horrendous dimensions, through every period in history, ancient, medieval and modern.

Widows were considered inauspicious, barred from festivities and forbidden all comforts and pleasures. Even laughter and entertainment were taboo, and life became in essence, 'a double wilderness'.

The death of the husband was construed as punishment for sins committed in a previous birth; in order to atone for those sins and ensure that she would not suffer widowhood in her next birth, the unfortunate woman had all kinds of austerities and flagellations prescribed for her.

Unlike the widower who was urged to remarry in order to keep the family line alive, a widow was led to believe that for all practical purposes her life had come to an end with the death of her husband.

Relentless, lifelong penitence and self-mortification was enjoined by every authority, right from Manu who decreed that a widow should "emaciate her body by subsisting on flowers, roots and fruit", to Parasara who declared that "wearing perfume, flowers, ornaments and dyed clothes, adorning her hair, chewing betel nut, applying collyrium and taking two meals a day" were all to be avoided by a widow; only one meal a day was permitted and she had to wear only white and sleep on the ground on a mat of *kusa* grass. Most of these injunctions are still followed.

A widow who slept on a cot was supposed to make her husband "fall in hell". The very sight of a widow was supposed to jeopardize one's chances of success in whatever undertaking one was setting out on; and a wise man was advised to "avoid even their blessings like the poison of a snake".[18]

The injunction that a woman whose husband is dead should eschew the use of a bed and should sleep on the ground finds a mention in several texts. The emphasis was on self-scourging; if denial was held up as the desirable norm for all women, it became doubly so for widows.

Several authoritative writers including Manu lists the kind of foods that a man ought not to eat—food prepared or served by one suffering from incurable diseases, an unchaste woman, an enemy, an outcaste, a *patita* (a fallen woman), and a woman whose husband was not living. Manu prescribed an expiatory fast of three days for Brahmins who had unwittingly partaken of food thus prohibited. The son of a Brahmin widow could not be invited to a *shraddha* (death anniversary) ceremony.[19]

A widow's life-span was considered to be a "waiting period", to be spent in prayer so that when she eventually dies she might in the after life be reunited with her husband. Under the circumstances, it is hardly surprising that a woman often burned herself to death along with her husband's corpse.

A pregnant mother was supposed to be surrounded by "auspicious women whose husbands were alive". Even grass widows (*prosita-bhartrka*) whose husbands were away were forbidden to wear ornaments.[20]

In fact, the female form itself was considered a punishment for sins committed in a previous birth. Various rituals and penances were therefore prescribed for women so that they could be spared another cycle of birth as a woman.

Small wonder, then, that the tenth century scholar Alberuni observed
that Hindu women chose to burn themselves to be spared the horrors of
widowhood.[21] In a similar vein, the fifteenth century traveller, Nicolo
dei Conti wrote:

> The widow herself, if she had no young children might well prefer even a
> painful death, in the hope of reunion with her husband, to a dreary life of
> hunger, scorn and domestic servitude.

An English merchant travelling in India at the end of the sixteenth
century recorded that "Wives here doe burne with their husbands when
they die; if they will not, their heads be shaven and never any account is
made of them afterwards".

And the situation had not improved much 300 years later. Fanny
Parks, a British traveller, recorded, in the mid-nineteenth century:

> A Hindu widow is subject to great privations. She is not allowed to wear
> gay attire or jewels, and her mourning is eternal.[22]

The widow of Maharaj Daulat Rao Scindia, who was a former queen of
Gwalior and whom Fanny Parks met, "always slept on the ground,
according to the custom of a widow, until she became very ill from
rheumatic pains; after which she allowed herself a hard mattress which
was placed on the ground. . . Her Highness mentioned that all luxurious
food was denied them. . . and their situation was rendered as painful as
possible".[23]

What added an extra dimension of wretchedness to these attitudes and
customs was the fact that thousands of child-brides were condemned to
such a life before they had even reached adulthood. Child marriages were
common and were not outlawed till 1929, when the Child Marriages
Restraint Act was introduced. The statistics for Bengal in the early
nineteenth century lists twelve and thirteen-year-old widows burning on
the pyres of their deceased husbands. At the last census of the nineteenth century, there were 10,000 widows under the age of four, and
over 50,000 between the ages of five and nine in and around Calcutta
alone.

Rammohun Roy in his tract on sati emphasized this wretchedness
that life as a widow meant. "Widows are left only three modes of conduct to pursue after the death of their husbands. First, to live a miserable life as entire slaves to others, without indulging any hope of support from another husband. Secondly, to walk in the paths of unrigh-
teousness for their maintenance and independence; thirdly, to die on the
funeral pile of their husbands, loaded with applause and honour of their
neighbours".[24]

He also mentioned the "subtle and sinister" compulsions on widows to burn, "confronted with the certainty that as widows they would be condemned to a life of constant misery and humiliation—on the other, the delusive hope of future reward is held out to them beguilingly, and under this combined ministry of fear and false hope they become not only resigned but reconciled to the horrible act of suicide".[25]

A widower was not bound to any vows for the spiritual welfare of his dead spouse, nor was he shunned as unlucky the way a widow was and continues to be; and there was no policing of his lifestyle to ensure that he did not stray from the path of righteousness.

These proscriptions still apply; a widow is often, even today, held morally responsible for the husband's death—"her ill-luck killed him". She is considered inauspicious and barred from participation in festivities. A report published in Calcutta's *Telegraph* in October 1987 quoted a widow who confessed that she had been reprimanded for trying to embrace her twelve-year-old son on the day of his *upanayana* (thread ceremony). As an inauspicious woman, she was not supposed to pollute the boy with her touch. A widowed mother is not normally permitted to be present at—much less participate in—the sacred ceremonies of her own son's or daughter's marriage.

Soubhagyavati (one who has *soubhagya* or good fortune) is the term used for married women whose husbands are living. The moment the husband dies, she is no longer referred to as *soubhagyavati*. Identification of good fortune with the husband—even if he happens to ill-treat her—is in itself a very deeply entrenched and pervasive attitude.

This attitude, and the response it evokes in women even today is typified by the example of one metropolitan woman I knew who died recently. Several years ago, suddenly one morning, her husband deserted her. She was then not yet thirty. She brought up her three children, all by herself, suffering untold hardships in the process. Twenty years later, when the children were grown up and settled in life, a message was brought to her one day saying that her husband was very ill and dying in a town far away. Her children, who had no memories of the father, recall the frenzied manner in which the woman ran to the prayer room and daubed her forehead with huge patches of *kumkum* (the auspicious red mark worn by Hindu women other than widows), with feverish pleas to God not to wipe that *kumkum* from her face. For two days she was like one possessed, praying and crying by turns, till the news of the man's death was brought. "She cried as we had never before seen her cry in all those years, not even when she went through some terrible times", her daughter said. Apparently, even the terrible privations of life as a deserted woman were preferable to the ignominy of widowhood, for it signified a fall in her status in society.

An extract from an autobiographical account written by a leading Indian actor and reproduced recently in *Manushi* illustrates similarly, the pervasive exaltation of *soubhagya* for a woman even in death. This woman, the narrator's sister, was ill-treated, beaten, starved and continuously abused by her mother-in-law. She "went through all these ordeals with the determination of a true Hindu woman", the account says. A daughter was born to the woman and soon after, the husband developed diabetes. The newborn child and her mother were accused of bringing ill-luck. When the man's condition turned critical and it became clear that he would not live long, she jumped into the well in the courtyard of the house. A few moments later the husband too breathed his last. "The news of the double tragedy spread like wild fire in the town. . . . Everybody said, 'blessed woman' when they saw the dead girl's body". A friend who wrote a letter of condolence to the girl's mother said, "When I think of her behaviour, I say to myself, 'What meritorious action!' I think she acted in a way which is very very creditable to our family. As the poet Moropant has said, 'What a great good fortune that a woman should die before her husband'". The letter went on to urge the mother to "think of her daughter as an ornament to the family".[26]

In the Kannada, Tamil and Telugu languages, the word for widow is an insult and a curse that is flung even at men; in Tamil euphemism, a widow is referred to as a woman "who does not live anymore" (even if she is alive). In Marathi there is a word that is used to denote both a widow and a prostitute; it is used when one wants to show contempt for a widow and defame her.[27]

Some communities impose food restrictions on widows—among the Bengalis, for instance, fish is a symbol of prosperity and auspiciousness; widows are therefore forbidden to eat fish. Almost all communities observe dress restrictions; widows cannot wear jewellery, bright coloured clothes or finery. Green or red glass-bangles worn by the women of the north as a sign of *suhag* (auspicious married status) are ceremoniously broken on the death of the husband. In orthodox families and in the interior, a South Indian widow still wears only white, unrelieved even by a coloured border on the sari. Till two generations ago it was common to give up the blouse since it was considered an adornment, and cover oneself only with the single length of white sari. The idea behind these curbs was not merely the prohibition of adornment but also the denigration of the woman as a consequence of her 'fallen' state.

The red *sindur* mark in the parting of the hair applied for the first time by the husband at the time of North Indian and Bengali weddings, is wiped off on the death of the husband, never to be put on again, just as in south India, the red *kumkum* is wiped off the forehead the moment a woman is widowed. An unadorned forehead bereft of that mark, is considered inauspicious and disagreeable.

The *thali* (chain and pendant worn round the neck by South Indian women from the time of marriage, day and night, never to be taken off even for a moment) is removed ceremoniously when a woman becomes a widow; a bare neck is another sign of a widow. There are no similar ways either in dress or in accessories, to distinguish a widower.

A small number of urban-upper-class women have broken these taboos in recent years, but they are still very much the exception. Widows are not invited to *haldi-kumkum* (turmeric and vermilion, symbols essentially associated with married women) functions where women traditionally get together on festive occasions. Betel-nut and flowers, offered at these get-togethers along with *haldi*, are forbidden to widows.

Some of the most poignant, first person accounts I have heard are from widows. Said one woman, "It (sati) would have been an easy way out, it would have been very easy to throw myself into the fire, that would have resolved all problems; the greater courage was the one required to live on, knowing what the future would be like for the rest of my life. What gave me this greater courage was the thought of my two little children". (And yet, those eulogizing 'voluntary' sati and claiming that a woman deserves veneration because of her extraordinary courage, never concede any courage to those widows who 'voluntarily' decide to face the problems that they are fully aware will beset them). What gave this woman courage was her children. If she had not had children, or knew that they would be looked after, or had been brain-washed by myths of afterlife, she too would have taken the 'easy way out' and jumped into the fire.

At a state-level seminar on working women's problems a few years ago, a woman in her thirties, employed as an officer in a metropolitan bank, spoke about how, although her colleagues at work respected and liked her and invited her home on ordinary days, they never included her when there was special (usually religious) function in their homes, because she was a widow. Their disapproval was heightened, she said, by the fact that she sometimes put a red *bindi* on her forehead even though her husband was dead. These symbols of the married status had assumed, for her and for her women colleagues—all college graduates— such an exaggerated importance and mystique that they became contentious even though they were mere symbols. Such are the emotional overtones associated with the idea of the "auspicious married state" and its manifestations. As she put it, "Only a woman whose body is legally and sexually owned by a man is respected in our society". It was a crude, but nevertheless a true statement.

Women of many communities observe periodic fasts and perform special prayers for the long life of their husbands. Thousands of urban-middle-class women who commute long distances by bus or train to work, also keep these fasts, in spite of the strain placed on them by a contemporary lifestyle. However, there are no festivals for men to fast for the long life of the wives.

Until a generation or two ago, the tonsure of widows was common—long hair being one of the attributes of female beauty—depriving a woman of this asset to make her look unattractive was part of the denigration of widows. (One explanation offered is that all one's sins are supposed to rest in one's hair, and therefore shaving the hair is part of a widow's expiation of her sins, for sinner she must be, if not in this birth then surely in an earlier one, or else she would not have been punished with a calamity like widowhood). Tonsured widows of the older generation can still be seen today.

To add insult to injury, the denial of all kinds of adornments for widows was sought to be justified "as in their own interest"—if widows looked attractive, they would become the victims of men and go astray; and that would mean dishonour for the family. Therefore, to keep her chaste, she had to be disfigured, secluded indoors and condemned to misery, both physical and emotional. Such an argument amounts to punishing the victim rather than the perpetrator of wrong, and yet, under patriarchal mores, the power-equation was loaded so heavily against women and in favour of the male who drew up, interpreted, as well as administered the rules, that women had no say in the matter.

The crux of the issue was, evidently, not just chastity as a general concept but specifically, control of female sexuality by the male.

Widows were not allowed to remarry. They were forbidden to turn to religious learning; as social outcastes they could not immerse themselves in jobs or interests outside the home. With nothing to do, if the future stretched out bleak and barren, the fiery pile assumed, in comparison, if not an attraction then at least a semblance of an escape hatch, with the possibility of religious merit thrown in as a bonus—as the Shankaracharya of Puri said in his recent defence of widow burning, "According to Hindu shastras and Vedas, the only choice before the widow is to suffer throughout her life or to commit sati; out of the two, sati is a better way out because the agony of burning would be short-lived, compared with the agony of life-long widowhood".[28]

What about the choices before the men when their wives die—should they also set themselves on fire? "No", the religious leader declared, "a man has to keep the fire of *agnihotri* burning. He needs progeny and for that he has to marry again".

Sati immolations among women of the Jain community, it is useful to note were negligible. This is because Jainism allowed widowed women to become nuns; for Hindu women even this option is closed.

The Widow Remarriage Act came into effect in 1856. Even after the legal sanction came through, social sanction for widow remarriage took a long time in materializing because of the ingrained prejudice of centuries. Ruler Zalim Singh of Kota, for instance, two centuries ago, imposed a "heavy tax on widows who remarried".[29] (Kota, incidentally, lies in the state of Rajasthan).

When the well-known social reformer and educationist, Dr Karve married a widow in the closing years of the nineteenth century, it is said that the street was "lined with people who spat on him in disapproval as he passed". Even today, remarriage for a widow is not seen in the same light as remarriage for a widower.

The British authorities were conscious of the connection between the condition of widows and the incidence of sati. Lord Amherst, while shelving a suggestion for the introduction of a prohibitory law, observed, "I wish that it were possible to take any means of bettering the condition of widows so as to take away at least all the inducement to concremation which arises from the forlorn and destitute existence to which a widow is condemned. These are slow but I think sure means of bringing the barbarous custom to desuetude".[30]

Even during the time (till around 300 BC) when widows were said to have had a choice of lifestyle—passing their remaining days in widowhood, resorting to niyoga or marrying again—"the first was of course the most honourable course" as Dr A.S. Altekar, the well-known twentieth century scholar, describes it. The question of honour has thus run right through history, from antiquity to modern times, but with reference to female sexuality alone.

The practice of niyoga was approved, suggested and practised in ancient times and this fact is often offered in support of the argument that the position of widows was not one of denial, and that society was generous towards widows in those times. Niyoga, however, was not the same as remarriage; the emphasis was not on offering a widow a renewal of conjugal life, but on the assurance of a place in heaven for the dead husband—for which it was necessary that a son should offer libations. If he had died without fathering a son, the widow was required (permitted) to have sexual relations with the brother of the dead man, for the sole purpose of begetting a son. There was to be no pleasure in such a union for her; this was explicitly spelt out. And once the purpose was served and a son was born (some scriptural authorities permitted two sons) she had to terminate the relationship—she was no more required as a procreating machine.

At best niyoga prolonged a woman's life, for it has been pointed out that as niyoga went out of fashion, the number of sati immolations increased.

The woman was everywhere regarded as a species of property which passed into the husband's family on her marriage. She was married no doubt to a person, but also into a family. (*Kulaaya hi stree deeyate*—a woman is given to the family, not to the husband alone). So if her husband died, his brother or any other near relation would take her to wife and raise children by her. This usually happened when a person died without leaving any male issue behind. To die without a son was regarded as a great spiritual calamity, and it was the sacred duty of a brother to see that a son was born of his sister-in-law to perpetuate his brother's memory and to ensure him a place in heaven. If this was not done, there was also the danger of the widow marrying a stranger and being lost to the family.[31]

Several heroes of the *Mahabharata* and the Puranas were born through niyoga (Dhritarashtra and Pandu, for instance). The custom was also resorted to when a man, though alive, could not father a child. Niyoga was thus not remarriage in the conventional sense but a specific adjustment for the birth of a son.

Even among those who frowned upon the custom, the objection was usually not so much that the widow's personal preferences were disregarded as that it violated the concept of chastity.

So we have the two factions, one for and the other against niyoga— one approving of the practice because she had a duty to her dead husband (to ensure his salvation by producing a son), and the other disapproving of the practice, again because she had a duty to her dead husband (to remain chaste and faithful to him). Either way, her life was seen as no more than a means to *his* ends.

The issue of invalidating a woman's life except as a procreating machine, illustrates the attitude to barrenness in the Indian tradition. The word for a barren woman is, like the word for a widow, an insult. The blessing traditionally showered on a bride is that she should bear many sons. A woman who does not conceive is cause for worry and anguish. Pilgrimages and expiatory rites are prescribed; if she still remains barren, the husband is considered justified in taking a second wife for the sake of progeny. A barren woman is prohibited from participation in certain festivities and she is either shunned or pitied for not being able to attain motherhood. Without progeny, her existence is considered incomplete.

The practice of niyoga became obsolete nearly 2,000 years ago, but the emphasis on self-abnegation as an essential quality in a "good woman" has persisted to this day.

Even those who condemn sati as barbarous and uphold a widow's right to live, betray the effects of this indoctrination: She can live on, but apparently only as an ascetic, judging by the pronouncements of some of those who take an anti-sati stand.

"Sati is a waste of energy", says Swami Prabhupada, leader of the Hare Krishna movement, adding that "widows should become *sanyasins* (nuns) to serve society selflessly".[32] "Why should a widow want to die?" Swami Harshananda, a monk of the Ramakrishna Mutt of Allahabad declares. "By leading a life like a monk, she can attain spiritual bliss". Even the preamble to the 1829 regulation legally banning sati said, "(The practice of sati) is nowhere enjoined by the religion of the Hindus as an imperative duty; on the contrary a life of purity and retirement on the part of the widow is more especially and preferably inculcated. . . ."

The issue was the *burning alive of a woman*, not what kind of life she had to live after becoming a widow. The law was against forcing or persuading a woman to burn herself alive; and yet, the authorities thought it necessary to add a reference to "a life of purity and retirement".

*

"By 1800 AD, the less attractive aspects of the Hindu concept of the place of women in society were dominant", observes Vincent Smith in *The Oxford History of India*. Women were seen as burdens, and forming a part of this larger canvas of oppression were other practices like female infanticide, child marriages, *purdah*, dowry and the ultimate manifestation, sati. Running through all these aberrant customs like a common thread was the fact of the trivialization of women's lives. Smothered or poisoned at birth, given away in marriage at a tender age, bargained over like some commodity by dowry hungry in-laws, secluded in the name of chastity and religion, and finally burned for the exaltation of the family's honour, or shunned as inauspicious widows, the burden of oppression took different forms at different stages of a woman's life, from birth to death, in a chain of attitudes linked by contempt for the female.

The birth of a son is, in every community, an occasion for rejoicing. The birth of a daughter is, in contrast, greeted at best with reactions of a lesser joy, disappointment or silence, and at worst as a calamity. Female infanticide has been known in India for a long time, especially in certain parts of the country, like Rajasthan and Gujarat. Rajasthan is the region where sati incidents continue to be reported to this day, while the communities of the state of Gujarat are said to account for the highest number of cases of female foeticide following sex-determination tests.

The British outlawed infanticide in 1804 and declared it to be murder, but a tribal chief who protested against the British edict is on record as having claimed that the practice was "4,900 years old".[33]

As with other enactments that sought to wipe out customs rooted in deviant social attitudes, passing a prohibitory law did not ensure that female infants were no longer shunned. Thanks to the severity of the clutches of the dowry system, certain communities in different regions of the country (parts of Tamil Nadu, Rajasthan) have seen, even in the 1980s, the systematic infanticide of girl babies because the families could see no way of mustering enough savings to facilitate the girls' marriage when they grew up. More recently, there have been allegations of female infanticide in the family of a member of the state legislative assembly of Rajasthan (an investigation was ordered by the crime branch). The law notwithstanding, reports of female infants being given poison berries or being abandoned to die keep surfacing.

As long as women's lives are trivialized, even modern technology cannot help getting hijacked to serve culture-based prejudices. Thus, with amniocentesis techniques becoming available in recent years, and abortion made legal, the clamour to know the sex of the unborn child has led to a medical procedure meant primarily to discover foetal abnormalities being used for large-scale selective abortions of female foetuses. In one survey that is often quoted, out of 8,000 foetuses aborted following sex-determination tests, 7,999 were reported to have been female, the lone exception being that of a Jewish woman who wanted a daughter. In 1987, following demands from women's groups for a ban on these tests, the state of Maharashtra made it illegal to use pre-natal diagnostic techniques for ascertaining the sex of the unborn child. The root cause of female foeticide, however, remains—the stranglehold of the custom of dowry and the very strong cultural preference for sons in certain communities. A nationwide ban on sex-determination tests is yet to be imposed, so all that a family in the state of

Maharashtra need do to circumvent the law is to step across into another state and get the test done. ("Better pay Rs 500 now than Rs five lakhs later on"—as dowry—is how these sex-determination tests are promoted).

Giving birth to daughters is in fact considered no less than a crime in several communities and the mother pays a heavy price for it, although science has made it clear that the sex of the offspring is not determined by the mother.

A letter in *Manushi* referred to the murder, in June 1988, of a woman and her two daughters by her husband who was a ticket-collector at Gorakhpur railway station. Her crime was that she had given birth to two girls in two-and-a-half years. The husband had postgraduate qualifications, but it is quite common for even educated families to exhibit this kind of prejudice against females.[34]

The Dowry Prohibition Act passed in 1961 made it illegal to demand gifts in cash and kind from the parents of a girl in consideration of marriage. Twenty-nine years later, the custom still persists, and has in fact worsened because of the spread of a materialistic outlook among the people. Brides whose parents are unable to meet extortionist demands (a few thousand rupees, fancy household goods and so on) from the groom's family are burnt in 'kitchen accidents'. The grooms marry again. No witnesses can be produced for an act that takes place in the privacy of the home, behind closed doors, and the law remains impotent, in spite of protests from women's groups and the families of the hapless brides.

During the decade of the '80s, dowry-related deaths have proliferated to such an extent that they are no longer considered news. Several citizens' panels have been formed, protest marches have been taken out, seminars arranged and anti-dowry cells opened by voluntary agencies as well as the police, but fresh cases keep hitting the headlines with relentless regularity. Delhi alone is said to record at least one death per day that can be attributed directly to harassment by the husband or the in-laws. In almost all the cases, dowry demands are at the root of the problem, or these are made the peg on which to hang other grievances. Deep-rooted conditioning ensures that however atrocious the demands made by the groom's family, it is always the girl's family that cowers and cringes. Delhi even has an association of parents of dowry victims.

In a recent case that was much discussed by the print and television media, three young sisters of a middle-class family of Kanpur in February 1988 hanged themselves in their home, because they could no longer bear the trauma of being rejected by one prospective suitor after another, since the father could not afford to pay the kind of dowry that was required if they had to find suitable husbands. Nine months later, in November 1988, four sisters in the Palghat district of South India hanged themselves to death, to spare their parents the problem of raising funds for their marriage. The girls, aged eighteen to twenty-five, were said to have been distressed by the frequent discussions at home about the financial problems caused by the marriage of their eldest sister; the debts incurred by the family at that time were reported to be still outstanding.

The roots of a pernicious custom like dowry can be traced to the fact that a woman is perceived as a burden, which in turn reflects the fact that a woman's work within the family, being unpaid, is not recognized as work. When she goes from her father's house to her husband's, the latter expects to be compensated for taking on a burden—and this takes the form of dowry demands.

Added to this is the cultural conditioning that insists that a girl's place after marriage is with her husband till her death, and that it is shameful for her to return to her natal home, whatever the provocation. In several recent dowry death cases, it has been reported that the women repeatedly complained to the parents of the ill-treatment in their marital homes because of inadequate dowry; some even sought refuge with their parents but were persuaded, either by the parents themselves or by other elders of the community, to "try for a reconciliation" and to "adjust" to life at the husband's, because that was what custom decreed. Vanita Khera, who was married in 1976, was driven out of her home a year later by her in-laws who confiscated all her jewellery and other items that she had brought as part of her dowry. She returned to her parents', acquired a degree in law and set up practice as an advocate in Jabalpur. She had a promising career and supportive parents, but the elders of the community urged a reconciliation, and after a gap of eight years, she returned to her husband who gave her a written assurance that she would not be harassed. The ill-treatment was however resumed and soon her father was informed that she had died of extensive burns caused while "heating water on a kerosene stove". The father filed a case in court, pointing out that this could not have been an accident and that the family had a gas-stove in the kitchen and that there was no need to heat water for a bath since it was the height of summer. However, the Khera family is said to be influential and the husband, brother-in-law, mother-in-law and father-in-law are all out on bail. At the age of thirty-one, a woman who could have been an inspiration to other women in distress, burned to death because the community felt that as a married woman her "proper" place was with her husband even though it was known that he had ill-treated her.

This is but one of several hundred cases that have been reported. According to the figures given by the then minister for home affairs in parliament, 1,319 women died during the course of 1986 in dowry related incidents. In 1987, the number went up to 1,786. Several hundred more such incidents are dismissed as suicides, even though it is known that constant harassment over inadequate dowries is the primary cause of young women taking their own lives.

In another case in December '87, twenty-five-year-old Shashikala Ramaswamy of Tiptur, who had a postgraduate degree, died after severe harassment by her doctor-husband and in-laws. She had reportedly asked a shopowner near her home for a loan of twenty rupees to buy herself a bus-ticket to go to her parents' home, on the day she died. The loan was refused. The neighbours were aware of the torture she was undergoing, and yet, there was no one she could turn to in moment of distress.

Dowry deaths and sati burnings are both psychological offshoots of male hegemony, with this difference that one takes place in the privacy of the home and the other not only takes place in the presence and full view of onlookers but also gets glorified as an exalted death. Both have their roots in perceptions that see women as dispensable commodities not deserving of dignity and respect as individuals in their own right.

In the name of religion, a widow is encouraged or forced to die as a sati. In the name of materialism, brides are burnt as dowry deaths. The equation that a woman finds herself in, in both situations, vis-a-vis her environment, is the same.

In this context, mention may be made of a practice known as *koorh* which was outlawed in the Bengal presidency two centuries ago. This was a practice based on the idea of the expendability of the female.

The Bengal Regulation XXI of 1795 describes this custom—men who wished to force a concession of their demands by the authorities sometimes erected a circular enclosure known as *koorh*, and raised a pile of wood inside. Within this enclosure an old woman was also placed, "with a view to sacrificing her by setting fire to the *koorh* on the approach of any government representative to serve the offender with a process".[35] The regulation prohibiting *koorhs* records that these Brahmins "also sometimes put to death with swords, females of their families *or some aged female procured for the occasion*" (italics mine). The regulation further observes that these women were not always unwilling victims; "On the contrary, from the prejudices in which they are brought up, it is supposed that in general they consider it incumbent on them to acquiesce cheerfully in this. . . .either from motives of mistaken honour or of resentment and revenge believing that after death they shall become the tormentors of those who are the occasion of their being sacrificed".

The penalty for offences under this regulation ranged from a fine equal to a year's income, to banishment of the family and capital punishment. Apparently, the victim chosen was invariably a woman, never a man.

Dowry deaths and sati are but two manifestations of the phenomenon of social hostility and rising crimes against women that have marked recent years. According to statistics provided by the home ministry, the number of crimes against women registered in India in 1986 was 42,581, as against 34,470 in 1984. In one year alone (1986) the number of rape cases registered in the country was 7,321; this is believed to be just a fraction of the total number of rapes that take place but do not get reported. In this grim scenario, the onus of proof of innocence is often on the woman, even if she is the victim—the assumption is that she must have "done something to merit such treatment" (this attitude applies equally to battering by the husband, rape, or molestation). And often, even when legal statutes for the protection of the woman exist, the police and other authorities prefer a policy of non-interference on the premise that this is something "between man and wife".

There is also a pervasive belief that a husband has the right to beat his wife—and thanks to the copious infusions of indoctrination right from birth, even women sometimes subscribe to this view. ("I have never thought of my husband as a criminal because I never considered his beating me a crime. How could I? My father always slapped my mother when he was angry. I thought it was just a male habit", said one victim who added that she was confused when she was asked to file a case against him. The woman was worried that going to the police could mean imprisonment for the husband who had "cracked two of her ribs and badly bruised her child" in his frenzy).[36]

The emphasis in newly formed cells in police department for women in distress and in family courts that are supposed to help women receive succour is not on the primacy of her interests but on 'preserving the institution of the family at all costs', in the debatable belief that this would serve society's interests best. Even legal judgements have taken this stand in some cases: This is what a senior judge of the Delhi High Court recently said:

> Introduction of constitutional law in the home is most inappropriate; it is like introducing a bull in a china shop. It will prove to be a ruthless destroyer of the marriage institution and all that it stands for. In the privacy of the home and the married life, neither Article 21 (the right to life and personal liberty) nor Article 14 (equality before the law) has any

place. In a sensitive sphere which is at once most intimate and delicate, the introduction of the cold principles of constitutional law will have the effect of weakening the marriage bond. . . and strike at the very root of the relationship (between man and wife). . . . [37]

The supreme court upheld this view.

Likewise, the law on restitution of conjugal rights was upheld as serving "a social purpose as an aid to the prevention of the break-up of marriage".[38] In other words, the constitutional guarantees of liberty and equality are valid for women only in so far as they are within the patriarchal cultural parameters governing their responses as eternally subservient to the male.

*

Folk-tales, ballads, epics and proverbs all reinforce the image of women as worthy of only a very low place in society:

> The drum, the village fool, the shudra, animals and woman, all these are fit to be beaten.

A Tamil proverb runs, "*Kallaanalum Kanavan, pullaanaalum purushan*" (Even if he is only a piece of stone or a bit of grass, he is still the husband).

A lullaby from Bengal runs:

> Do not cry my beautiful baby
> I shall bring a wife for you
> Her skin will be like gold
> Her lips will be nipples of red
> I shall fill huge drums with *ghee*
> I shall cook very fine rice
> My son will eat his fill
> His wife will lick his empty plate.[39]

Religion, mythology, social conditioning, folklore and even law thus underscores the inferior status of women and trivializes their lives as individuals.

Within the wider issue of the diverse manifestations of adversities confronting women, four specific areas can be identified as having a bearing on the custom of widow immolation—economic factors, religious pressures, education and male chauvinism.

*

Under the Dayabhaga system of inheritance (one of the two standard authorities for Hindus on the division of property among heirs) which was followed in Bengal, a widow was entitled to inherit the property of the deceased husband, overriding the claims of his other relatives. The entire property of a man dying without sons went to his widow who became as much a coparcener as the male. In addition, under Dayabhaga law, a widow could not gift away her property or sell or mortgage it; which meant that she could not distribute it to Brahmins for performing rites to ensure her husband's passage to heaven. The Bengal region recorded the highest number of sati cases, running to over 600 per year, till the abolition of the practice in 1829, and it is possible that in some of the cases, the family of the deceased man had an interest in the removal of the widow, using religion to this end.

While the province of Bengal officially recorded 7,941 sati cases during 1815–28, the adjacent region of upper provinces, where the Mitakshara system of inheritance was in operation, saw a far smaller number of 203 sati cases in the same period. In 1829 alone, the upper provinces recorded forty-three cases while the lower provinces of Bengal recorded 420. Under Mitakshara, the rights of a widow were limited and amounted to no more than a lifetime maintenance. Under the circumstances, the relatives did not stand to gain much through her death.

There is a further aspect of the inheritance issue that standard explanations in terms of Dayabhaga and Mitakshara laws have not taken into account. Even under Mitakshara law, the widow got the husband's property if he happened to be separated from his co-heirs and did not have sons—that is, whatever protection the Mitakshara offered the widow against avaricious instigations to immolate herself held good only as long as the joint family system remained intact. With the erosion of this lifestyle in the face of increasing exposure to the alien ethos of the colonizers, even this dubious protection was perhaps whittled away.

There is also the larger economic motivation which is a modern phenomenon—over the last decade or two, it has been seen that a sati immolation in a village or a town has immediately enriched the community through donations from those who contribute cash towards the glorification of what they consider to be a supernatural occurrence. The erection of a commemorative temple leads to offerings which add up to a tidy sum. Conducting an annual fair in glorification of the event adds to this enrichment by way of stalls, visitors, souvenirs, coconut and incense sales and sundry receipts.

One transport company owner claims to have made "at least a million" by ferrying pilgrims to Jari village where a woman burned to death in 1979. Coconut dealers likewise, are said to have made a lot of money from sales to visitors making the customary offerings at the site of the immolation. In fact, the sharing of the money derived as income from the site is said to have become a matter of dispute between the temple management committee of the village and the woman's in-laws.

Estimates of the money collected as donations in the wake of the Roop Kanwar incident put the amount at an incredible seventy to seventy-five lakh rupees (seven million to seven-and-a-half million rupees). In an adjacent village, the villagers reportedly urged a widow in their midst to burn herself as a sati "because there has not been a sati in our village so far".

Another aspect of the prosperity angle is that several leading industrialists of the country (the Birlas, Modis, Goenkas, Somanis, Jains, Podars) hail from the Shekhawati region of Rajasthan (where sati is recorded more frequently than anywhere else). The Birlas for instance, built an imposing temple in commemoration of a fourteenth century sati at Jhunjhunu, with 350 rooms for the use of visitors and an annual fair that reportedly attracts over 2,00,000 people. Following the Sati Prohibition Act of 1987, the fair was banned in 1988. Yet even with the truncated, 'private' prayers of 1988, the collection was estimated to be 1.57 lakh rupees.

If that is one side of the economic aspect, the other is that of economic distress forcing indigent widows to mount the pyre.

A study of the profiles of widows who burned themselves in Bengal in the years before the Sati Abolition Law was promulgated in 1829, shows that many of the women came from impoverished families; of the forty cases reported from Burdwan in 1822, only three or four of the deceased left any substantial property; the greater proportion were in fact in a state of poverty. Likewise, out of seventy-nine cases of satis in Hooghly, forty-one were in poor and thirteen in middling circumstances. For the year that followed, out of eighty-one cases in the area, fifty-three came from poor or middling circumstances. Clearly, in these cases, economic distress must have played a significant part in their decision to end their lives on the death of the husband, faced as they were with a "double jeopardy"—considered not only inauspicious but also an economic drain on the family's scarce resources. For many widows in the early nineteenth century, the virtue of becoming a sati lay in the deliverance that it promised from a life of certain misery.[40]

A letter written by a judge of the Calcutta Court of Circuit to the Nizamat Adalat (the central law courts) in 1819 observed that sati cases were found "more among the most ignorant and poor", and reiterated this point of economic compulsions. So did Rammohun Roy who pointed out that husbands often failed to provide for the maintenance of their wives. In such cases where the decision to mount the pyre was based on economic pressures, sati was in fact ritual suicide.

In 1819 again, William Chaplin, commissioner of Poona received a communication from the political agent in Dhulia (in Bombay presidency) saying that a widow of Svangheir had sought permission for becoming a sati, and that she had been persuaded to desist from the act by the assurance of a life pension of seven rupees per month. The governor-general had authorized such subsistence grants to widows as a measure towards fighting the practice of immolation. Also relevant in this context is the fact that the Kerala region of South India, where matrilineal traditions were followed has recorded no sati incidents at any time.

The modernizing of India too has contributed in a way to the worsening of the economic conditions of women; where once women had specific tasks assigned to them in production from which they could expect some returns, however small—in agriculture and crafts, for instance—modernization has meant, on the one hand, mechanization of some of the basic processes which used to be performed by women and on the other, the shifting of the technological base of production processes into the hands of the men. In this way, modernization of agriculture and industrial growth or 'rationalization' have themselves widened the economic chasm between the men and the women, and caused what has come to be known as the 'feminization' of poverty, along with greater insecurity and powerlessness.

Economic distress is the reason why hordes of widows flock to places like Varanasi (Benares) and Brindavan even today. These are considered holy places of pilgrimage and there are a number of charitable alms-houses and *dharmashalas* catering to the indigent pilgrim. According to the 1981 census of India, there were 80,000 widows under the age of twenty, out of a total of twenty-three million widows in the country. Of these, over 20,000 destitute widows are estimated to be in Benares (one estimate puts it as high as 60,000). Although, compared to the situation a generation ago, more widows are economically independent today, the lot of a widow is still largely unenviable.

To die in Benares is believed to bring special merit, therefore widows driven out of their homes or with no means of support congregate here in their thousands, to eke out a miserable existence, poorly fed, poorly clad, unwanted, uncared for and unloved. They beg or subsist on the crumbs doled out to them as charity, live in inhuman conditions, and die unlamented. Given no choice, they consider this wretchedness as punishment for the offence of having outlived the men they were married to.

Cities like Benares and Brindavan are said to be "not just dumping grounds for widows but recruiting grounds for brothel keepers". Preyed on by relatives, cowed down by priests and persecuted by society, many widows have been driven to prostitution to keep body and soul together. In contrast, when one upholds the values of chastity and prefers immolation as a sati, she commands admiration for her "courage"—small wonder, then, that some widows not only went to the pyre apparently voluntarily but even insisted on their right to burn with the body of their husbands.

*

An illiterate class is at a disadvantage in sifting facts from the law books or other authoritative texts and arriving at its own conclusions about contentions and even routine matters. Women as a class were traditionally denied access to learning, particularly esoteric knowledge as handed down in the scriptural texts. Whatever the pundits declared to be decreed in the books was accepted unquestioningly as religious injunctions, for in the absence of personal familiarity and knowledge, there could be no questioning or verification of pronouncements. As far as Vedic and Sanskrit learning was concerned, women were illiterate. In terms of general literacy, too, women have always lagged behind the men (and still do) because learning was considered only of secondary importance in their lives—housekeeping, child-care and related skills took precedence. When girls of four and six were given away in marriage (as was common in the nineteenth century and the first few decades of the twentieth) it was no wonder if formal education for most of them terminated at that age and the dropout rate was around eighty per cent. Out of a population of some hundred million at the end of the nineteenth century, of which females formed roughly half, the number of women who could read and write in India was just over 543,000[41] and only 1.8 per cent of girls of schoolgoing age were actually in school. This worked out to one girl for every forty boys in school.

At the time of independence in 1947, only seven per cent of women were literate. A number of socio-economic handicaps were responsible for women lagging behind men in literacy rates. (Girls, for instance, are forced to drop out of school as in other Third World countries, because they are needed to look after younger siblings at home while the mother goes out to work to supplement the family income. Also, education for boys is considered an "investment" and worth the trouble and expense, whereas for a girl it is considered either a luxury or a waste, since she would be going away to another family after marriage and would be lost to the natal family).

The imposition of *purdah* was another reason why girls were not sent out to acquire an education. Backwardness, large-scale illiteracy and blind faith in outmoded beliefs and superstitions form a package that even today reinforces women's vulnerability to male manipulation, bigotry and the sway of obscurantism. As a result, if the community— which was led by men, naturally—decided that sati was decreed and enjoined, the woman was in no position to argue.

Rajasthan has one of the lowest literacy rates in the country today— and this is the region that has seen the largest number of sati incidents in the last 150 years. Only one in ten among the urban women is literate; for the rural areas the figures are even lower. (In contrast, Kerala state boasts the highest literacy rate for women, at 65.7 per cent). While the correlation of education with sati incidents may not be the full explanation, illiteracy does play an important part in the general oppression and marginalization of women.

                                    *

While social indoctrination by itself would not have been such a strong inducement to immolation, in conjunction with religious backing, it certainly makes a potent combination. Those who had access to the scriptural texts and could interpret them were very few in number; their word had to be taken for religious sanction or taboos in codes of conduct.

Given male dominance and the exaltation of the concept of heavenly bliss, merit for the departed soul and absolution of sins not only for the dead man but also for the entire family and for several generations to boot, the belief (wrong as it turns out) that Hindu religion enjoined sati, resulted in many widows 'voluntarily' burning themselves. "The stimulant of religion requires no aid even in the timid female of Bengal who, relying on the promise of regeneration, lays her head on the pyre with the most philosophical composure. . . ."[42] observes Lt.Col. James Tod (political agent to the western Rajput states during the nineteenth century), adding that the notion of metempsychosis which has a strong following in Hindu beliefs, assists in this nexus of religion and indoctrination.

This nexus is illustrated by an incident reported by the acting magistrate of Midnapore (now called Midnapur) in his letter to the governor-general at Fort William in 1797. Describing an immolation by a nine-year-old widow, he said, "Her aunt used her endeavours to dissuade her from the act but the higher order of Brahmins filled her head with such notions of propriety. . . ."[43]

Sati, from this perspective becomes a 'prescribed conduct', with religion shoring up the effects of indoctrination. Fanny Parks in her chronicles during the first half of the nineteenth century, likewise, described another incident of 1828 in which the magistrate tried to prevent an immolation by offering money to the woman but she was adamant and threatened to hang herself in the court. In a bid to dissuade her, an official had her husband's body kept for two days, hoping that hunger would break her resolve (since, by custom, the widow could not touch food or water from the time of the husband's death to the time of the immolation); even so, the woman was firm in her resolve and finally lit the pyre herself and died in it. When the fire caught for the first time, she jumped out but returned stubbornly to it a second time. When the magistrate tried to stop her, she declared that all the women of her husband's family had been satis. "Why should I bring disgrace upon them? I shall go to heaven. . . ."[44]

*

Under patriarchal lifestyles, where male domination denies women access to religious knowledge, education and the means of economic independence, male chauvinism becomes a common dimension in every facet of life. Its emphasis over and above these manifestations has been one of the reasons for the incidence of sati, as it has been in other variants of crimes against women in general.

Commenting on a sati incident in 1931, Mahatma Gandhi traced the genesis of the self-immolation of wives to male chauvinism. "If the wife has to prove her loyalty and undivided devotion to her husband, so has the husband to prove his allegiance and devotion to his wife. Yet, we have never heard of a husband mounting the funeral pyre of his deceased wife. It may therefore be taken for granted that the practice of the widow immolating herself at the death of the husband had its origins in superstitions, ignorance, and blind egotism of man".[45]

Gandhi also referred to Diodorus Siculus, a Sicilian contemporary of Julius Caesar, who stated that the custom of widow burning was devised by some men among the nobility to ensure that the wives did not poison their husbands (if they did, they would have to burn to death too, along with the husbands).

But why would wives want to poison their husbands in the first place? Because of unhappiness in marriage, the explanation goes. But then unhappiness in marriage afflicts the men too; why was there no move by the women to "protect" themselves from poisoning plots by devising similar rites for the men? Clearly, because women were not in a position of authority where they could devise or decree "safeguards" for themselves the way the men supposedly did.

Commenting on how the undeniable element of coercion in sati immolations has been glossed over (as in the argument that turns the premise into one of 'tradition vs. modernity') it has been pointed out that "men's deep-set insecurities about women and their obsession with proving to themselves that their women can have nothing worthwhile, literally not even a life, beyond them, is at the root of the horrible practice of widow immolation".[46]

In a patriarchal pattern where one group has control over the destiny, life and death of another, urging women to give up their lives on the death of the husband becomes part of a logical sequence. Widows endangered family honour; therefore to forestal molestations, or temptations, widows were burnt along with the husbands; if that amounted to penalizing the victim instead of the culprit, there was always justification enough for the chauvinists in the fact that when celestial males like Indra and Krishna were not above an escapade or two, mere ordinary male mortals could be forgiven their weaknesses.

"Since male honour is primarily concerned with the sexual purity and exclusiveness of women within a kinship group, the death of the woman is preferred to loss of patriarchal honour through possible sexual misadventure on her part".[47]

"It is the same all over the world, civilised or uncivilised", observed Fanny Parks, describing her reactions on coming upon a sati memorial—"The laws of England relative to married women and the state of slavery to which those laws degrade them, render the lives of some few in the higher, and of thousands in the lower ranks of life, one perpetual sati or burning of the heart, from which they have no refuge but the grave, or the cap of liberty—the widow's—and either is a sad consolation. It is this passive state of suffering which is most difficult to endure and which it is generally the fate of women to experience. . . ."[48]

Even the law on adultery in India today typifies the concept of woman as one of the "possessions" of the male who marries her. Under Section 497, a man who has sexual intercourse with a woman who is the wife of another man, is liable to imprisonment and fine. (The adulterer is reckoned to have "helped himself" to something that did not belong to him). The woman, even when she is a consenting partner to this adultery, is not liable to punishment; morality is not so much the issue as the fact that the adulterer has violated the sexual rights of the husband over the woman. The supreme court upheld this view in a judgement in 1985. A married woman, in contrast, cannot prosecute a woman who has had intercourse with her husband, because, the wife does not have, in the eyes of the law, rights over her husband which the other woman can be accused of having usurped.

In this kind of environment, any attempt by a woman to reach for independence of any kind—intellectual, physical, economic or social—is invariably seen as a threat. In the West, this took the form of witch-hunting—"a woman with a mind of her own who dared to defy the norms of the period was cast as a witch and burnt at the stake—woman as a witch really meant woman as a threat".[49]

Each one of these factors—education, religion, economic compulsions and male chauvinism—offers an explanation only in part. Nonetheless, if illiteracy is a contributory component, Roop Kanwar certainly was not illiterate, nor was she from an illiterate family. She had finished school and was a city girl; her father-in-law had a master's degree in arts and a bachelor's degree in education and was a teacher in a high school. The village of Deorala itself is not an isolated, backward or secluded place; her husband was a graduate too and was planning to study medicine.

Moreover, many of those who justify sati now as a glorious tradition of Hinduism are not illiterates but respected professors, leaders in their professions and politicians. And even Radhakanta Deb who received a knighthood and was known in the forefront of the pro-sati move opposing Lord Bentinck's law in 1829, was known as a pioneer in women's education and a scholar. Education in the formal sense and condemnation of the practice of sati do not seem to have an automatic correlation.

If educational backwardness was the cause, then there is no reason why Calcutta which was a metropolis with a cosmopolitan culture and a centre of administration, should have seen so many immolations. In fact Calcutta contributed more than half of all sati incidents for the whole of British India during the year before the practice was prohibited by law.

Some of the most staunch sati traditions have been in the well-to-do royal families of Rajasthan. Neither economic causes nor illiteracy and backwardness in the conventional sense could have been a contributory factor. As for religion, the Bengal region was not particularly religious during the time when sati cases were taking place by the hundreds. In fact, in a letter appended to the text of John Poynder's speech at the

court of the proprietors of the East India Company in 1827 pleading for
the abolition of sati, one finds the remark that "In Bengal Hindoos are
far less tenacious of their religious tenets and ceremonies than in almost
any other part of India; they are far less careful respecting caste. . .and
Brahmins are. . .guilty of actions which according to the strictness of
the law. . .would degrade them. . . ."[50]

While individually none of these factors might suffice to explain a
sordid rite like widow burning, in combination they take us closer to an
understanding of why and how, in a culture ostensibly rooted in the
basic tenets of compassion and non-violence, thousands of widows
whose only crime was that they happened to be alive at the time of
their husbands' deaths, came to be burnt to death, with the overt and
covert sanctions of a large section of the community.

4

Crime and Punishment

Name: Boodul. Age: 25. Caste: Chuttry.
Date of burning: 4 August 1822.
Remarks: The woman burnt along with the corpse of her husband. She had only one child, a girl 13 years old, well provided for, and she was not pregnant. The *darogah* and other police officers were present and I myself saw and spoke to her a few hours before the sacrifice. There was no legal impediment to her being burnt. . . .

—Extract from the official records relating to sati, 1822

The practice of burning or burying a widow along with her husband's body was outlawed in British India in 1829. During the preceding quarter century, there had been intermittent appeals to the administration to have the rite prohibited. But the British authorities demurred because they were apprehensive that any attempt to ban the practice could be construed as interference in the religious customs of the Hindus and cause resentment among the community.

Instances of British officials intervening to save widows from a fiery death were recorded even in the closing years of the eighteenth century. M.H. Brooks, the collector of Shahabad, after saving a widow from immolation in 1789, sent a report to the governor-general, Lord Cornwallis, seeking approval for his initiative in preventing a woman from burning to death. The governor-general in his reply declared that the administration did not consider it advisable to authorize him to stop sati immolations in his official capacity; it was, however, suggested that he could use his influence unofficially to dissuade widows from burning. This official response is believed to have influenced other magistrates in restraining themselves from interfering when they came to know of plans for an immolation.

In 1803 William Carey, a British missionary working in Bengal, set about collecting statistics on the number of women who burned to death in sati rites, in order to urge the administration to stop the gruesome practice. According to his estimates, 438 widows had burned to death within a radius of thirty miles around Calcutta in the span of a

year. The following year, he had ten men help him in the task of collecting data from different areas, and passed on his findings to the then
governor-general, Lord Wellesley, who in turn referred the matter to the
supreme court in 1805.

This year was a landmark of sorts, for it saw the first few instances
of official intervention in sati incidents. In February of that year, J.R.
Elphinstone, the collector of Gaya, stopped a twelve-year-old widow
from mounting the pile. In another incident, a girl named Ghoorna was
being taken in a palanquin to the cremation ground for immolation
when the magistrate of Benares forbade her to proceed with the rite. The
girl returned home. In both these cases, the records note, the widows
were "grateful" for having been saved.

In the wake of an attempted immolation by another twelve-year-old
widow, which the magistrate of Bihar stopped, a letter was addressed to
the Nizamat Adalat. As a result of this the members of the council
suggested that sati burnings be banned by law.

The colonial administration was dependent on Hindu pundits for the
interpretation of native customs and jurisprudence; besides, the British
policy was "to allow the most complete toleration in matters of religion to all classes of its native subjects". The official response to the
suggestion that sati should be prohibited was therefore characterized by
indecisiveness and inertia, and more than seven years were to pass
before an official regulation on sati was announced in December 1812.

Under this regulation, a widow was to be permitted to immolate
herself in cases in which it was "countenanced by (her) religion"—that
is, if she was not under sixteen, and if her decision to burn was voluntary and not made under the influence of stupefying drugs, she could
commit sati. A woman who was pregnant was not to be allowed to
burn.

These guidelines were drawn up on the basis of an interpretation of
Sanskrit texts by a pundit named Ghansyam Sarma when the Nizamat
Adalat sought clarification from him on the scriptural position on sati.
Subsequently this regulation was amended to specify that women with
children under the age of three could not become satis unless someone
undertook to guarantee their maintenance. Also, Brahmin women were
forbidden to commit *anumarana*. A police officer was required to be
present at every immolation to ensure that these regulations were not
flouted.

As several commentators on the social scene have pointed out, this
regulation virtually amounted to legalizing sati because an official
presence at the immolations came to be construed as an authorization
for widow burnings. The Nizamat Adalat and the governor-general con-

ceded subsequently that the regulation meant to discourage immolations, in fact "augmented rather than diminished" the practice and that people performed the rite with greater confidence under the impression that the official presence signified endorsement.

From the time the regulation came into force, the annual records maintained by the administration on sati showed an increase in widow burnings—the presidency of Bengal registered 378 cases in 1815, 442 in 1816, 707 in 1817 and 839 in 1818. (There must have been many more that did not get recorded, as Warren Hastings, who was governor-general then, himself conceded in a letter to a friend). Apparently, clothes and wood (for the cremation) used to be sanctioned and this, along with the granting of land similar to the provision for the descendants of sepoys killed in service, amounted to reinforcing the belief that the administration was legitimizing sati.

Among the Jogee tribe, a widow used to be buried alive rather than burnt. Three months after the regulation of 1812 came into effect, an eye-witness recorded that a sixteen-year-old girl was buried alive with her husband's corpse in a grave six feet deep, with her mother and friends present during the interment. This incident took place some twenty miles from Calcutta.

By 1818 the official and legal position on sati was one of considerable confusion. First, the steadily rising figures (378 to 839 in three years) jolted the authorities. Second, several magistrates from different districts, among them those of Hooghly, Jessore and south Concan, connected the annual increase in sati incidents with the introduction of the prohibitory regulation. The magistrate of north Concan in fact refused to promulgate the regulation in his jurisdiction. Likewise, when a proposal was put up during that year for the extension of the regulation to Madras, the governor in council at Fort St. George described the move as "mischievous". The confusion that the regulation brought in its wake was typified by responses like that of the collector of Ahmednagar, Captain H. Pottinger, who gave his consent for an immolation but refused to defray the expenses on clothes for the widow and wood for the pyre, and forbade official supervision of the rite. While he disapproved of widow burning, he also felt that it would have been "a breach of Brahmanical law and custom" if he had stopped her.

A circular order issued in 1817 had made it obligatory for the relations of a widow contemplating immolation to inform the police. Under this order the magistrate could sentence offenders to imprisonment and a fine. However, the penalties applicable for violations of the order were not spelt out but left to the discretion of the individual magistrates.

In two cases reported in 1817, fines of ten rupees were imposed for not giving prior intimation to the authorities about a proposed immolation. In another case, the penalty was five rupees. And in spite of the regulation forbidding the burning of widows with children under the age of three, in at least twenty-four cases that came to be recorded during that year, the mothers of infants had burnt. In Gorakhpur and Ghazipur that year, two widows aged ten and twelve respectively were among those who mounted the pyre. So was a eleven-year-old widow to whom the magistrate of 24 Parganas had given permission for immolation without even ascertaining her age; she had been earlier denied permission by another magistrate. The magistrate's justification for allowing her to burn was that he thought she would otherwise starve herself to death.[1]

The magistrate of Ghazipur, on noticing twenty-three cases listed on a single page of the official records as having taken place "without previous notice" is reported to have remarked that the practice of burning before notice given to the police seemed "very prevalent" in the district.[2] That was as far as official reaction went, in enforcing even the limited prohibition on widow burning.

If the penalties for offenders were not spelt out, neither was the disciplinary action to be taken against the police for not preventing 'illegal' immolations. Policemen were mostly Hindus or Muslims and often allowed immolations because they hesitated to interfere in what they thought was a religious ritual.

In one case, for instance, where a woman was held down on the pyre with bamboo placed across her, and had died after making violent efforts to escape, the *darogah* officially supervising the event "remained aloof" since he was a Muslim and therefore could not get close.[3]

John Poynder in his impassioned speech before the court of the proprietors of the East India Company in 1827, chronicled several such cases in the years following the introduction of the prohibitory regulation. One of these referred to an incident in Faruckabad (now called Farukhabad) where the magistrate reported a sati immolation involving a Brahmin woman who was under-age and whose marriage had not been consummated; she resorted to *anumarana*. On every count, it was an immolation that should have been forbidden, but the Nizamat Adalat considered it "not fit that criminal cognizance be taken" to punish those involved.[4]

In another case where the son had set the pyre alight without obtaining official clearance and presence, the authorities released him on the assurance that he "would not do it again" (that is, not burn his mother again, as Poynder sardonically observed).

In Ghazipur again, an eighteen-year-old widow with a six-day-old child burned to death on her husband's pyre. The heirs, the magistrate recorded, pleaded ignorance and were therefore not penalized.

A typical entry in the official records relating to sati includes, besides the name of the widow, her age, her caste, the name of the deceased husband and the date of burning, also a column marked 'Remarks':

> The *darogah* was present. There was no legal impediment to her burning. Nothing was urged, in conformity with the *shaster*, against the performance of the ceremony. . . .

One entry picked out at random reads:

> Age 14. Bhant caste. Burned at Aurangabad. This sacrifice took place by the ceremony of *sahamarana*. The widow's father was committed for trial before the court of circuit on strong suspicion of encouraging or at least permitting her to burn herself, and was acquitted.

If the official attitude to the regulation was lackadaisical, that of those for whom it was meant matched it in terms of scant regard. The magistrates of Chittoor and Nellore recorded in their remarks in 1819 that even when permission was sought for immolation, often it was clear that the parties had "no intention of abiding by the decision of the authorities" in the event of permission being denied. And under the entries in the official statements on sati the following year, is the eloquent remark made by an officer in charge—"As usual, no notice given". As one British administrator commented subsequently, all that the regulation which he described as "evil" did was "to separate the horrid suicides from the still more horrid murders".[5]

Perhaps not even that—among the cases recorded in 1819, for instance, was one in which a man was reported to have pushed a widow's hand with a bamboo in order to thrust her back into the flaming pyre. The magistrate ruled that he was not guilty of any legal crime since he was merely expediting the ceremony. (Poynder in his chronicles records that the court of Nizamat Adalat observed while commenting on this case that the man should have been punished for "misdemeanour").

When a widow with three children and a fourth on the way burned to death, a fine of twelve rupees was levied on the *darogah* and three rupees on the *jamedar*. (The price of two lives, as Poynder remarked). The difficulties of checking whether a woman was pregnant (or menstruating, since a woman during her period was supposed to be forbidden immolation) must have added to the gross ineffectiveness of the 'legal' position.

Likewise, there was no way of ascertaining whether those who came forward to vouch for the maintenance of the orphans carried out their obligations or not. No penalties were spelt out in the regulation for defaulters.

Where individual officials were keen on preventing sati, they did manage to save some lives—several magistrates recorded, during these years, incidents where the woman was rescued from a fiery death. The magistrate of north Concan was one such official; in Benares, two widows with infants were successfully dissuaded from burning during 1815. The magistrates of Burdwan, Bellary, Cuddapah, Tinneveli (now called Tirunelveli), Trichy (now called Tiruchirapalli), Verdachalam and Madura (now called Madurai), likewise recorded instances where they were able to prevent widow burnings.

Cuddalore was another place where the threat of a fine stopped a planned immolation in 1819. The same year, the magistrate of Guntoor recorded two occasions when a widow's life was saved. In the same year, permission was sought for a sati rite in Masulipatnam. The magistrate of the area sent a reply that while he was not forbidding her immolation, he would immediately arrest those who assisted her in the rite and charge them with being accomplices in murder. That sati did not take place, and "her relations appeared pleased at her having obtained a decent pretext for avoiding the horrid ceremony".[6]

In one case mentioned in the Parliamentary Papers, a widow was asked to first burn her finger. This expedient effectively squashed her intention to mount the pyre. In Ghazipur alone, during a single year, no less than sixteen sati cases were reported to have been prevented by the magistrate.

For that matter, even before the administration took a stand on sati by drawing up the regulation, there were instances of Englishmen rescuing widows from imminent death by fire. Job Charnock, who served as governor of the East India Company towards the end of the seventeenth century, and is known as the founder of Calcutta, erected a memorial to his wife whom he had first seen as she was about to burn on the funeral pyre of her husband. (This incident is believed to have taken place around 1678–79). He had her rescued and subsequently married her, and the couple had three daughters. This memorial is said to be the oldest standing masonry in Calcutta today.

Benjamin Walker, in *Hindu World*, mentions a similar case—in 1705 Nicotao Manucci rescued a woman who was about to perish as a sati; she too subsequently married a European.

One incident that is quoted often is that of Sir Charles Napier (the British general who supervised the annexation of Sind and became its governor) who confronted a sati party and tried to stop the rite. The priests protested, declaring that widow burning was "our custom and it is sanctioned by your laws". The Englishman is said to have retorted, "My nation also has a custom. When men burn women we hang them. Let us all act according to our customs". That widow did not burn.

A particular case of 1823 merits mention because it added to the regulation a specification about the nature of the pile to be constructed. The Parliamentary Papers relating to the East India Company's affairs record that on 27 September of that year, a woman named Radhabyee fled twice from the burning pile. According to the evidence given by one of the two officers of the Tenth Regiment who were eye-witnesses to the event, the first time she ran out of the fire she was only scorched on the legs and would have survived had she not been forced on to the pyre a second time by three men who flung wood at her to keep her there. When she escaped again, this time with "almost every inch of skin on her body burnt" and plunged into the river (cremations were mostly performed on the banks of a river) the men followed her and held her under the water in order to drown her, till the two officers came to her rescue. The woman died in hospital the following day and the three men were charged with murder. The commissioner, who described the incident as "unfortunate", observed that the men had probably acted "under the mistaken notion of the legality of this brutal act and therefore did not merit the full penalty". The court acquitted one of them while the other two, although "found guilty to a certain extent" were released because the pundit whom the court consulted declared that the Shastras specified no punishment for preventing a woman from escaping.[7] Official indignation over this woman's death led to a suggestion in the all-India conference of Brahmin priests a few weeks later, that the pile prepared for concremation should be modified and made lighter with grass in order to allow a woman greater chances of escaping from the fire if she did not wish to burn. (The collector of Poona, however, reported in December of that year that in spite of the 'modified pile', a Brahmin widow had perished. So much for official and 'legal' facilities for ensuring that widows did not burn to death!)

One of the suggestions put forward during the year that followed was to sanction a pension for widows who refrained from burning. This suggestion was turned down. Someone, identified only as a writer in the *Asiatic Observer*, and quoted by Poynder, suggested that same year (1824) that mercantile houses and similar agencies should dismiss those who burnt their mothers, from their employment. Apparently nothing came of it. Various other suggestions were put forward—for instance, the one that even if sati was not officially banned, the relations of the woman and the officiating priest could be prosecuted for homicide. Yet another suggestion came from the magistrate of Dacca that forbade sati for all but those of the pure caste (very few would qualify, he thought; as a result nine out of ten immolations could be prevented).

These pressures on the government to abolish sati by law intensified as the years passed. In the mean time, Rammohun Roy, a wealthy Brahmin intellectual of Bengal, who had been deeply shocked by the immolation of his brother's wife which he is said to have tried to stop, launched a crusade against widow burning and published two pamphlets, one in Bengali and the other in English, pleading for the abolition of sati. The first of these two tracts appeared in 1818 and was titled "Conference between an advocate for and an opponent of the practice of burning widows alive". The second tract followed two years later. Roy argued that sati was nowhere enjoined in the sacred texts and that a rite that caused innocent blood to be spilt was a blot on Hindu society. A man of liberal leanings, Roy had founded newspapers and schools and wrote in Persian, Bengali and English condemning practices like caste discrimination and blind adherence to rituals. He later also founded the Brahmo Samaj which sought to propagate a non-sectarian concept of religion. In 1830 he became one of the first Indians to travel to England, where he died three years later.

At the time of the publication of his two pamphlets on sati, on an average one widow was being burnt to death every day in Calcutta alone. It is said that in subsequent years, Roy often went to the cremation grounds to try and stop widows from perishing on the pyre.

The appearance of his two tracts led to a polarization of views among the Hindus of Bengal, with one faction joining him in condemning the practice and the other insisting that sati had a religious sanction. Rammohun Roy subsequently also published an essay supporting inheritance rights for women. His crusade against sati added to the pressures on the British administration to bring in a law banning the practice.

Among the factors that hastened the introduction of a legal prohibition on sati was the sudden rise in the number of widow burnings in 1825—639 recorded cases in Bengal, compared to 572 the previous year and 328 in 1815. One opinion attributed this increase to a cholera epidemic in which many men perished (as a result, the number of widows burning with them also went up). Even allowing for the effect of the disease, the administration found the figures disquieting. Since 398 out of the 639 cases in the year—or more than half—were in the Calcutta region alone, these statistics flew in the face of the theory entertained in some quarters (and Lord Amherst who was the governor-general before

Lord Bentinck, was among those who subscribed to this theory) that the practice of sati was confined to the rural, backward, illiterate sections of the populace and that the spread of education would automatically lead to the disappearance of the custom. Contributing to the gathering disgruntlement over the government's procrastination in the matter was the reproduction of two articles on the gruesome rite in the *Oriental Herald* published from London which pointed out that on an average two women were burnt to death every day in Bengal. The March issue carried a further exhortation for abolition from an Englishman who identified himself as an old inhabitant of Bengal.

Finally on 8 November 1829, Lord Bentinck, who had taken over as governor-general the year before, issued the official minutes in which he observed that to consent to the consignment "year after year of hundreds of innocent victims to a cruel and untimely end where the power exists of preventing it, is a predicament which no conscience can contemplate without horror . . . every day's delay adds a victim to the dreadful list which might perhaps have been prevented. . . ." Pointing out that the judges of the Nizamat Adalat had unanimously recommended the abolition of sati and that the opinion of the army officers had been ascertained on the question of abolition in order to make sure that there would be no uprising if a law prohibiting sati were to be passed, he submitted the draft of the enactment which came into force as Bengal Regulation XVII on 4 December 1829. Under this law, sati became a cognizable, criminal offence punishable with a fine and/or imprisonment.

The preamble to this proclamation observed that the practice of sati was revolting to the feelings of human nature and was,

> nowhere enjoined by the Hindu religion as an imperative duty. On the contrary, a life of purity and retirement on the part of the widow is more especially and preferably inculcated and by a vast majority of the people throughout India the practice is not kept up nor observed; in some extensive districts it does not exist; in those in which it has been most frequent it is notorious that in many instances acts of atrocity have been perpetrated which have been shocking to the Hindus themselves. . . . The governor general in council, without intending to depart from one of the first and most important principles of the system of British government in India that all classes of the people be secure in the observance of their religious usages, so long as that system can be adhered to without violation of the paramount dictates of justice and humanity, has deemed it right to establish the following rules which are hereby enacted, to be in force from the time of their promulgation throughout the territories immediately subject to the presidency of Fort William.

All zamindars, talukdars or other proprietors of land, all suddar farmers and under-renters of land of every description, all dependent talukdars, all naibs and other local agents, all native officers employed in the collection of the revenue and rents of lands on the part of government, or the court of wards, and all munduls or other headmen of villages were, with this law, declared "especially accountable for the immediate communication to the officers of the nearest police station, of any intended sacrifice" in the form of sati. Any wilful neglect or delay in doing so made one liable to be fined by the magistrate up to 200 rupees or imprisonment which could extend to six months.

All persons convicted of aiding or abetting in the sacrifice of a Hindu widow "whether voluntary or not" were to be deemed guilty of culpable homicide, and the penalty, fine or imprisonment, was to be at the discretion of the court of circuit. The plea that he or she was "desired by the party sacrificed to assist" in the rite was "not acceptable".

The introduction of the law brought Lord Bentinck a "Hindoo Congratulatory address" from the native supporters who included Rammohun Roy; in the effusive style of the time, it began:

> My Lord, with hearts filled with the deepest gratitude and impressed with the utmost reverence, we the undersigned Native inhabitants of Calcutta and its vicinity beg to be permitted to approach your Lordship to offer personally our humble but warmest acknowledgements for the invaluable protection which your Lordship's government has recently afforded to the lives of the Hindu female part of your subjects. . . .
>
> Excessive jealousy of their female connections . . . operating on the breasts of Hindu princes rendered those despots regardless of the common bonds of society and of their incumbent duty as protectors of the weaker sex, in so much that with a view to prevent every possibility of their widows forming subsequent attachments, they availed themselves of their arbitrary powers and under cloak of religion introduced the practice of burning widows alive under the first impressions of sorrow, immediately after the demise of their husbands. . . .

A similar address of thanks, signed by 805 Christians, was also presented the same day, on behalf of that community.

Six months later, the statute was extended to Madras and Bombay presidencies, with modifications in the latter where the offence became murder if the woman was under eighteen.

From the time that the administration began to maintain mandatory records of sati in 1815, till the time Lord Bentinck abolished the practice in 1829, a total of 7,941 widows had burned—not counting those cases that did not come to the notice of the officials—in the province of Bengal alone. Of these, 1,150 incidents had been in the Benares area, and 700 in the Patna region.

The act was promptly challenged by a group of orthodox Hindus, led by men like Radhakanta Deb, a Sanskrit scholar and a champion of education for girls. An appeal was sent to the privy council in London seeking a revocation of the law on the grounds that it amounted to unjustifiable intervention in the religious matters of Hindus. An attorney named Francis Bathie was entrusted with the task of arguing their case against the law in London. A counter-petition was introduced in the House of Lords by Lord Landsdowne urging that the petition against the enactment should be dismissed.

Defending the enactment was the Company's standing counsel, Sergeant Spankie. The hearing which began in June 1932 ended on 12 July 1932, with the dismissal of the petition. Finally, with the signing of a proclamation by William IV, sati came to be prohibited.

The Reformer, a weekly publication, hailed Lord Bentinck's enactment as one of the "noblest triumphs ever achieved in the cause of humanity". The editorial went on to say, "No longer shall legalised murder stalk through the land, blasting the fair forms of those beings whom heaven gave us for our comfort and solace through the pilgrimage of life. . . ."

But it did, continuing to rear its head now and then, with execrable persistence. The practice of keeping an official tally of the number of immolations ceased with the passing of the law banning the rite, but incidents kept cropping up: 1830—a sati in Ratnagiri, and another in Chibotu in Patna; 1831—a sati at Madhurikhand near Agra; 1832—a sati near Gaya; 1833—a sati at Mathura, and so on. Widows not only burned to death but those responsible often went unpunished. In the Madhurikhand incident, three men were awarded sentences of seven years each for violating the law and two others were sentenced to five years' imprisonment. The case however ended with the governor-general awarding a pardon. In 1832, the first case in Bengal came up for trial under the newly enacted Sati Abolition Law. Lord Bentinck again awarded a pardon to the accused.

Although the law prohibited sati in British India in 1829, the native princely states were required to introduce legislation of their own since these states had entered into individual treaties with the British. Jaipur became the first princely state in the former Rajputana (as Rajasthan was then known) region to proclaim a law prohibiting sati according to a gazette notification of 1846. By year end, eleven out of eighteen Rajput states and five others had banned sati.

In the same year, Gwalior state proclaimed that zamindars who failed to give information in time about planned sati immolations would be criminally prosecuted. Under this law, a conviction was recorded six years later in 1852, when the person guilty was sentenced to twelve years' imprisonment, along with forfeiture of property. Mewar too prohibited sati but the law was not very effective and immolation incidents continued to be recorded in 1854, 1860 and 1861..(In the first of these, a eleven-year-old girl had been burned to death). Likewise, in Oudh, the rite was forbidden in 1833 but two incidents were recorded the following year. Sawantwadi and Tanjore (now called Tanjavur) were two states that had sought to prohibit sati before Lord Bentinck's legislation. (Tanjore, however, 'relapsed' subsequently and became one of the 'bad' centres for sati cases). Hyderabad, Alwar and Faridkot followed suit in the later years. In 1846, the raja of Mandi agreed to prohibit sati; twelve women were said to have burned to death along with the ruler of this state, in the years after the British enactment.

In the meantime, following the death of the ruler of Ahmednagar in 1840, the British agent used troops to foil a sati bid and the resulting confrontation led to a decision by the Bombay government to attach any place in the Ahmednagar area where sati took place.

Between the latter half of 1847 and the first half of 1848, several states including Patiala, Kota, Bilaspur, Jhind and Chamba resolved to forbid sati. The state of Nabha fell in line in 1860. Jodhpur, Bikaner and Udaipur all prohibited sati during this period; however, incidents of immolation continued to be recorded.

The year 1846 saw the widow of Sardar Sham Singh burn to death after he was killed at Sobraon; in 1853, the widow of the Waghela chief in Kuri (Gaekwar's district) became a sati.

1859 witnessed sati incidents in Lucknow and Alwar and three years later the funeral of the Thakur of Rewa in Sirohi was the occasion for yet another sati (which resulted in a conviction). The year 1864 recorded a sati by the widow of the son of the Thakur of Begun in Udaipur.

In 1883, the widow of the Thakur of Utarna burned to death in Jaipur; the sons and brothers were sentenced to seven years' rigorous imprisonment while the minor accomplices were awarded a sentence of three years.

The trend continued into the twentieth century too—a sati in Gaya district in Bihar in 1903, another in the Patna district the following year and yet another in a Kanpur district two years thereafter.

In a case that came up before the Allahabad High Court in 1914, it was decided that those who contributed ghee for the immolation thereby becoming abettors in the act were to be declared offenders. The Patna High Court in 1928 likewise, convicted those who had not only induced a widow to enter the pyre but also prevented the police from rescuing her when she tried to save herself by jumping into a river.

Stray cases of widow burning continued to be recorded in the post-independence years too—one at Madhav ka Vas in 1954, another in 1957 (when the wife of Brigadier Jubbar Singh burned on his pyre in a much publicized event). The Rajasthan High Court the following year ruled that members joining in a sati procession were to be considered as abettors.

Two cases were recorded in Shewara in 1960–61; there was one in Surpura and another in Mawda kalan village in 1975 and at least three in 1980 (including one in Jhadli village, one in Nangaur district and one near Barnala), three more in 1983 (two in Bilaspur, one in Madhya Pradesh which the police prevented), yet another in 1984 and one more in 1986 near Jabalpur. All of these got reported in the newspapers but only as small, insignificant items. Although Rajasthan is said to have had nearly thirty sati cases since independence, no one has been convicted in any of them. The sati incident in which Roop Kanwar perished at Deorala on 4 September 1987 also got reported only as a small item in the newspapers at first. But it captured the limelight when women's groups in the state capital demanded action against the offenders. In the wake of the furore over, and publicity in the press, for the incident, the government promulgated on 1 October 1987, the Rajasthan Sati (Prevention) Ordinance under which an attempted sati immolation became punishable with imprisonment ranging from one to five years and a fine of 5,000 to 20,000 rupees. Those abetting directly or indirectly became liable to a death-sentence or life imprisonment along with a fine. Abetment under this ordinance was defined as,

- any inducement to a widow to get her burnt or buried alive along with the body of her deceased husband, or with any object or thing associated with him irrespective of whether she was in a fit state of mind or was labouring under a state of intoxication or stupefaction or other cause impeding the exercise of her free will;
- making her believe that becoming a sati would result in some spiritual benefit to her or her deceased husband or general well-being of the family;
- encouraging her to remain fixed in her resolve and thus instigating her to become sati;
- participating in any procession in connection with sati or intentionally aiding the widow in her decision to commit sati by taking her along with the body of her deceased husband to the cremation ground;
- obstructing or interfering with the police in the discharge of its duties in taking effective steps to prevent the commission of sati;

- preventing or obstructing the widow from saving herself from being burnt or buried alive;
- being present at the site of the immolation or participating in any ceremony connected with it.

Under the ordinance any act that glorified sati became punishable with imprisonment for a period of one to seven years and a fine of five to thirty thousand rupees.

The statute empowered the collector and the district magistrate to demolish temples or structures erected for the glorification of sati and seize any funds or property collected for the purpose of glorifying the act.

Offences under this ordinance were to be tried under a special court set up by the state under a district and sessions judge. This court would be empowered to take cognizance of an offence upon receiving a complaint and without the accused being committed to it for trial. Powers were also granted to the special court to attach the property or funds collected for commemorating a sati, irrespective of whether any punishment had been awarded or not. Under the ordinance, the burden of proof that an offence had not been committed would lie with the accused; the in-laws of the widow would be held suspect till they could prove that they did not coerce, abet or participate in the burning of the woman.

The police officers and village officials who had information about an impending incident of sati or about one that had taken place would have to report it to the nearest police station; failure to do so would invite a penalty in the form of imprisonment up to two years, along with a fine.

Originally the ordinance also provided that temples or other structures constructed for the glorification of sati which were already in existence at the time of the promulgation of the ordinance would not be liable to demolition, nor would the continuation of ceremonies in such temples be affected. However, following a plea by a patron of the National Federation of Indian Women to have this section declared unconstitutional, Justices Lodha and Jain of the Rajasthan High Court struck down, on 1 December 1987, the clause exempting sati structures already in existence.

This ordinance was criticized by those who pointed out that the Criminal Procedure Code and the Police Act already in existence were adequate to prevent and punish those guilty of perpetrating sati. (Under the Police Act of 1861, abetment of suicide is a cognizable offence and the police are authorized to arrest without a warrant). Sections 141 of the Indian Penal Code—IPC (forbidding unlawful assembly with

Crime and Punishment 75

mischievous intent) and 129 of the Criminal Procedure Code (powers to disperse an unlawful assembly) were also already available to deal with situations foreseen under the new ordinance. Besides, under Section 302 of the IPC, even conspiring to murder is punishable; introducing a separate legislation for sati, the critics pointed out, amounted to investing widow immolation with a special status and mystique, instead of treating it as just another activity leading to the loss of life. However, these critics were ignored.

Subsequently the union government also introduced a Commission of Sati (Prevention) Act 1987, under which attempted immolation would be punishable with imprisonment of six months and/or a fine, and abetment of sati in any manner direct or indirect would invite the death penalty or life imprisonment along with a fine.

Abetment under this law included inducements to a woman to get burnt with the body of her husband (or any object associated with him) irrespective of whether she is in a fit state of mind or is labouring under intoxication or other cause impeding the exercise of her free will. As in the earlier Rajasthan ordinance, making a widow believe that the act of sati would result in some spiritual benefit to her or to her deceased husband or relatives or the general well-being of the family would also be construed as abetment. So would participation in any procession in connection with the rite, or being present at the site or preventing a woman from saving herself, or obstructing the police from taking steps to prevent an immolation. Besides conferring on the collector or district magistrate powers to remove temples or other structures glorifying sati and to confiscate funds or property collected for the purpose of glorification, the statute also specified that offenders would be disqualified from inheriting property that (they) would have become entitled to on the death of the person whose death had led to the sati incident.

Those convicted under this law would also be barred from standing for election for a period of five years from the date of release; in addition, using sati as a part of election propaganda was also prohibited. Section 3(B) of clause 19 of this law says,

> the propagation of the practice or commission of sati or its glorification by a candidate or his agent or any other person with the consent of the candidate or his election agent for the furtherance of the prospects of the election of that candidate or for prejudicially affecting the election of a candidate would be an offence.

Women's groups and activists were quick to point out several flaws in the new legislation.

For one thing, a widow saved from a fiery death would be, under this statute, accused and sent to jail instead of receiving sympathy, succour and protection. It also lumped together as abettors those who intoxicated a woman so that she would burn, as well as those who watched the proceedings as bystanders—the former, lawyers pointed out, must be in fact treated as murderers and not merely as abettors.

While the provisions of the act acknowledged the element of pressure or persuasion in a widow's immolation, it still equated sati with suicide; in fact the official approach, according to one opinion, was confused between suicide and murder—the penalty spelt out was for murder, but the act was treated as suicide. (In the Roop Kanwar case, the FIR was recorded under Section 306 referring to abetment, and only after the storm that the media raised was this changed to Section 302 which made it murder). In addition, as in the case of the state ordinance, the promulgation of a special law to deal with sati invested the event with mystique and elevated what should be a murder case to that of a conscientious offender status. "Sati is murder most foul," declared Justice Krishna Iyer, formerly of the Supreme Court, pointing out that the rite was part of a continuum of issues from female foeticide, infanticide and dowry deaths to widow immolation.

Another point is that since the pyre is lit by someone other than the widow herself, it can hardly be classified as suicide under the law.

The act also comes under fire for reversing the burden of proof on to the accused; under criminal law, an accused is believed to be innocent till proved guilty, whereas under the Sati Prevention Act, the family will have to prove that they did not abet or force a burning. One opinion holds that if the new law had been in the form of an amendment in the homicide section of the IPC (to make all sati burnings equal to murder unless otherwise established by the defence) the problem of "women killers getting off lightly for merely abetting suicide would have been solved".[8]

Justice Sujatha Manohar of the Bombay High Court said that sati could not be equated with suicide or euthanasia, because the decision to burn was made when a woman was in shock and under psychological stress.

She also suggested making landowners responsible for communicating immolation attempts to the police (as under Lord Bentinck's law). Lawyers, judges, legal and social activists have all declared that sati is murder, and yet the law has fought shy of acknowledging this.

Although the supreme court ruled that the fair held annually at the Jhunjhunu sati temple in August–September would not be permitted in 1988, it decided in favour of the family trust managing the temple in the matter of continuing the rituals of worship inside the temple and declared that "prosecution against those performing puja within the temple should not be initiated under the Commission of Sati (Prevention) Act". The court made a distinction between "holding an annual fair outside the temple" and "offering puja inside", on the grounds that the former could be a "law and order problem".

Would offering prayers at the temple amount to glorification of sati? Even the supreme court judges said it was difficult to answer that question.[9]

Emboldened by the ruling in this case, in Deorala the Dharma Raksha Samiti went ahead with preparations to mark the first anniversary of Roop Kanwar's immolation, although the law enacted in the wake of that incident was specifically meant to prohibit the glorification of a widow's death on the pyre of her husband. Employing devious strategies, the Deorala observance took the shape of a religious discourse that nonetheless ended up keeping the sati issue in unarticulated prominence. (The *acharya* who delivered the week-long discourse made statements like: "Deorala is sacred ground. You know why" and "I had come to Deorala on September 20 last. You know why. Then, it was an ambition of mine to conduct a discourse in this sacred land").

About 4,000 people attended the session, with women making up half that number. The police arrested forty-six persons for raising slogans glorifying sati and the truck in which they were travelling— belonging to Roop Kanwar's father—was impounded. (A portrait of Roop Kanwar was displayed on the truck, and the discourse itself was conducted a short distance from the *sati sthal* where she burned to death).

Given the loopholes in the government act, some women activists came up with a more comprehensive bill, for the prevention and abolition of crimes perpetrated against women in the name of religion or custom, which would cover not only sati but a wider canvas including polygamy, *purdah*, witch-hunting, the practice of dedicating girls to temples which is prevalent in certain regions (forcing them into a life of ignominy as virtual prostitutes, although they are ostensibly wedded to the deity) and similar aberrations affecting women's lives.

Under this proposed alternate bill, any torture, cruelty, inhuman or degrading treatment of women, would be illegal and punished as such.

The bill recommends life imprisonment and fines for those responsible directly or indirectly for burning or burying a woman alive; those abetting such an act would become liable to a minimum of ten years' imprisonment and a maximum of a life sentence, along with a fine. Being present at a place where such an act is to take place would also constitute abetment. Glorification and promotion of the custom or rite would also be an offence; glorification would include being a member of a trust (or donating to a trust) which has as one of its aims the perpetuation of the memory of a woman killed in the name of religion.

The withdrawal of income tax concessions to those trusts that donate money to projects glorifying sati is another suggestion that has been made.

Any person holding political or public office who organizes support or collects funds for any religious practice or custom related to torture, cruelty, inhuman practice or degrading treatment of women would invite imprisonment and a fine; in addition the offender would be debarred from seeking office for a minimum period of seven years.

The bill also authorizes the collector or district magistrate to impose a collective fine on a community that is found guilty of promoting or staging an act of this kind. Vigilance committees, which would include women, would submit reports to the legislative assembly every six months, on offences recorded. It is difficult to predict whether this bill will ever become law. More pertinently, activists concede that merely passing legislation will not make for change; it is how the law is implemented that determines the extent to which practices like sati can be curbed. It is the will of the government—and of the people—that ultimately decides the effectiveness of attempts to excise offensive accretions from the social fabric.

5

Lamb to the Slaughter

... My husband accompanied the magistrate to see the suttee: about 5,000 people were collected together on the banks of the Ganges. . . After having bathed in the river, the widow lighted a brand, walked round the pile, set it on fire and then mounted cheerfully. . .

As the wind drove the fierce fire upon her, she shook her arms and limbs as if in agony; at length she started up and approached the side to escape. A Hindu, one of the police who had been placed near the pile to see she had fair play and should not be burned by force, raised his sword to strike her, and the poor wretch shrank back into the flames. . . .
—Fanny Parks, *Wanderings of a Pilgrim,* Vol. I

The arguments of those who have opposed the law banning sati are built round certain basic contentions. The first one—and the most strongly articulated defence—is that sati is a purely voluntary act and therefore not to be equated with murder. The other is that, considering the size of the population, it is a minuscule and insignificant number of widows who receive the "inspiration" to go through such an awesome act and because of this, legislation is neither called for nor proper. The third premise is that the law is an infringement of an individual's fundamental right to faith guaranteed under the constitution, and hence objectionable.

While condemning the use of force as wrong, the pro-sati argument insists that sati is "always a voluntary act", one that calls for great courage and therefore worthy of veneration. Bal Singh Rathore, father of Roop Kanwar who burned to death in September 1987, said at a meeting with the press a year later that he was convinced that his daughter had not been coerced into burning and that she had decided quite voluntarily to end her life in this manner in spite of attempts by her aunts and in-laws to dissuade her. (He was not present at the immolation).

The Shankaracharya of Puri who has been vociferously condemning the introduction of legislation prohibiting sati has likewise declared that sati is always voluntary. Vijayaraje Scindia of the royal family of

Gwalior, now a prominent political leader of the Bharatiya Janata Party, has defended sati and maintained that "a voluntary act of self-immolation by a widow in dedication of her husband does not constitute an offence".

A journalist from Bombay is among those who have filed petitions in the supreme court against the Sati (Prevention) Act; he too insists that sati is a voluntary gesture deserving respect. He points to the title under which the papers relating to the East India Company affairs on the subject of sati were published: "Hindu widows and voluntary immolation". The use of the word voluntary, he declares, is significant.

If sati was indeed a voluntary act, what does one make of the several eye-witness descriptions recorded by different persons at different places and at different times, giving graphic details of the use of force?

The French traveller Francois Bernier recorded a sati incident at Lahore when a "twelve-year-old widow, trembling and weeping bitterly", was forced onto the pyre by three or four Brahmins and an old woman, after they had tied her hands and feet. He also witnessed another sati where the widow was "struggling to leave the funeral pyre when the fire increased around her, but was prevented from escaping by the long poles of the diabolical executioners".[1]

This was during the seventeenth century. Another account from the eighteenth century says: "She was fastened on the pile and the fire was kindled but the night was dark and rainy. When the fire began to scorch this poor woman, she contrived to disentangle herself from the dead body, and creeping from under the pile, hid herself among some brushwood. In a little time it was discovered that there was only one body on the pile. The relations immediately took the alarm and searched for the poor wretch; the son soon dragged her forth and insisted that she should throw herself on the pile again or drown or hang herself, (urging) that he should lose his caste (if she did not)".[2]

The son and the others present proceeded to tie her hands and feet and flung her into the fire where she quickly perished, the account adds. This incident occurred near Calcutta.

Thomas Twining, a civil servant of the East India Company at the turn of the nineteenth century, saw a widow burning on his way from Calcutta to Shantipore. She was around twenty years old; seeing her preparing to mount the pyre, he attempted to dissuade her but she was lifted onto the pyre and tied down and two long green bamboo poles were fixed to pegs on either side before the pile was set on fire. (Green bamboo, so that these poles would not burn away quickly and become ineffective in holding the woman down).

The use of force by means of bamboo in this manner was "universal throughout Bengal", says one report.[3]

At Arrah in 1804, the collector's wife and one Mrs Julius rescued a widow when their approach in a coach led to the dispersal of the crowd. The widow told the Englishwomen that her ascent of the pyre was "not voluntary" but the consequence of being terrorized by the Brahmins who had also given her large quantities of opium and *bhang* to stupefy her. Seeing the women's carriage drawing near, the men had been hasty in cutting down the canopy of dry faggots over the bodies, with the result that it fell on to the edge of the pile instead of over her, and she had been saved.[4]

Fanny Parks' chronicles of her stay in India also mention that bamboo levers were often clamped over the whole pile to hold down the woman and the corpse of her husband, and "several persons are employed to keep down the levers while others throw water upon them that the wood may not be scorched".

In the early years of the nineteenth century, Mr Bird, the magistrate of Ghazipur recorded an event in which,

> perceiving the legs (of the widow) hanging out, they beat them with a bamboo for some time in order to break the ligatures which fastened them at the knees, so that the limb could be bent upward and thrust into the fire. . . .[5]

Another eye-witness account from 1826 describes how men with swords took positions at the four corners of the pyre, and after the wood was set alight hacked the cords which supported a canopy of faggots over the pile so that it fell on to the woman and smothered her. The woman's shrieks were heard, in response to which the priests chanted the prayer, "Narayana, Narayana".[6]

In 1835, six years after the British had prohibited sati, five queens in Ahmednagar were dragged to the cremation ground despite their protests, and burnt to death on the pyre of the deceased ruler. The British agent's intervention in this case led to a violent confrontation.

In Gwalior, a widow escaped from the fire; the spectators struck her with sticks and when she hid among the reeds by the riverside, they dragged her out and drowned her. This was in 1860.[7]

How does one reconcile accounts like these with the claim that sati is always voluntary?

"These are exaggerated reports that were deliberately distorted by the British", insists the journalist who filed a writ petition in the highest court of the land today, against the Sati (Prevention) Act. "Not a single woman has been forced to become a sati", he avers. "And even if the woman screamed", he argues, "it is not unnatural. Is it not a fact that sometimes one shrieks in the state of ecstacy? Do not women scream violently at the time of childbirth? Just because they scream at that time, those acts are not shameful", he says. "The real reasons they (the British) banned sati was to wipe out the higher ideal of self-sacrifice and unbelievable courage from the hearts of the Hindus".[8]

But then not all such accounts are from the British days. An officer of the IAS recalls that when he was the collector of Ajmer between 1958 and '60, he received information that a young widow was being compelled to burn herself on the *thervee* (thirteenth day) of her husband's death. Along with the superintendent of police, he drove to the village with two truckloads of armed police and managed to whisk the girl away from a crowd that was strongly fanatical.[9]

A friend of mine who toured the country extensively during the 1950s in connection with her job recalls that she came upon a half-burnt woman who had been lying under a tree for two days on the outskirts of Jaipur, after escaping from the pyre of her husband. Her relations had refused to have anything to do with her since she had disgraced the family by being unable to go through the "ceremony". The woman lay in agony, unable to move, for over forty-eight hours before death mercifully put an end to her suffering.

In the Roop Kanwar incident of 1987, first reports from those believed to have been eye-witnesses claimed that her steps had been unsteady on the way to the cremation ground, and that she had been frothing at the mouth. (Others insisted that she had been smiling and calm, but no one will come forward to corroborate details one way or the other for fear of being charged with participation in an illegal act). She is also said to have shouted "Mummy, papa," and flailed her hands when the flames caught; this, the "voluntary theorists" claim, was a gesture of benediction to the crowd present, and not one of agony.

Incidentally, the journalist who has filed a case in the supreme court against the Sati (Prevention) Act also told me that he is convinced that Roop Kanwar's father was telling the truth (about her voluntary decision to immolate herself) and adds that he had this corroborated by a friend who has experience in lie detection and was present at the meeting with the press where Rathore made the statement.

Arguments about whether a widow walked "voluntarily" to the pyre or was coerced into burning, lose sight of the fact that even when actual physical force is not employed to push or drag a woman to her death, the threat of force brings about a similar result. The French scholar Abbe Dubois, for instance, describing a sati immolation noted that "Brahmins holding lit torches formed a ring around the pyre while a second ring was formed by relatives and friends who held swords and other arms".[10]

It is known that at the Roop Kanwar incident in 1987, sword wielding Rajput youths surrounded her as she set out for the cremation ground, and formed a ring round the pyre.

The picture that these accounts build up is one that is far from the romantic vision of a devoted, love-lorn wife voluntarily snuffing out her life because of unbearable grief over the death of the husband. A letter sent by the Nizamat Adalat to the government in England during the time when the introduction of legal sanctions against sati burnings was being debated, said the same: "The most unwarrantable means are sometimes used to give the appearance of a voluntary act to that which the woman neither intended nor consented to".[11]

To be sure, the records also include accounts where the woman did in fact seem to commit herself to the flames quite voluntarily, without any outward trace of agitation. And some even "voluntarily" returned to the pyre after running away in agony the first time. (One example is the account narrated of a woman by Fanny Parks of an incident at which her husband was present. The widow in this instance refused to be dissuaded by offers of money and threatened to dash her head on the ground if she was refused permission to burn; she ascended the pyre "cheerfully" after lighting it herself. A crowd of 5,000 watched all this. When the fire became fierce, she made a move to escape when a Hindu policeman— whose presence was meant to ensure that no force was used on her as per the prohibitory regulations then in force—pulled out his sword. "She shrank back into the flames, but once again fled into the river. After drinking some water, she decided to ascend the pyre again. . ."[12])

If overt, physical compulsions are absent, there are still the social, psychological and acculturizing forces. A widow's life in society being one of unrelieved abjectness, opprobrium and denial, a glorified immolation offers, at a moment when she is psychologically vulnerable, a very strong and delusive release in the name of salvation. Economic distress at times intensifies this covert pressure (a majority of those who became sati in Bengal in the years prior to Lord Bentinck's law were, according to the figures available, indigent women for whom "the virtue of becoming a sati lay in the deliverence it promised from a life of misery and hardship".[13])

Another "willing" widow who declared that she would dash out her brains against a wall if prevented from burning, abandoned her decision to burn when a friend deputed to dissuade her declared that he would have the pensions for her children annulled so that they would starve.[14]

Indoctrination rather than any grand affection for the husband was more often than not behind a "voluntary" decision to burn to death. And while the official regulations and statutes looked for physical intoxication, no account was—or is—taken of the inducements of psychological intoxication which often generates, upholds and impels a "voluntary" decision in favour of immolation.

"Every girl", observed Francois Bernier more than four hundred years ago, "is taught by the mother that it is virtuous to mingle one's ashes with the husband's, and that no woman of honour will refuse compliance with the established custom".[15] Even if the injunction is not spelt out in quite so many words, the thrust even today is the same—the ultimate exaltation for a virtuous and faithful woman lying only in the context of her husband's existence.

It is in this light, rather than that of exalted love for the husband, that sati incidents involving child-widows (nine and ten-year-olds) must be seen. The Parliamentary Papers of the nineteenth century record several instances of girls of such tender years immolating themselves. At least one instance is on record where the widow was eight years old. These 'widows' had not even begun life with their wedded spouses. If grief and loyalty was what impelled them to a "voluntary decision" of immolation then it was more grief at their own pathetic conditions as widows, and loyalty to the idealized concept of marriage instilled into them by indoctrination, rather than love for the husband in the usual sense.

The relations contributed to this psychological duress with talk of "honour for the family"; they "sing songs telling her that she is going to join her husband and she answers also in singing, that so she will do. . . ."[16]

What lies at the heart of the rite, whether it is "voluntary" or forced, suicide or murder, is the subordination of women and the inauspiciousness of widows; these are the common denominators in both situations, irrespective of whether a woman was a willing martyr or a victim.

A widow, being a sinner, must seek expiation and offer recompense through sacrifice, the indoctrination implies; and the ultimate sacrifice earns veneration, while dereliction is equated with damnation along with imputations of depravity, so that a psychotic dimension gets added to the "voluntary or forced" debate.

A missionary at Cuttack making a plea for the suppression of sati shortly before Lord Bentinck's law was passed, recalled one instance that took place near Serampore. Two wives aged thirteen and sixteen were widowed on the death of a man at Konanagar, and both wished to become satis. The elder, being pregnant, was advised to postpone her immolation till after the confinement, and deeply unhappy over being thus prevented, she resolved to burn herself a month after giving birth, and went to her parents. At the end of the time, however, she flatly refused to burn herself, having considered the matter at leisure, and continued to live on with her parents. So much for "voluntary" immolation!

Imitation had a hand in indoctrination too—if sati was, to begin with, practised among the nobles and the royalty, whatever the nobles did, the citizenry wanted to emulate too.

Rajput women in particular received this kind of indoctrination so that burning oneself came to be looked upon as a "privilege attaching to their blue blood" and consequently, Rajput immolations were, in a sense, "more voluntary". Not just married women but even betrothed girls saw such a gesture as *de rigueur*.

Quoting the magistrate of Trichy who observed that "the act I apprehend is always voluntary, provided a being in a state of stupefaction and delusion can be said to possess the power of volition", Edward Thompson adds that "the worst of all compulsions is that of society pressing with a weight of training and of expectation on those who, as slaves were, are forced down to a sub-personal level".[17]

Such indoctrination in the exaltation of a woman's capacity to exult in a "sub-personal level" (the more effacing, the more meritorious) is so complete that women themselves can show hostility towards those of their sex who do not fit the mould. Women who believe in and look for selfhood, women who seek an identity of their own apart from their roles as their husbands' wives, women who want economic independence and question the sexual status quo, are derided as "strident, unfeminine feminists" (in the same manner that feminists are denigrated in other regions of the world too). On my way from Bombay to Jaipur in August 1988, a fellow passenger on the train, had told me that there was a temple at Deorala which was over two hundred years old. When I arrived in the village and asked my way to "the temple", it was the *sati sthal* (where Roop Kanwar had burned to death) that I was directed to. After I had spent some minutes at the *sati sthal*, one of the women present suggested that I go inside the "temple"; as I went inside the small structure to a side where incense sticks were placed before a large picture of Roop Kanwar, a cluster of curious onlookers followed me and watched my movements. As I was coming out, I heard one of the women remark sharply "She has not come to offer puja to *sati mata*". I had not offered obeisance, nor brought flowers and coconuts as offerings, and that seemed to add a shade of hostility to their responses thereafter.

It is interesting to note that when Rammohun Roy was invited to attend the hearing of the pro-sati petition before the privy council in London in 1832, he accepted the invitation with the remark that he would "not fail to be present there at eleven o'clock to witness personally the scene in which an English gentleman of highly liberal education, professing Christianity, is to pray for the re-establishment of suicide and in many instances actual murder".[18]

The use of the word "suicide" is worth noting, indicating as it does that he saw even the so-called voluntary satis for what they were—suicides motivated by forces other than physical coercion.

"The widow persisted" has been a line of defence right through the years; it came in handy if there were pangs of conscience. So it was before the legal statute of 1829, and so it continues to this day. A woman's fiery immolation is still regarded by the pro-sati faction as a meritorious deed, and this stance itself makes for insidious pressures on a widow and colours her perceptions.

The superintendent of police of the Bengal presidency, W. Ewer once said: "It is generally supposed that a sati takes place with the free will and consent of the widow and that she frequently persists in her intention to burn in spite of the arguments and entreaties of her relatives. But there are many reasons for thinking that such an event as a voluntary sati very rarely occurs; few widows would think of sacrificing themselves unless overpowered by force or persuasion. . ."[19] Even their own persuasion, sometimes, as it seems—on the death of the Rajput potentate Ajit Singh (d. 1724) when several queens set out to burn themselves and the ministers expostulated with them suggesting a life of religious devotion, the chief queen is said to have replied, "Kunti, wife of Pandu, did not follow her lord; she lived to see the greatness of the five brothers, her sons; but were her expectations realised? This life is a vain shadow, this dwelling one of sorrow; let us accompany our lord to that of fire and there close it".[20]

It is the foreseen futility of the life remaining, rather than love of the husband, that persuaded this "voluntary" sati, even though as royal women they would have been materially well off.

Fifty years later, much the same response born of indoctrination was remarked upon by the magistrate of Burdwan, Mr Molony who observed in 1818 that "ninety nine out of a hundred women sacrificed themselves under the influence of the infatuation poured into their ears. . . than from any conviction of their own minds".[21]

And a century-and-a-half further on too, a Rajput woman echoed again the same sentiments of resignation in her comments after the Roop Kanwar sati. Speaking to a social worker who was present at the *sati sthal* on the thirteenth day after the immolation when the *chunari* ceremony was held, a widow named Uma Devi said that sati was not a voluntary act. "I am a widow", she said, "I know what it is to lose one's husband. You go insane. It is cruel to term an act of insanity as an act of voluntary bravery. It is the womenfolk in the household who use a moment of weakness and madness to encourage you to die. . ." The Rajput women sitting around and listening to her conversation with the social worker frowned upon Uma Devi and started a spirited defence of sati. "Our husband is our God, when he is gone it is best to go with him"[22], they said.

How a combination of indoctrination, resignation, economic distress and the threat of familial and social contumely urges a widow to end her life is illustrated by yet another incident that took place in the Sirhat district of Rajasthan in 1980. The man had been bedridden for several months and was a burden on the family which was not well-off. The wife was being "constantly nagged and belittled" by her sister-in-law, and life apparently "held no rewards for the unhappy woman—she must have regarded death as a welcome release". When the husband finally died, the woman dressed herself in her bridal sari, asked the priest to recite from the scriptures and burned along with the corpse. The event has been graphically preserved in photographs.[23]

That such a situation has no correspondence for the male to infuse his "voluntary death" with veneration is one of the cardinal points in the sati issue that the arguments about "voluntary" immolations does not confront. Although sati has been equated with dare-devil voluntary death for the men on the battlefield in defence of the country, the parallel is a spurious one, for a woman is never required to show this fealty during the life of her husband. Her exaltation consists not just in giving up her life, *per se*, but in being of service to him as long as he is alive and considering herself "finished" thereafter; her exaltation is within a matrix limited by a specific, sex-related happening—the husband's death—over which she has no control.

The "voluntary immolation" argument goes on to point out that terminating one's life for a pious purpose is allowed in the Hindu dharma. Saints and monks too, it is pointed out, gave up their lives voluntarily. Here again, the correspondence sought to be shown between sati and such suicides loses sight of the fact that "for a pious purpose" comes to be interpreted for the woman *only in the context* of her husband.

Sati as a voluntary act has also been likened to the Japanese act of hara-kiri, but again, while the circumstances of hara-kiri vary, those of sati are pegged specifically to the death of the husband, which whittles away at the element of self-volition claimed for it.

The lobby fighting the sati prohibition law points out that even Rammohun Roy, who had played a decisive role in the introduction of Lord Bentinck's enactment, was not against voluntary sati. This argument ignores the fact that he went on to add, in the same sentence, that "as a rule, sati was not voluntary but manipulated".

The entire argument about the voluntary nature of sati is raised on the premise that a woman's reaction to her husband's death is—and ought to be—typified by the sentiment: "I loved him so much that I cannot conceive of a life without him". This contention splices two separate statements in a way that has made for an incendiary extension in logic. "I cannot conceive of a life without him" is the reaction that is incontrovertible, but not necessarily for the reasons adduced in the first clause. That too, yes, to be sure, but making it the principal clause has resulted in a blurring of two different perspectives. She cannot conceive of a life without her husband because her life as a widow is expected to be, and will be, a fate often worse than a quick, even if horrible, end. *Ergo*, she "voluntarily" chooses a fiery death—even "cheerfully" insists on it sometimes—abetted in her response by the heady mystique that has come to be associated with sati.

The genesis of this sense of mystique is the original legend of Sati which provides a "divine example of wifely devotion and loyalty"; although she did not immolate herself on her husband's pyre, she reduced herself to ashes in an expression of connubial fealty. With the accretions of metaphoric extensions, the myths have proliferated—that the woman about to become a sati acquires *sat* (divine inspiration), that her body burns to the touch and her eyes redden and glow, and that she works miracles. Accounts of such miracles are numerous but none have unauthenticated claims.

In one such incident, where the police had not been given prior intimation of a planned sati (as required by law), the friends of the widow claimed that before they could inform the authorities the woman had spontaneously broken into flames, so they merely supplied the required wood to feed it. (This explanation was apparently accepted, as no punishment was awarded to those who put up this defence).[24]

When the widow of Ramlal who died in Jarauli village in 1913 burned to death on his pyre and five persons were convicted, their defence was that they feared her curses for she had shown her "chastity" that morning by performing several miracles, among them one of stopping the rain. And when the accused had refused to light the pyre, she had whispered into the ear of the corpse and raised her arm and the pyre had burst into flames.[25]

According to the Shankaracharya of Puri, who says he had a team investigate the Deorala incident of 1987, "When Roop Kanwar was trying to commit sati and her father-in-law tried to save her by holding her back, there was a lightning effect from her body and he was thrown back".[26] (And yet, according to another report, the same father-in-law claimed to have been "unconscious" throughout the event).[27]

The decking up of the woman in her bridal finery as she sets out to immolate herself, the music and pomp, procession, the flowers, sandal-paste and incense, and the reverence with which the ritual dispensation of rice grains or coins from her hands is accepted before she mounts the pyre, are all part of this mystification which helps mask the frightening and ugly aspects of the rite. In fact, the gruesomeness of the event itself lends it mystique—if death as such evokes feelings of awe, mystery and fear, then violent and premeditated death is even more awe-inspiring. (Public hangings, for instance, had large crowds thronging to the spectacle not because everyone who turned up was bloodthirsty but because of people's instinctive fascination for the macabre). In the case of a widow burning, the overtones added to the proceedings in the name of religion via mythology have made for a beguilement that goes looking for miracles and, feeding upon itself, spawns more myths. This is as true today as it was two millennia ago.

Recording an account of a sati in the Punjab in 317 BC Didorus Siculus said: "She was set upon the pyre by her own brother, and was regarded with wonder by the crowd that had run together to the spectacle, and heroically ended her life, the whole force with their arms thrice marching round the pyre before it was kindled".[28]

More than two thousand years later, those who saw Dip Kanwar ("the last distinguished sati in Bikaner") go to her death in 1825 spoke of her "radiant heroism" as long as they lived.[29]

And a century-and-a-half later still, when a sati incident took place in Jhadli village in Rajasthan in 1980, the Inspector General of Police is reported to have said that "religion and the law aside, one will have to admit that it was a courageous act".[30]

This image of sati as a glorious invocation of courage and idealism has spawned myths galore, with details straddling the divide between fact and fiction; and contributing to this corpus of extraordinary lore is the Hindu belief in transmigration and rebirth, and the concept of marriage as an eternal continuum of a bond between a man and a woman.

One such example is the story narrated to Lt. Col. W.H. Sleeman in the 1830s by a college principal and recorded in his chronicles—two

serpents reportedly crawled into the burning pyre when his great grandfather died and, convinced that the reptiles did so because they had been
the wives of the deceased man in a former birth, the family performed
obsequies not just for the four women who burned with him but for six
souls, including the two serpents.[31]

In a village near Deorala, the site where a male and a female cobra
were co-cremated is said to be drawing worshippers in the same way as
Roop Kanwar's *sati sthal*. The *chunari* ceremony performed for this
'sati' reportedly drew 500 persons.

Another story that Sleeman records is that of a banker at whose death
a Lodhee woman claiming to have been his wife in three previous
births decided to immolate herself; her husband was alive and she was
forbidden to burn along with the banker's body but she gathered some
of his ash and burned nonetheless, with her husband himself applying
the torch to her pyre. A memorial is said to have been erected to her at
Khittolee and perhaps still exists.

It is often claimed that the family or friends could not dissuade a
widow from burning because she threatened to pronounce a curse on
those who prevented her from carrying out her "divinely ordained" act.
A sati's curses are greatly feared because they are supposed to be pre-
monitory, and belief in this aspect of the sati mystique has been
responsible for several women not being saved from a fiery death. The
lore on curses is as plentiful as the other myths—in 1845, Jawahir
Singh's widow is said to have predicted the overthrow of the Khalsa,
which came about shortly thereafter. A Rajput woman whose husband
had died during a spring hunt had pronounced a curse that all future
spring hunt expeditions by the two families would end in death; and for
four generations, this dire prophesy is said to have come true.[32]

Likewise, another woman who mounted the pyre in 1813 predicted
some calamitous event "in four hours". Reportedly there was a great fire
in the city at the specified hour.[33]

One Rajput family which had incurred the wrath of a sati remained
childless for "fifteen generations", claims another story. (One won-
ders—if a couple had no progeny, where is the question of fifteen
generations?)

One story about a sati's curses relates to the imprecation by two
satis in Cutch that whoever cultivated a field in Murlah would come to
grief. Generations later, James Tod records, the land still lay sterile
adding "such is the implicit reverence for the injunctions of a woman at
this moment of aweful inspiration when about to take leave of this
world".

A sati gets deified the moment she resolves to burn herself and even before she mounts the pyre. "All the relatives and friends bring her, one a letter, another a piece of cloth, this one flowers, that one pieces of silver or copper, asking her to give this from me to my mother, or to my brother or whoever the dead person may be whom they have most loved while alive. . . ." And all the relatives and friends "congratulate her beforehand on the good fortune she is about to acquire in the other world and the glory which all the members of the caste derive from her noble resolution. . ."[34]

In a recent publication, *Fruitful Journeys—The ways of Rajasthani Pilgrims* by Ann Grodzins Gold, there is a mention of nine sati memorials in Ghatiyali village, south of Jaipur. The author records that satis are considered "posthumous wielders of power" because they represent exceptional self-sacrificial deaths like those of the warrior *jhujharjis* (souls of those who died an untimely death). It is therefore believed that veneration of a sati can bestow all kinds of boons.

At Deorala, the myths woven around Roop Kanwar's death include stories of sick persons getting miraculously cured by a visit to the *sati sthal*. The bits of details that surfaced in the media reports, about her "piety" even as a child and her preference for idols rather than dolls, and her frequent visits to the sati temple so that she was "inspired", stories about how she whispered in her husband's ear to seek his permission (for her immolation) and how he had come alive for a moment to grant it, were all part of the interleaving of fact and fiction that has always gone into the making of the sati mystique. (Other reports, for instance, discount the pious girl theory and say she was a fun-loving girl who wore modern clothes and painted her nails bright red).

For the first time, one report claimed, she had removed the *ghunghat* (veil) in front of her in-laws while declaring her intention of becoming a sati; and for the first time, another said, she pronounced the name of her husband (which wives brought up in a conservative tradition would not normally do). There is no way of confirming whether these details were fabrications or had any factual basis but they spotlight not so much on a supranatural take-over of the widow as the interpretation of gestures like removing the veil or pronouncing the name of the husband as supranormal impulses worthy of wonder. A woman removing her veil in front of her in-laws in a conservative family would probably be rebuked for being disrespectful; the same gesture in a different context becomes part of a reaction of exaltation because of the aura around such a death?

A few months after Roop Kanwar's death, I was at Deorala village where the immolation took place. As I approached the *sati sthal* and came upon the clearing with the fenced off cremation platform in the middle, an eerie, high-pitched wailing assailed my ears. There were some forty men and women standing around or moving about in the clearing but there was no other sound in the hushed mid-morning air except this loud, unnerving lament.

It came from an elderly, frail looking woman, middle class judging from her clothes; like almost every woman present there, she too had her sari *pallu* drawn over her head in the traditional style. She was sitting on the ground in front of the enclosure and crying and talking by turns, as if she were addressing a plea to someone.

I had thought at first that she was perhaps someone from Roop Kanwar's family mourning the girl's death, but it turned out that this was a visitor seeking the *sati mata's* intervention in ridding herself of the spell of black magic that she seemed to be convinced some evil antagonist had cast on her family. After a while she got to her feet and, assisted by two men who supported her one on either side, circled the *sthal* once, raising a loud supplication all the time, addressed to the deified *sati mata* who was, in her reckoning, capable of granting all kinds of favours and boons.

Had Roop Kanwar perished in a fire some place other than the pyre of her husband, she would not have been deified and no supramundane powers would have been attributed to her, however virtuous and devoted she might have been as a wife. This mystification of the death of a woman along with the corpse of her husband has a great deal to do with the persistence of the custom, its fascination and impassioned defence. Like the clouds of coloured *gulal* powder flung by the bystanders at an immolation that obscure the sight of her dreadful death by fire, the layers of mystique that sati has been clothed in also veil the natural feelings of horror and moral opprobrium normally associated with violent death.

Roop Kanwar's father had said in an interview that he was convinced that his daughter walked voluntarily to her death. Could they not have stopped her physically? I put this question to the journalist who had been present along with the father when he made the statement (he is the one who has filed a writ in the supreme court against the Sati Prevention Act). No, the journalist insisted, they could not have restrained her for fear of being cursed by her. (It is because of the belief that a sati's curses will prove prophetic that the funeral party always raises a clangorous din as she ascends the pyre, to drown her words). I asked the journalist if it was not irrational to let the fear of a curse get the better of one's compassion and concern over the brutal burning alive of a woman, and he declared that it was perfectly understandable that one could be afraid of curses. "If I have a fear of lightning and wish to protect myself by staying indoors, no one can force me to get out in the storm saying that my fear is irrational", he argued. (This journalist, incidentally, claims that from the time he began to write in praise of sati, he has had an unexpected run of good fortune. He also claims that when the sati ordinance came up for arguments in court, the lawyer who was to plead in favour of the prohibitory statute was suddenly taken ill for two weeks just as the case was coming up).

Even the Shankaracharya of Puri has said that "ever since this anti-sati law was enacted, nature has been revolting. Today, when we should be feeling the heat of summer, it is cold. The monsoons bring no rain. And untimely rainfall has destroyed crops ready for harvest. All because sati has been insulted".[35]

It was because of Roop Kanwar's sati that Rajasthan had good rains in 1988 after a long spell of drought, the pro-sati faction claimed!

A sati is said to work miracles before, during and after her immolation. Even the *chunari* was supposed to rise up and disappear into the heavens during the thirteenth day ceremony, according to the myths about sati. No such miracle, however, took place, as one witness regretfully conceded. Roop Kanwar's parents have said that the message about the planned immolation did not reach them in time at Jaipur ninety minutes away "because the vehicle bringing the message broke down" and this breakdown was interpreted as divine intervention, to ensure that the parents did not try to prevent the burning. (In actual fact, another vehicle had had a breakdown).

When Francis Bathie, the lawyer entrusted with pleading the case for annulment of the Sati Abolition Law before the privy council set sail for England, in 1830, he is said to have been shipwrecked. This was interpreted as "retribution for undertaking a mission for the continuance of widow burning", by one group, while Bathie himself is said to have believed that the fact that he survived the shipwreck proved the legitimacy of his mission!

One of the objections that women's groups have raised against the Sati (Prevention) Act of 1987 is that that it fails to steer clear of this mystification of sati. By adding the clause in its wording "Whereas sati or the burning or burying alive of widows or women is revolting to the feelings of human nature and *is nowhere enjoined by any of the religions of India as an imperative duty*", (italics mine) the rite acquires a separate significance that distinguishes it from other kinds of murder or suicide. The death of a widow in a secular, constitutional light must be seen for what it is—the death of a human being. Treating sati on par with the existing legal position on murder or suicide would have facilitated its deterrence.

The brainwashing of a widow about the supreme felicity awaiting her in heaven is one aspect of the mystificaton which has contributed in no small measure to the "voluntary" decision of many a widow to end her life. "Dying with her husband, she sanctifies maternal and paternal ancestry of her husband's family too", she is made to believe.

A conversation that Sleeman recorded with a "native gentleman" of Jubbulpore (now called Jabalpur) is worth recalling here. This worthy said, "The knowledge that they cannot unite themselves to a second husband without degradation from caste, tends strongly to secure their fidelity to the first, sir. Besides, if all widows were permitted to marry again, what distinction would remain between us and the people of lower caste? We should all soon sink to a level with a lowest!" "And so you are content to keep your caste at the expense of the poor widows?" Sleeman asked him. "No", the gentleman replied, "They are themselves as proud of the distinction as their husbands are, therefore they burn, to become reunited with the husbands in paradise, to escape the troubles of this life, temptations and suspicion".

His answer exemplifies all the extraneous pressures that are brought to bear on a widow, in the name of a religious custom—the trivialization of her life in favour of "retaining caste", the sexual chauvinism ensuring her "fidelity" through death, and the admission of "escape from the troubles of this life".

The mystique of heavenly bliss is thus both derived—and offers an escape—from a widow's vulnerability and weaknesses, both real and attributed. This gentleman, incidentally, was a Rajput and Rajputs are among the most staunch believers in the myth of sati.

If celestial felicity is the allurement for the woman, those lending her moral support are not left out of the reckoning either. As a woman mounts the pyre, "the bystanders throw on butter and wood: for this they are taught that they acquire merit exceeding ten million-fold the merit of an *ashwamedha* or other great sacrifice. Even those who join the procession from the house of the deceased to the funeral pile, for every step, one is rewarded as for an *ashwamedha*".[36]

And those who could not be present and share in the bonuses of the hereafter could nevertheless rake in some of the rewards through objects connected with sati which became invested with magical properties. Thus "Mothers collected the cowries strewn by the suttee as she walked round the pile before she fired it and hung them round the necks of their sick children as a cure for disease".[37]

Likewise, the bamboo poles used to hold a widow down on the pyre were "sometimes fashioned into bows and arrows and incantations recited over it. The arrow would then be shot into an image of some enemy whereupon that enemy, it was believed, would be immediately seized with chest pain".[38]

In Calcutta, a widow set herself on fire inside the house in 1911, and there was a rush of hysterical women to the place to pick up relics.[39]

In another case, a woman put on her bridal finery and burned herself at home in Tinneveli some years earlier; if unbearable grief at the death of her husband was the sole reason, why the bridal finery? Because this kind of female immolation has been surrounded with a numinous mystique—a woman setting out to perform the sati rite is always decked out in what one pro-sati proponent describes as "*soubhagyalankar*" or the auspicious symbols of conjugal life that are decreed for women: henna or vermilion (both forbidden to widows), the *bindi* or red mark on the forehead, turmeric (all considered auspicious and prohibited for a widow) and flowers (likewise taboo for widows). This proponent who is the head of a research institute, and organized a "tutorial on sati" in January 1989 to expatiate upon the great Hindu tradition that sati forms part of, argues that describing sati as "widow burning" is a "monstrous insult to her great sacrifice" because the sati is not a widow. "The basic conception in sati," he declares, "is linked with the Hindu view of marriage as a religious sacrament postulating a permanent union as husband and wife not only in this life but in all previous births and in all births to come".[40] This mystification of widow burning (to quibble over semantics is to obscure the incontrovertible fact that when the husband is dead, a woman is by definition a widow) offers no explanation why, under this concept of everlasting conjugal union, a husband whose wife has died does not exalt himself by following her into the hereafter to perpetuate their bliss in togetherness.

So, back we are again, with the premise of one set of values, codes and morals and their manifestations for women, and a different one for the men.

That this champion of the 'burning of married women' is a medical practitioner is an irony that seems entirely lost on the proponent himself.

Given this kind of pervasive mystification of the burning of a widow, the controversy over "voluntary or forced" immolation assumes an additional dimension of covert inveiglement—if in Bengal it was physical force and intoxication, in Rajasthan it was a conspiracy of the spirit through mystique and myth—what Edward Thompson called psychological intoxication. The impalpable weight of this mystique can be just as crushing as the weight of the logs and coconuts heaped on her on the pyre. While regulations and statutes take care of the latter, the former and more insidious burden remains. Part of the mystique is the belief that once a woman has set out to immolate herself, if she changes her mind it would bring bad luck; fear of this "bad luck" was the reason for several incidents in which the woman fleeing from the fire was physically forced back into the flames. In this heady mix of mystique and menace, the fact of the loss of life which is central to the occasion apparently gets completely eclipsed by delirious other-worldly excitement.

That this kind of burden in the shape of mystique born of indoctrination is still as strong as ever is exemplified by a comment that one widow made in the wake of the Roop Kanwar sati. "It is because some widows do not observe all the penances prescribed for them that the rains fail these days", she said. If a woman brave enough to burn to death is deified, lesser beings living on as widows, by extension, become contemptible—even in their own guilty estimations, such is the seduction of the sati mystique.

The concept of *soubhagya* itself is part of a mystique that has no parallel for the male—a woman whose husband is not alive is not a *soubhagyavati* however exalted her personal capabilities. Denied greatness or merit in other ways, a woman's sole chance of exaltation and praise lay in a fiery death—and this is the crux.

There are, however, a couple of sati incidents where the mystique served to rescue the woman. Near Benares, a woman had been goaded by her family into a decision to burn a year after her husband's death; she ascended the pyre with some relic of the husband's, but sought refuge in a river when the flames became unbearable, and was picked up by a police boat downstream. "The whole city was in an uproar" because of the rescue of a Brahmin widow and thousands of angry citizens surrounded the magistrate's house. Her father was in the crowd, demanding that the official hand over the woman since the father could not support her and it was better for her to burn. When the magistrate's remonstrations were of no avail, he hit upon the expedient of pointing out that since the sacred river had rejected her and not drowned her although she could not swim, it meant that divine providence had decreed that she should not sacrifice herself. The crowd dispersed and the father took her back. This was in 1816.

More recently, in March 1985, the deputy superintendent of police came upon preparations for a sati at Devipura in the presence of some 20,000 spectators. He declared that if she was a real sati, the pyre would break into flames on its own, and therefore forbade the relatives to apply the torch. An hour later there was still no miraculous flame, and the immolation was prevented. (In consequence, the story goes, the officer soon lost his son. This has been denied by others and shown to be a fabrication).

Some incidents do, indeed seem to surpass understanding in terms of mystique and myth. A former officer of the administrative cadre records a case during the 1950s in Rajasthan in which a woman from the village of Chittorgarh came to Ajmer claiming that she had become a sati there in her previous birth. No memorial stone could be located in the area she indicated, but a piece of stone that was being used by a washerman as a scrubbing block turned out to be a sati memorial.

There are also cases where ostensibly no valid explanations are available for the way a widow gives up her life. I was told about two such incidents that occurred, one in Benares some sixty years ago (when my informant was a girl of ten) and the other in Kothari village (in the U.P. state). In the former, the widow had wished to end her life with her husband's corpse but was forcibly prevented by her family who locked her in a room while they went to the cremation ground to burn her husband's body. When they returned, she was found dead inside the room with no evidence of violence or poison. In the other incident, a woman named Savitri had gone to her natal village where she suddenly dreamt one night that her husband had been bitten by a snake and died. She asked her brother to prepare a *chunari*, applied henna on her hand to leave an imprint on the lintel, and borrowed five rupees to travel back to the husband's place where it was found that he had indeed just died of a snake bite. She died on his pyre. These incidents may defy explanation and indicate the possibility of responses beyond the parameters of the rational; however, it is unfortunate that they are used to coerce and brainwash other victims, who might otherwise have wished to live, to become satis.

*

In the wake of the Roop Kanwar sati, a monk of the Ramakrishna Mutt of Allahabad who condemned sati was prompted to add: "What one has to admire—whether the practice itself is right or wrong—is the tremendous courage displayed by these noble ladies who cared more for their cherished ideal than for their lives. Honour and chastity were everything for them and life was like a straw when compared to these".[41]

This kind of exaltation of a woman's sacrifice has its roots in "men's obsession with proving to themselves that their women can have nothing worthwhile, literally not even a life, beyond them. . . ."[42]

And it is precisely this praise and exaltation of what is seen as a meritorious act that lends support to indoctrination through precept. "Can one not appreciate at least the courage to die," Gandhiji asked himself in the context of a sati incident in the 1930s; and his reply was "No, in all conscience. Have we not seen even evildoers display this sort of courage? Yet no one has ever thought of complimenting them on it. Why should I take upon me the sin of even unconsciously leading astray some ignorant sister by my injudicious praise of suicide? Satihood is the acme of purity. This purity cannot be attained or realised by dying".[43]

A measure of the consummate influence of the mystique of sati on the psyche is the jargon of the pro-sati argument—"Every widow is not required to become a sati by burning. If she is unwilling to burn herself, she should lead the pure life of a *brahmacharini* (celibate). She should not become a sati. If a *weak woman wants* to burn herself, her husband's brother should stop her. He should pick her up from the pyre and take her home. If he cannot stop her, her husband's disciple should carry her away. But the weak should not be allowed to commit sati. . . ."[44] says the Shankaracharya of Puri.

On the face of it, this argument seems to validate the existence of choice for a widow; but the way it is phrased, one who does not burn becomes by inference, "weak" and found "wanting". More insidiously, even a weak woman is expected to want to burn herself, even if she is permitted to be stopped by her brother-in-law. On the one hand, the theory justifies sati as a heroic gesture by women possessed of extraordinary courage; on the other it talks about "weak women not being allowed" to burn, implying that even a weak woman should want to try to burn herself. A strong woman's strength lies not in asserting herself but in self-sacrifice, in not just giving, but giving up. Draupadi of the *Mahabharata* was a high-spirited woman, but she is not held up as an ideal for Indian womanhood. It is Sita who goes through a trial by fire and a second banishment whose endurance and loyalty is held up to women as a model for all times.

The elaborate directions and ritualistic etiquette is also part of the mystification of sati—who should try to save her first, and who should make the attempt next, what expiation is necessary and sufficient if she is in the prohibited category and still wants to burn.

Ananda Coomaraswamy in a much-quoted passage has said, "This last proof of the perfect unity of body and soul, this devotion beyond the grave, has been chosen by many of our western critics as our reproach; we differ from them in thinking of our suttee not with pity, but with understanding, respect and love. So far from being ashamed of our suttee, we take pride in them; that is even true of the most progressive among us".[45]

However, he went on to add that it was "true that in aristocratic circles sati became to some degree a social convention, and *pressure was put on unwilling individuals* . . . and from this point of view we cannot but be glad that it was prohibited by law in 1829" (italics mine).

He thus conceded that use of force was wrong, but the question of force is complicated when seen in the broader perspective of indoctrination born of mystique.

One argument puts it this way: "Because of westernised ideas we call womenfolk as (the) weaker sex. But according to Hindu tradition and mythology, our women were called 'Shakti'. No wonder they ascended the funeral pyre deliberately and steadily into the centre of the flames, sat down (and) leaned back in the midst of it as if reposing on a couch".[46]

"The martyrdom of Queen Padmini never ceases to inspire us", another journalist has said. Inspire us to what? In similar vein, an American has said, "Sati is the resort of a new widow who, unable to imagine living without her husband, follows him to the other world, a sort of ultimate expression of faith and courage of a Hindu wife. The Hindu villager knows this instinctively and acts with deep respect and honour for satis like Roop Kanwar, while the middle class Indian, infected by western culture and frightened by what the white man might think of him, rejects this native wisdom".[47]

If that betrays the seduction of mystique, even the rebuttal, by another American does no less: "It is one thing to have had such practices in the past. Indian culture is unimaginably rich and needs no apologists. We should not expect the people of a thousand or two thousand years ago to have modern views. But surely it is wrong to tolerate such practices in the modern world?"[48]

This reasoning equates sati (barbaric) with tradition, and anti-sati (compassionate) with modern, so that the debate is made out to be one of tradition vs. modernity, instead of one about the morality of violent death, whether traditional or modern. Likewise, another argument holds that "sati had a legitimate place in the cultural milieu in which it had its origin" and that "sati in the mythical past was a rare, fearsome but moving ritual that symbolised the reaffirmation of the purity, self-sacrifice, power and dignity of woman".[49]

This kind of description, with words like "moving", "heroic" and "inspired", has constantly added to the mystification of the rite of widow burning.

"She sat on the pyre like a queen on a throne, and her face was radiant as she stepped forth to join her lord" is one example of the kind of lyrical hype that the media has added to the mystification of the event

> The queen made the sixteen *shringars*. Her hair was flowing like liberated snakes. The strings of pearls worn round the neck knock each other. Carrying a garland of flowers in her hands, the queen walked with a graceful gait and the multitudes cried, '*Khama, khama*' (well done) in deep reverence. Sati Musi embraced death with the dead body of the Ravraja. The sun, with a feeling of affinity and esteem, stopped his chariot to view the sati.[50]

is another example of this. Even those who insist they find sati abhorrent concede its exaltedness, "under spiritual influence". (The Vishwa Hindu Parishad, for instance, is opposed to sati; however, "under spiritual influence it cannot be prevented by society" its president has declared).

This spiritual influence that lends sati its credence makes for pedantry of the kind that seeks approval for the event (*ghatana*) but condemns it as an institution (*pratha*) or practice. While in theory, it makes a distinction between the inspired impulse on the one hand and the premeditated enjoinment on the other, it risks forgetting the boundaries of those areas of reasoned response which help retain within sight the central fact—that a live woman, who has committed no crime meriting the ultimate punishment, dies in the act. What has happened is that *ghatana* has been appropriated as a stepping stone in establishing a *pratha*, and this is at the core of the sati issue today.

This partly explains the kind of semantics that has made possible "discussions" of whether the woman should mount the pyre "after it has been lit" or before. (She is supposed to jump "into the pyre" which is *already* alight, since otherwise, her son who applies the torch will be guilty of killing a Brahmin!) Semantics was again involved when the pundit who interpreted the scriptures for the British law courts used the phrase "It is the *inheritance* of every Hindu woman" (italics mine)— inheritance can mean a right as well as something that (willy nilly) devolves on one. The ambiguity was fraught with mischief.

Radhakanta Deb likewise argued, in his defence of sati during the plea that was sent to the privy council after Lord Bentinck's law, that a woman "being wedded to the soul of the husband", could not be widowed.

Apart from all else, the basic etymological confusion between the Sanskrit word sati, the name of the Hindu goddess, and the practice of widow immolation created a nexus that could be—and was—usurped for specific ends—those of promoting a particular social attitude to women at particular times.

And this has made for the muddled logic in the responses of those who eulogize sati—the Shankaracharya of Puri reiterates that Hinduism seeks the well-being of all living creatures so that "a dog will not even bite any one, nor a snake or scorpion—our religion is such that the lion and the goat will coexist peacefully. . . ."[51] But not, apparently, a widow and her fellow citizens in her community! This, then, is the crux—the vulnerability that social, religious and economic pressures thrust on a widow. Seen from this perspective and setting aside the few freak cases that fall beyond the pale of rational explanations, there is no such thing as a voluntary sati.

A classic instance of how circumstantial coercions in combination can make for what on the face of it seems like a voluntary immolation is the account of a sati incident recorded by Sleeman. In September 1829, a sixty-five-year-old widow in Jubbulpore district sought permission to burn herself on her husband's pyre. Sleeman refused, but she remained adamantly by the water's edge without food or water for four days till he finally felt obliged to retract his stand. Had she lived, he says, she would surely have been cherished by her family; and yet, a combination of factors resulted in her decision to burn—there was indoctrination, for one. Her mother-in-law and aunts had all become satis in the family and, looking at the temples erected for them, she had decided, years earlier, that she would become a sati too. Besides, she had, at sixty-five and as a widow, very little to look forward to by way of a future, even if her family had been supportive.

A study of the socio-economic profiles of the women who resorted to sati in Bengal during the fourteen years preceding the introduction of the prohibitory law similarly shows that a majority were not young women with bleak and long years of widowhood stretching before them but women forty and over (the life expectancy at that time was around thirty-two). Most of these women were of poor means (unlike Rajput queens) but they saw no point in continuing to live. This idea of worthlessness that acted as a decoy to their deaths finds no correspondence for the male, although clearly there must have also been males in similar circumstances.

It is in recognition of the power of indoctrination and precept that the law on sati promulgated in 1987 includes a ban on all kinds of glorification of the rite and forbids the erection of temples or other memorials in honour of women who became satis. Under this enactment, all speeches or actions eulogizing sati become offences liable to punishment; congregations for the purpose of glorifying sati are also forbidden. This has been challenged on the grounds that such a law contravenes the freedoms guaranteed to an individual under the fundamental rights of the constitution. One of those who subscribe to this theory that the law infringes upon citizens' rights to faith, free speech and action, argues that if he believes in the power of sati he should be free to glorify it.

But would that not lead to indoctrination and, through indoctrination, to a perpetuation of the rite? No, he insists. Sati immolations are not the result of indoctrination.

The Rani Sati temple at Jhunjhunu, he argues, draws tens of thousands of visitors throughout the year and yet these multitudes of women have not gone on to burn themselves as satis—and therefore glorification cannot cause indoctrination. And prohibiting it amounts to unconstitutional curtailment of one's rights. In support of this stance, he offers also an analogy—"Just because you erect statues of Gandhiji, you cannot guarantee that Gandhi's ideals will be spread among the populace. In the same manner, the mere erection of sati temples will not mean encouraging sati because sati is a rare, inspired impulse that possesses only a very few".

Such a discounting of the indoctrination theory can be demolished with a counter-analogy—if one person gets knocked down in a traffic accident every week at a particular spot where 10,000 persons pass by, it would hardly be admissible to argue that preventive action is unnecessary in view of the small number of victims among those passing by.

A petition filed in the supreme court on behalf of the Shankaracharya of Puri, claims that the law violates Article 19 of the constitution which guarantees freedom of speech and expression, and the right to assemble peacefully. The prohibitory enactment is, therefore, in his view, "an insult to democracy" and "against religion, civilisation, culture, ethics and morality".[52] "Every Hindu" he has urged, "should die opposing the law". (The Shankaracharya was to give an address on "Sati dharma is an ancient Vedic tradition", on 28 March 1988 at the Annual convention of the Akhil Bharatvarshiya Dharma Sangh—The All India Religious Association—of which he is president. Swami Agnivesh went to the supreme court declaring that this would amount to a breach of the law under the section prohibiting glorification of sati, and the supreme court issued a restraining order, so that the Shankaracharya had to call off his address).

A Hindu woman seeking permission from Akbar's son, Prince Daniyal, to become a sati

Lord William Cavendish Bentinck (1828-1835), who passed the Bengal
Regulation XVII of 1829 prohibiting sati

Rammohun Roy (d. 1833), the first Indian to publicly denounce sati

Roop Kanwar who became a sati on 4 September 1987

Roop Kanwar with her husband Maal Singh

Armed Rajput youth keeping a nightlong vigil at the *sati sthal*
(site of sati)

Woman paying obeisance at the *sati sthal*

Roop Kanwar's brothers at the *chunari* ceremony on the thirteenth day after the sati

Rajasthani women at a pro-sati rally in Jaipur in October 1987

Swami Agnivesh, who took an anti-sati stand
after the Roop Kanwar sati in September 1987

The Shankaracharya of Puri, a vociferous advocate of sati

A sati memorial tablet preserved at the Shashwati Museum, Bangalore

The spirit of the law prohibiting the glorification of sati is clearly lost in this contention by the Shankaracharya that under democracy citizens must have the liberty to say and do what they want even if it amounts to incitement to behaviour that would contribute to a violation of another clause of the constitution which forbids discrimination on grounds of sex.

Article 25 of the constitution guarantees freedom to all persons to profess, practice and propagate religion. By declaring that widow immolation is sanctioned by textual reference and is part of the Hindu religious practice, the Shankaracharya insists that the ban on sati amounts to an infringement of a widow's right to become a sati. But these textual references do not include the main Vedas which are pre-eminent among the scriptures, nor does Manu's code which takes precedence over other texts mention—much less enjoin—sati. Sati has acquired religious backing only because commentators from the sixth century onwards drew up interpretations that reflected, and in turn reinforced, the social trends in each period, and these trends included a fall in the status of women in the society.

The same "freedom to profess" argument is used by other pro-sati proponents too. "I am against sati as a practice", says Kalyan Singh Kalvi, president of the Rajasthan state Janata Party, who spearheaded the pro-sati movement in 1987. "It should be punished as suicide. But once it is done, what is the point of harassing innocent people? Again, once it is committed, there are certain rites which must be done. No one can interfere with these rites", he had said.[53]

This stand too offers a spurious logic that could be applied to every illegal act (murder included) claiming *de facto* immunity. The Bharatiya Janata Party leader, Vijayaraje Scindia has also criticized the law on similar grounds. The Indian constitution, her argument points out, recognizes an individual's right to faith, and sati is part of the Hindu faith, she says. "No woman, wishing to be a sati after her departed husband, could therefore be deprived of her right to that faith". Like the Shankaracharya of Puri she too has declared that she would oppose such a curtailment of rights even in the face of the possibility of imprisonment. However, any element of coercion in the act, she says, would defeat the "sublime purpose" of immolation and would be an offence.

Again and again, this is the argument put forward against the legal ban on sati—that compulsion is to be condemned, but that sati is always voluntary and that for a woman who thus wishes to end her life voluntarily, the law is an encroachment on her fundamental right.

The president of the Institute for Oriental Study at Thane on the outskirts of Bombay, Dr V.V. Bedekar, has described the enactment as "the blackest bill ever passed"; he has declared that it is only in communist and autocratic countries that ideas are regimented and people are compelled to believe in doctored thoughts and ideologies.

"By this bill women in India have lost their freedom to die of their own free will. Male chauvinism has won again", he states. In this hijacking of the feminist perspective for ends other than the amelioration of the conditions of women, the fact that the element of free and true volition is more myth than manifestation is completely and thoroughly bypassed.

Bemoaning the loss of the "freedom to die" is to lose sight of the fact that most Indian women still do not have the freedom to marry the person of their choice, take up jobs of their own choosing or, in general, pattern their lives according to their own inclinations. When the freedom to live in a manner consistent with one's preferences is not available, how valid is it to clamour for the "freedom to die?" Worth noting in this context is the fact that those opposing the legislation on the score of "freedom to die" are all men; women have not protested against this loss of freedom. By contending that force was never involved and that the act connotes "the valour and courage of a woman", the medical practitioner who organized a series of tutorials on sati has lent credence to the momentum of the myth of inspired death. In a telegram to the president of India challenging the legislation on sati, he has said that the act "in its legal and social spirit under-estimates and fails to realise the strength and power of human devotion, love and sacrifice to the beloved. To deny any sacrifice and to categorize it as unbelievable, impossible and unthinkable is imposing one's own limitations on others".[54]

While not discounting the very rare instances of a divine urge to give up one's life on the death of one's husband it is at the same time sufficient to recall that when the Mewar ruler died in 1861, a slave girl was persuaded to mount the pyre with him, obviously not for the sake of showing conjugal love for the beloved, but as a prestige issue for the male potentate (in that he did not go to his death alone, without any women following him!) What the legislation seeks to ensure is that instances of "divine urge" are not made the ideal in the name of which pressures, overt and covert, manifest and subtle, devious and direct, psychological and circumstantial, are brought on other widows to "conform or else".

To argue further, as he has done, that "a progressive society always has the least regulations" is again to confuse cause with effect—while it may be true that a progressive milieu and minimal regulations find a correlation, the absence of regulations does not automatically foster a progressive milieu. The Charter of the UN Declaration of Human Rights to which India is a signatory, guarantees, under Article 6, the voluntary right to life, he points out in his letter to the minister for home affairs, adding the familiar refrain that he possesses "deep reverence and respect for all those women of the past who committed sati voluntarily".

A recent judgement of the High Court in Bombay which ruled that the right to end one's life through suicide had to be respected, is cited in support of this pro-sati stand. Here again, we see an inherent confusion derived from the fact that while both sati and suicide result in death, there is a difference between the two in that the former is specifically connected to a particular event (the death of the husband) and a particular ideology (*pativrata* or chastity as typified by immolation), while suicide is not constrained in this way. And yet, Dr Bedekar's stand is that he would have "no hesitation in supporting a woman if she chooses consciously and voluntarily to die by the act of sati, howsoever cruel, illogical and irrational one may consider it to be".[55]

"If she chooses consciously and voluntarily"—that in essence is the issue, in the light of the pressures of indoctrination, mystification and sometimes even force, that confront a woman.

So consistently has suffering been held up as a test of a woman's devotion that the issue of voluntariness becomes largely meaningless.

Perceive then, the scenario of options before the woman who has just been bereaved—on the one hand, the life of widowhood, typified by physical, financial, social and psychological misery stretching out for the rest of her days; on the other, the delusions of some mystified approbation, glory and veneration that would put an end to the threat of being found wanting in those virtues of self-negating devotion to her spouse that have been held up to her as the ideal right from childhood on, an ideal fashioned by precept, socialization and infixion. Even the wisest man in a similar situation, caught between two such options, would be forgiven for confessing to a sense of confusion. For an ordinary, mortal woman with normal human weaknesses for whom sexual vulnerability adds an extra dimension of handicaps, the odds are loaded hopelessly against a rational response. Even the questions of fealty and purity become secondary, if not irrelevant, in her reckoning in the face of such trauma.

The threat of curses keeps sympathizers away; the prospects of economic liability urge her—and her male relatives—even if only in the subconscious layers of responses, to give credence to mystique.

And there is that pile of heaped wood, exerting literally a fatal fascination, even if she were not under physical compulsion to enter it. . . .

*

Bangalore city in south India boasts a unique museum, perhaps the only
one of its kind anywhere, devoted to the artifacts connected with
women's lives. At the entrance of this museum is a pair of black stone
tablets, with human figures chiselled on them in bas relief. These are
mastikals put up in memory of women who became sati. Such stone
memorials used to be raised wherever a woman immolated herself with
her husband and became a *maha sati*. (The word *mastikal* is a distortion
of *mahasati-kallu, maha* meaning great and *kallu* meaning stone).
About a foot high, these stones usually had carvings of a woman's
hand, or the sun and moon (representing her devotion, as eternal as the
sun and moon); sometimes they also showed a man on a horse or on an
elephant (to signify his status) with the figure of a woman underneath.
Stone tablets of this kind can be seen in several places in different parts
of the country. The ones at the museum were reportedly being used as
drain covers somewhere in the town, when they were discovered, identified and brought to the museum.

These memorial stones were also known as *devli, satikkal* or
virakkal (*vira*: courageous) particularly in south India; in the northern
regions these often took the form of a platform with a canopy over it,
or cairns topped by a symbolic lamp or a miniature dome. In places like
Bikaner and Hampi (Vijayanagar empire of the fifteenth and sixteenth
century) where a number of immolations took place, the memorial
stelae took the form of upright pillars of stone with engravings.
Travellers of the eighteenth and the nineteenth centuries have recorded
coming upon such memorials by the wayside, on the river banks and in
the jungles. In Gujarat, these memorials were known as *paleeyos*.

The earliest such epigraphical evidence available is the one at Eran
near Sagar in central India, which mentions a date corresponding to AD
510. How common was the custom? Was it rare, sporadic or pervasive?
This question becomes relevant in the context of the argument advanced
by some of those frowning upon the legislation banning sati that since
sati is only a very infrequent occurrence, and since laws are enacted only
to control an offence that is on the increase, there is no need for legal
prohibition.

Seen as a percentage of the population, the number of women who
burned on the pyres of their husbands may be insignificant, but it is not
the numbers but the significance attached to the beliefs that eulogize the
rite that is the issue. Estimates of the number of women who perished
on the pyre range all the way from "a handful of scattered, rare incidents" to "25,000 per year". The only kinds of figures available are

those recorded officially in the years from 1815 to 1829, till the law abolishing the custom was promulgated by Lord Bentinck. These figures put the number of widows who burned as sati at a few hundred per year (7,941 for the fourteen years.) Altekar estimates the incidence as one in a thousand at the height of the custom. For Rajasthan, he put it at one in ten.

The earliest recorded sati in India was in 317 BC which was chronicled by Alexander's soldiers in the Punjab. The latest recorded one was in 1987 at Deorala in Rajasthan. In between these two lie several thousands of immolations, known and unknown.

About the origins of the custom there is no unequivocal evidence, although it is traced all the way back to pre-history. Since history and mythological elements are found interwoven, and peopled with celestial as well as legendary historical figures, information about this early period of history is based on conjecture or deductions.

Although the dictionary defines sati as a Hindu custom, the practice of widow sacrifice at the husband's funeral was not unknown in other cultures. It was known in ancient times among the Gauls and the Goths. It was also known among the Slavs (who were influenced by the Goths), the Greeks, Celts, Scythians, Thracians and the people of Oceana. The Egyptians too had the custom of burying a woman in her husband's tomb along with his armour, chariot and other favourite possessions. In ancient China, even favourite courtiers were expected to affirm their loyalty to the deceased emperor through suicide; and wives who committed suicide on the death of their husbands had gateways erected in their honour by imperial command.

. In Babylon and in Celtic Britain, a man's slaves and attendants were often interred with him on his death. The explanation for such a custom was the belief in pre-historic times that the life and needs of the dead in the next world are similar to those in this world, and therefore it was the duty of the surviving relations to provide the deceased with all the things that he used while he was alive—his servants, horses, wives and so on. Had such a belief been the explanation for the custom, logically the husband too should have been buried or burned with the wife, but given the pervasive pattern of patriarchy in all societies, "man was perhaps not prepared to sanction a custom adverse to his own comforts".[56]

One of the very few exceptions—if not the only one—recorded is said to be that of the king's sisters in Ashanti, whose husbands were compelled to end their lives on the death of their royal consorts.[57]

In Fiji and among the Maoris, widow burning was known. Some American-Indian tribes included in their funeral rites a ritual similar to that mentioned in the Vedas of the widow lying down beside the dead body before it was disposed of.

The custom of widow burning is believed to have travelled to Southeast Asian countries like Java, Sumatra and Bali presumably as a result of Hindu migration.

One opinion holds that sati was probably a Scythian rite introduced from central Asia; a parallel is drawn with Thracian funeral rites in which apparently the favourite wife was killed while the other spouses, being denied this privilege, bemoaned their disgrace.

Whether the number of widows who perished in such a rite was large or small, the custom is considered to have been once widespread. The consensus is that it had probably gone out of vogue by the first millennium BC.

Diodorus Siculus mentioned sati as a custom devised to stop unfaithful wives. According to his explanation, when couples married young and later regretted it, "many of the women became depraved and through incontinence fell in love with other men, and when at last they wished to leave the husband, they got rid of them by poison". Hence a law was passed ordaining that the wife should also burn along with the husband on his death. (This account was quoted by Gandhi in his comments on sati). This rather fanciful explanation of the origin of the custom does not address the question of what husbands did when they too repented their marriages (as they doubtless did) and wished to do away with their wives.

"The widow of a warrior among the Madra and Bahlika clans would even immolate herself with her husband's corpse", says one treatise on the ancient civilization and culture of India, adding that "this horrifying custom was completely unknown in the east and would so remain till early feudal time, say the 6th century AD".[58]

It is to this century that the earliest known sati stone of Eran belongs. It mentions Goparaja, a chieftain of Bhanugupta's reign, who was killed in a battle and whose wife immolated herself along with his body.

Most of the early historical references to sati are in travellers' accounts—Alberuni in the tenth century recorded that Hindu wives chose to burn themselves on the death of the husband "in order to be spared the miseries of widowhood". From the eleventh century onwards, the custom seems to have spread, with Brahmin women, who were previously excluded from the rite, also burning alive on the pyre. The fourteenth century traveller, Ibn Batuta is said to have fainted on witnessing a sati ritual. Nicolo de Conti, another traveller who left chronicles of the fifteenth century, recorded that 3,000 wives and concubines of the king of Vijayanagar empire had pledged to burn themselves on his pyre.

The *Akbarnama* mentions an officer in the Mughal court who was about to burn his mother on the pyre of his deceased father. Akbar saved her from the fire. He, it is said, also rode out a hundred miles to save a Rajput princess from immolating herself. "It is a strange comment on the magnanimity of men that they should seek their deliverance through the self-sacrifice of their wives", the *Ain-i-Akbari* quotes him as having said. His father Humayun was the first Mughal ruler to make attempts at preventing widow burnings. (According to the *sharia*, self-immolation is suicide and therefore a crime).

In the southern regions, the Vijayanagar empire recorded several infamous incidents between the fourteenth and the sixteenth centuries and a number of sati stones were raised to commemorate these events. In the Goa region, the Portuguese administration of Albuquerque banned sati in AD 1510 and put a stop to further immolations.

On the death of the Naik of Madura, 400 wives are reported to have burned to death in 1611. Another account mentions 11,000 as the number of women who immolated themselves with the ruler here. Some of these accounts may be exaggerated, but there is little doubt that a large number of women did in fact set themselves on the pyre.

The French traveller Bernier has described the incident of a twelve-year-old child-widow being forced to become a sati at Lahore, in spite of her protests and struggle.

One of Shivaji's wives became a sati in 1680; twenty years later, his daughter-in-law also burned herself with his son Rajaram. Sati incidents seem to have increased from around this time, till the rite was finally outlawed by the British in 1829.

"I have seen women burned in three different ways, according to the customs of different countries", says an account by Jean Baptiste Tavernier (seventeenth century). "In the kingdom of Gujarat, as far as Agra and Delhi, this is how it takes place: On the margin of a river or tank, a kind of small hut, about twelve feet square, is built of reeds and all kinds of faggots, on which some pots of oil and other drugs are placed in order to make it burn quickly. The woman is seated in a half reclining position in the middle of the hut, her head reposes on a kind of pillow of wood and she rests her back against a post to which she is tied by her waist by one of the Brahmins, lest she should escape on feeling the flame. In this position she holds the dead body of her husband on her knees, chewing betel all the time..."[59]

In Gujarat, "heavy cartwheels used to be placed on the woman and her limbs tied to them"; often, there would be a canopy of faggots and logs that was cut down to crush and smother the woman while she burned.

As mentioned earlier, amongst the Jogee tribes the custom was to bury rather than burn the widow. Along the Coromandel coast too, burials were known. In 1813, some twenty miles away from Calcutta, a sixteen-year-old widow was buried with her husband's body in the presence of her mother and friends. A graphic description of this interment is included in Edward Thompson's book *Suttee*.

Between 1815 and 1828, the Benares area saw 1,150 satis, and the Patna area 700; Ghazipur and Gorakhpur averaged two every month; in the Madras and Bombay presidencies, it was between three and five satis per month. Bengal had 7,941 officially recorded cases of immolations during this period, with doubtless many more unrecorded officially.

In the south, Tanjore, Trichy, Masulipatnam, Guntur, Bellary and Cuddalore were among the cities that recorded sati incidents during the nineteenth century while official records were being maintained.

In Kashmir, sati became common among the women of the royal family between AD 700 and AD 1000—on the death of King Sankaravarman in AD 902, three queens, two maidservants and one male servant all burned themselves on his pyre. In AD 1081, when king Ananta died, his queen, servants and litter-carriers are said to have immolated themselves. And on the death of Kalasa in 1089, a concubine joined the queens when they mounted the pile. G.T. Vigne in *Travels in Kashmir* recalls seeing "not fewer than twenty sati memorials" in neat rows, at each memorial to a deceased ruler of Mundi. Sikander, who ruled Kashmir (1389–1413) is said to have prohibited sati but his successor lifted the ban.

Among the nomadic Gaddi tribe in the Kangra region of the Himalayas, likewise, sati was known; one report mentions twelve *dheradues* (memorial temples).

Some accounts of the medieval period also mention death by the sword of ministers and faithful followers who had pledged to die on the death of the ruler. (During the time of the Hoysalas, for instance, Nayaka servants are said to have cut off their limbs and heads following the death of the king to fulfil vows).

Nepal continued to record sati incidents even after the British abolition of the act; in 1845 and 1877, for instance, sati immolations took place; in the latter, at the funeral of the ruler Jung Bahadur, three women burned themselves.

Rajasthan, of course, took top place in the number of sati incidents; Marwar alone saw at least twenty-seven sati immolations between 1842 and 1845, and at the funeral of the ruler of Bundi, no less than eighty-four women are said to have given up their lives by burning.

In Maharashtra, sati was practised among the Peshwas. The widow of Peshwa Madhavarao I became a sati on his death. Likewise, Rani Ahalyabai's daughter is said to have immolated herself on becoming a widow in 1792.

Among the Sikhs in the Punjab, Vincent Smith notes, sati burnings were "atrocious". When Ranjit Singh died in 1839, at least four queens and seven concubines burned with him. The third Sikh guru had condemned sati but "the Sikhs did not want to lag behind the Rajputs in time honoured martial traditions" (which enjoined sati). The possibility of Dogra influence (from Kashmir) in this rite is also mentioned.

One of the women who burned with Ranjit Singh reportedly did so against her will; the queens are said to have been led to their deaths between a double line of infantry. On his son's death the following year, a dozen women immolated themselves, including eleven slaves. With Naunihal Singh, who died at the age of nineteen, two women burned; when his successor was assassinated in 1843, he is said to have burned "with the usual sati rites". A year later, at Raja Suchet Singh's funeral, no less than ten wives and 300 concubines ascended the pyre. That same year, Hira Singh was cremated near Jammu with twenty-four women.

In the post-independence years, the Shekhawati region of Rajasthan alone is said to have recorded one sati incident every year. Madhya Pradesh and U.P. in central India also witnessed sporadic incidents (but far less than in Rajasthan). Altekar in *The Position of Women in Hindu Civilisation* mentions that his sister became a sati in 1946.

The seduction of the spirit of mystical martyrdom that widow burning signifies cannot be dismissed as insignificant, even if the actual number of sati deaths was small. Besides, this seduction holds even the intelligentsia—professors, journalists, professionals and politicians; who flaunt their adulation with defiance—in a thrall.

The place and relevance of legislation banning sati has to be therefore seen in the context not of the percentage of widows who immolated themselves or the actual number of immolations, but of the persistence of the custom as well as the beliefs that it is based on; what is significant is not just the statistical numbers of women burnt to death but the exaltation of such a rite and the ideology that promotes its glorification. Whether ten people starve to death or a thousand, the fact of outrage and unacceptability of the event remains; in the same way, what is worrisome is not the percentage of widows burning *per se* but the entire gamut of social, economic, psychological, cultural and political factors promoting an ethos where the giving up of a woman's life because her husband has died is seen as laudable and worthy of praise.

*

Sir John Malcolm in *Memoir of Central India* mentions the case of a mother immolating herself on the death of her only son in 1879 at a place called Amjherra; a similar case is also mentioned at another place called Katchrode. A few cases of *ma-sati* (mothers immolating themselves) have also been mentioned in the Punjab and Rajasthan. A stepmother immolated herself near Ajmer during the 1950s. In the case of some rulers, ministers and servants committed suicide on the death of the master but there was no mystique attached to the event in the way that a wife's sati is mystified.

On the death of King Ballala in AD 1220, for instance, his minister and general Kuvaralakshma killed himself along with his wife.[60] In Kashmir, in AD 902 and AD 1081, male servants gave up their lives on the death of the ruler. In Gujarat and Rajasthan likewise, slaves sometimes became *satu*—in 1818 when the maharaja of Jaipur was cremated, eighteen slaves are said to have burned. An attendant of Sawai Jagat Singh also burnt to death on the death of his master in 1819.

Instances of *sata*—men ending their lives on the death of their wives—are not unknown, though the number is exceedingly small. But no temples have ever been raised to their conjugal devotion, nor is a man deified for such fealty or even love.

6

The Beauteous and the Brave

The Chohani queen, with sixteen damsels in her suite, came forth. 'This day', she said, 'is one of joy; my race shall be illustrated, our lives have passed together; how then can I leave him?'

The Bhattiani queen proclaimed, 'With joy I accompany my lord. . .'

The Choara rani, Tuar queen and Shekhavati queen did likewise. For these five queens death had no terrors. . . The countenances of the queens were radiant like the sun. . . As the flames rose, the assembled multitudes shouted, '*Khaman, khaman* (well done). . . .'

—Lt. Col. James Tod, *Annals and Antiquities of Rajasthan*, description of sati by five queens of the Rajput potentate Ajit Singh, who died in AD 1724

Krishna Kumari was a sixteen-year-old Rajput princess who was known as the flower of Rajasthan. Jagat Singh of Jaipur and the Raja of Marwar fell in love with her and went to war to decide who would win her hand. The Raja of Marwar emerged victorious but her father could not bring himself to accept the Raja as his son-in-law (he preferred the other) and decided the only way to avoid complications would be for his daughter to die. He sent a functionary to have her beheaded but at the sight of that fair face the man could not bring himself to raise the sword. The father then had a cup of poison sent to her. She consumed it after remarking to her mother, "We are marked out for sacrifice from our birth". When the poison proved ineffective, her father made her drink the potion three more times until it killed her. The grief-stricken mother is said to have starved herself to death. This incident was recorded some 200 years ago.

In the same vein is the story of Korum Devi in the fifteenth century who first cut off one hand to be sent to the father of her lord as proof of her intentions, before burning herself as sati along with her betrothed. There is a lake named after this woman in Jaisalmer.

These two anecdotes typify the Rajput preference for death rather than what they saw as a dishonourable alternative. This exaltation of premeditated, even violent death underlies the attitude to sati in Rajasthan, and partly explains the persistence of the custom in that region.

The incidents in the rest of the country were isolated and sporadic occurrences, and certainly far more rare, compared to what Bengal and Rajasthan saw.

In the first decade of the nineteenth century, when official and public attention came to be directed to the custom of sati and estimates of the number of immolations were undertaken for the first time, Bombay and Madras presidencies averaged around fifty sati deaths per year. In comparison, the annual average for Bengal presidency was in excess of 610. Thus, of the total number of sati cases recorded in the three British presidencies, nearly ninety per cent took place in Bengal.

For the years 1815–17, Calcutta with four adjacent *zillas* recorded 864 sati immolations, while the rest of the British territory accounted for 663 cases. In 1819, no less than 421 out of 650 sati cases were from the Calcutta division alone. Likewise, in 1825–28, sati deaths in Bengal totalled 2,126 of which Patna, Benares and Bareilly accounted for 222, 185 and forty-eight cases respectively, while Calcutta division alone accounted for 1,368 deaths.[1]

J.O. Todd who was a judge in Masulipatnam in Madras presidency recorded in 1819 that "the practice (of sati) is by no means common in this part of the country". Sir John Malcolm who was the administrator in Central India before moving to Bombay as governor, observed in *Memoir of Central India* that "In the whole of Central India, there have not been, as far as can be learnt, above three or four sati annually for the last 20 years. They are much limited to particular tribes of Brahmins and Rajputs".[2] He added specifically that the incidence of sati is not comparable to that in "Jeypore, Jodhpur, Odaipur etc".

One estimate puts the number of widows who became sati in Rajasthan at ten per cent.[3] Bengal recorded the largest number of sati immolations in the three decades preceding the Sati Abolition Law of 1829, and Rajasthan has continued to record to this day sporadic incidents, a century-and-a-half after it was declared illegal.

Many of the sati cases outside Rajasthan also betray a Rajput connection—thus the state of Idar, a Rajput state near the former Bombay presidency, was the scene of several sati immolations. In 1833, in the presence of a vast crowd, the raja was cremated along with seven of his queens, two concubines, four female slaves and a man servant. Two years later, at the funeral of the raja at Ahmednagar a particularly gruesome sati immolation was performed. The British had passed a law against sati six years earlier, and the British agent moved in with a contingent 300 strong, to try and stop the event. The son of the deceased raja pleaded with the agent not to interfere, and in fact sent secretly for the Bhil tribals to assist in outnumbering and overpowering the British force. In the armed confrontation that ensued, casualties were heavy on both sides. However, during the night, the hapless women were reportedly dragged to the pyre and burned. Ahmednagar used to be part of Idar, and the ruling family was of Rajput descent, which perhaps explains the insistence on carrying on what they obviously thought was a "tradition". In Nepal, likewise, where sati incidents were known, the ruling family was also of Rajput descent.

The question naturally arises: Were there any peculiarities in the circumstances or ethos of the Bengal and Rajasthan regions that encouraged the practice of sati?

In Bengal, a confluence of cultural and economic factors offers one explanation for the frequency with which the region witnessed widows burning with their husbands. Between 1815, the year when official figures became available on sati, and 1828, the last year before sati was legally prohibited, a total of 7,941 incidents of widow burning had taken place in Bengal alone (not counting those that did not get reported officially). One of the explanations offered for this phenomenon of a few hundred widows burning year after year in the region was that in Bengal the Dayabhaga laws of inheritance were followed whereas in the rest of the country the Mitakshara codes applied.

As we've seen earlier under the Mitakshara system, women in joint families had no right to property; they were entitled only to maintenance, whereas the Dayabhaga school conferred on women the same property rights as their husbands had, and made them coparceners along with the men. This, as some social commentators have pointed out, must have frequently induced the surviving members of the family of the deceased husband to get rid of the widow, "by appealing, at the most distressing hour, to her devotion to, and love of, her husband".[4] Further, under Dayabhaga, a widow could neither gift away nor mortgage or sell the property she inherited, which meant that she could not, for instance, distribute it to Brahmins for performing the funeral rites of the departed husband.[5] Her continued existence after her husband's death could have therefore been seen as a threat to vested interests. Rammohun Roy too emphasized this point in his tract on what he described as a practice "abhorrent to nature, repugnant to reason and contrary to the most ancient and the highest legislative authority of the Hindus"; he argued that the practice of burning widows was motivated not so much by religiosity as by sheer human avarice.[6]

The Dayabhaga law can, however, offer only a partial explanation. For one thing, the same rules of inheritance applied in both Calcutta and Murshidabad divisions, and yet the number of sati deaths in the former was sixteen to twenty times higher than in the latter. (One possible explanation for this difference in incidence could be that Murshidabad was a predominantly Muslim area and hence the number of Hindu widows could have been small in absolute terms).

For another, an analysis of the details pertaining to the economic status of each case of sati shows that those in poor and middling circumstances were in fact in the majority. Inheritance could not have been a major consideration in these cases. However, the plight of widows in Bengal was (and continues to be) particularly wretched; and given the ethos that looked upon widows as ill-starred, inauspicious and deserving of only privations, impoverished widows had precious little to look forward to, if they outlived their husbands, except acute distress, both physical and emotional. Thus a widow would have been damned if she was well off, and damned if she was poor.

Lending credence to this theory was the fact—also pointed out by Rammohun Roy—that suicides among the women of Bengal were "almost ten times" than elsewhere. In this light, the economic factors under the Dayabhaga law could not have been by themselves an adequate explanation.

A study of the age composition of the women who became satis also show that nearly half the number were fifty or over. The fact that as widows they had, at that age, little to look forward to, in the remaining span of their lives irrespective of their economic circumstances, might have also added its weight to the other factors that promoted immolations.

The number of sati incidents in Bengal rose sharply in the last quarter of the eighteenth century and the first few years of the nineteenth. Connecting this to the British presence, two theories have been advocated—one is that the spread of materialistic culture in imitation of the English colonizers, who were headquartered in Bengal, enhanced the economic attractions of doing away with a widow who would only be a burden on the family if she lived. While increasing materialism may have had a hand in intensifying trends that already existed, this imitative factor was not sufficiently widespread by that time, to explain the number of sati deaths, nor—more importantly—their proliferation among the poor and destitute classes.

On the other hand, the British presence itself is believed to have resulted in a curious strengthening of the so-called orthodox customs, as the veteran freedom fighter Kamaladevi Chattopadhyay points out in *Indian Women's Battle for Freedom*. Because of the traditional position of eminence that the Brahmins (who had emigrated to the area in large numbers from the eighth century on because of offers of land and jobs) enjoyed, the colonial rulers believed in inducting Brahmins into their administrative machinery, in order to facilitate its acceptance by the people. This resulted in the Brahmins becoming exposed to western influence, and subjected them to "new inner conflicts between their traditional make-up and the new privileged status" that they acquired in the colonial set-up. In their anxiety to affirm that they had not in consequence jettisoned their orthodoxy in the face of their new status, they in fact began to reinforce customs like sati. Further, the respected position that they enjoyed as the elite of society invested them with a certain authority to proclaim that immolation of widows was, in fact, enjoined by religion. Lending credence to this theory is the fact that the incidence of sati cases were, in this period, the highest among Brahmin women—forty per cent.[7]

The practice of *kulinism* which permitted polygamy among Bengali Brahmins is considered to have been another contributing factor in the high incidence of sati in Bengal. Instances are mentioned of twenty or thirty wives burning to death on the husbands' pyres. Rammohun Roy also pointed out that the failure of husbands to make adequate provision for their wives resulted in economic distress that contributed to immolations.

In addition, the process of data collection must have also played a part in showing a rising trend of incidents—the first, very rough estimates of the number of sati deaths became available only around 1803–04; official statistics came to be recorded only after 1812; and it is possible that with each year thereafter, the extent of coverage was improved, so that more cases got reported than for the earlier periods.

*

The river Ganga has had an exalted and revered place in Hindu beliefs. Ganga water signifies purification, moksha and the ultimate liberation of the soul transcending all sins. Certain locations along the river's course are considered especially auspicious, and it is possible that cremations were shifted to such places from nearby areas, thereby pushing up the number of sati cases in those regions through which the river flowed (mainly Bengal). An account by Jean Baptiste Tavernier says,

"In Bengal I have seen them come to the Ganga after more than 20 days journey. . . ." The same account also mentions one woman who came all the way from near Bhutan in the north, in order to perform the cremation and sati on the banks of the Ganga.[8]

This again can offer only a partial explanation for the preponderance of sati cases in Bengal; for Benares which not only lies along the Ganga but is also considered the holiest of holy places, especially to die, did not record anywhere near as many sati deaths as Calcutta and its environs. (Out of a total of 8,133 sati deaths in the Bengal presidency during 1815–28, Benares division accounted for 1,153 as against Calcutta division's 5,199).[9]

Rajasthan, the other stronghold of sati, is said to have over 200 temples commemorating sati. Most of the incidents recorded in the years after the Sati Abolition Law of 1829 and in the post-independence years of the twentieth century have been in Rajasthan.

The Rajputs of Rajasthan are a warrior race; the word Rajput means 'son of the king', and most of the clans of the community trace their ancestry to the nobles and the high military officers of the various invaders who came into North India and established kingdoms or fiefs in the early centuries of the Christian era.

Not surprisingly, the military virtues of fearlessness and valour came to be highly valued; in addition, honour had always been an over-riding concept. A glorious death was to be welcomed—for the men in battle, and for the women in a fiery end through the rites of *jauhar* or sati. If death rather than defeat and dishonour, was the motto for the men, death rather than disgrace and dishonour through ravishment, was its equivalent for the women. A fearless disregard for one's own life in the pursuit of a higher national or spiritual exaltation marked this conception of "honourable" response. The Rathore clan of Rajasthan traces its descent from the sun, and the Chauhans and the Solankis from the mythical figure that rose from a sacrificial fire near Mount Abu (in south Rajasthan). They are for this reason known as *agnikula* (*agni*: fire, *kula*: clan).

Fire is seen by certain sects as a liberator rather than a destroyer, and has purificatory symbolism. If you combine this with the fact that in the Hindu tradition death is looked upon as a release or a new birth that sets the spiritual element free from the "superincumbent clay", you have the roots of the rationale that exalts and extols fiery death in the cause of honour.

According to the famous and oft-repeated story, when Allauddin Khilji attacked the city of Chittor in 1303, Rani Padmini burnt herself to death in a rite known as *jauhar*, rather than put herself at the mercy of the conqueror. Along with several hundred women, she is said to have descended into a cavern that was set ablaze before its opening was closed. The *kund* commemorating the event is still pointed out to visitors at Chittor.

The word *jauhar* is derived from *jatugriha* meaning a house made of lac or other combustible material. To protect their honour and avoid the possibility of molestation and rape by invaders, the wives of Rajput warriors often chose *jauhar* and leapt into the fire when defeat for their men seemed imminent. At the *jauhar* before the fall of Jaisalmer in 1295, for instance, no less than 24,000 women are said to have been burned to death. At Chanderi, likewise, when the Rajputs were in confrontation with an invading army, the wives resorted to *jauhar*. At the fall of Chittor again in 1569, 300 women burned themselves in the rite of *jauhar* rather than live on as wives of the defeated (and therefore disgraced) princes.

A princess of Mewar and wife of Jaswant Singh I is said to have ordered the gates of the fort shut on her husband when he returned defeated from a battle. Death to the valiant was the preferred objective, rather than a matter of sorrow.

If the doctrine of fealty was one attribute of the Rajput psyche, there was the other, the chivalric code which made the threat of dishonour to a woman a compelling reason for unsheathing one's sword—even if it was to kill her in order to "save her" from a fate worse than death as the Rajput code saw it.

James Tod in *Annals and Antiquities of Rajasthan* narrates a sixteenth century incident that typifies this attitude of the Rajasthanis. Once a Rajput ruler fell in love with the daughter of a Brahmin; to save her from "pollution" by the ruler, the Brahmin cut his daughter to pieces and burned her with a curse on the ruler that peace would desert him, and that he would die "in three years and three days". (The prophesy, Tod adds, did come true!)

Battles and feuds, sometimes carried on for generations, have been a constant theme in the history of the Rajputs; so were, in consequence, sati immolations.

When the ruler of Marwar died in 1562, twenty-four women became satis with him. At the death of his successors in 1594, 1619, 1638 and 1678, eight, twelve, ten and twenty-nine women respectively burned to death. In 1723, altogether sixty-six women including six queens, twenty-five concubines and thirty-two slaves perished. In 1803 and 1843, the rulers were cremated with twenty-eight and six women respectively. With Raja Budh Singh of Bundi, eighty-four women immolated themselves.

In Mewar, the most solemn of all oaths was that of the sati—*"Maha satian ka aan"* (By the great sati) was an adjuration frequently used in royal patents and records.[10]

Udaipur was "pre-eminent" in the number of sati deaths—at Maharana Bhim Singh's funeral in 1828, four wives and four concubines burned themselves. In 1838, when his successor Jawan Singh died, two queens and six concubines became satis.

Edward Thompson records that on this occasion the British authorities expressed their disapproval but "Udaipur shrugged its shoulders and went its blood-strewn way".[11] Jawan Singh's successor Sardar Singh was reportedly "unpopular" and in consequence, at his death in 1842 "only one woman", burned with him. Dip Kanwar, daughter of the Udaipur ruling family and the wife of Maharaja Surat Singh's son, became a sati in 1825; a fair in her honour used to be held every year at Devi Kund near Bikaner. An agent of the governor-general, reporting on a sati incident, described Udaipur as the principality where "ancient customs and usage are cherished more religiously than perhaps in any other state".

When Maharaja Man Singh of Jodhpur died in 1843, his queen, four concubines and a slave girl all burned on the pyre. Again, the widow of the son of the Thakur of Begun immolated herself in Udaipur in 1864. On the outskirts of Udaipur where the Ranas burned, and outside Bikaner, a number of memorials can be found, testifying to the number of women who went to a fiery death on the pyres of their husbands.

Behind the city palace in Alwar, near Jaipur, there is an elaborate cenotaph called the Moosi Maharani ki Chattri. Moosi was a concubine who immolated herself on the death of Maharaja Bakhtawar Singh, and came to be known thereafter as Maharani Moosi. Built in 1888, this monument is described as "one of the finest of its kind" and has a pair of marble footprints at which the locals offer water in the belief that this offering "protects children from the evil eye".

It is said that during the tenure of Lord Dalhousie (1848–56) there was a restraining influence on sati immolations in Udaipur, but after his departure the state again reverted to its dubious place at the top of the table of Rajput states for sati deaths.

Several of the royalty women who could not immolate themselves on the same pyre as their husbands', burned afterwards—Bimaladevi, queen of Rawul Gursi, waited six months in order to complete the construction of Gursi-sir lake which her husband had been building when he died, while queen Pushpavati who was widowed when she was pregnant ascended the pile after her son was born.[12]

At the cremation of the ruler of Mewar in 1861, when none of the wives came forward to burn on the pyre, a slave is said to have been finally persuaded to immolate herself, "to preserve the honour of the clan" ("a Sisodia never went to his death alone!"). Sawai Man Singh II was in favour of prohibiting sati, but at his death his wives nevertheless immolated themselves.

The link between members of the ruling dynasty and their subjects in the Rajput states had historically been very strong, and what the women of the royal families did came to be seen as worth imitating. As a result, "Rajput ladies burned more willingly than those of other parts of India".[13]

For Rajput women, thus, the precedent held up as the ideal and entrenched in their psyche as the highest in terms of glory was that of death on the pyre of the husband. "Woman, considered a lower caste (than the male) could attain salvation and be born a Rajput male in her next birth if she attained the glorious death of a sati".[14]

The practice and prevalence of widow burning in Rajasthan in the last few centuries was such that Thompson proffers the theory that Rajasthan had "almost certainly been the original home from which sati had spread over India millenniums before".[15]

That the Rajput concept of fiery immolation emphasized not so much the spiritual as the valorous, and not so much deliverance as sanguinary deliverance is evident from the number of practices other than *jauhar* and sati—*sogun, karga shapna* and *chandi* for instance, which seen in the light of their history, provide additional insights into their attitude to "honour". Trial by *sogun* refers to the rite of purgation through fire or water (washing the hands with boiling water, for instance). "Where justice is denied, the sufferer will challenge his adversary to the *sogun*", daring one to transcend the natural human responses to pain and punishment—if a man was willing to prove his point by going through such terrible trials, a woman should be prepared to prove her faithfulness to her husband by going through a fiery immolation too, the logic went. Humane responses and the courage to walk into the face of death are, perhaps, mutually exclusive.

While doubting that there could be such a thing as a "Rajput psyche" to explain the proclivity to glorify immolations, a former officer of the IAS who was posted as chief secretary of Rajasthan state and has personal knowledge of sati cases, points out that the Rajasthanis do not consider sati to be akin to suicide committed by weak-minded persons— "Most Rajputs consider (sati) to be a symbol of divinely bestowed power to create, strengthen, fight and die for loyalty . . . the attitude to sati is similar to the Japanese view on hara-kiri—an act of sacrifice with honour".[16]

Chandi is described as a singular kind of revenge through self-immolation in which maledictions are pronounced on one's opponent with one's dying breath (in a manner similar to the curses of a woman about to become a sati, which are greatly feared). Tod records that caravans, when faced with marauders, sometimes resorted to *chandi* "or even sacrificed a whole body of women and children whose blood the marauders were declared responsible for".

Karga (or *khanda*) *shapna* or the adoration of the sword, is a martial ritual performed during the annual Navarathri festivities, after which a Rajput is considered "free to indulge his passion for rapine and revenge".[17]

Every day's rituals during these nine festive days opened with the slaughter of buffaloes and rams after a visit by the Rana to the temple of the Devi, the goddess of destruction.

Grace Thompson Seton, who travelled extensively in India during the third decade of the twentieth century and recorded her impressions in *Yes, Lady Saheb*, says, describing her visit to Amber in Rajasthan, "Not far away was the blood-stained altar in the fort temple where a goat is sacrificed daily to Kali, the Goddess of Destruction, the practice of live sacrifice being maintained to this day".

Tod's volumes on Rajasthan are full of narratives illustrating how the Rajputs' impetuosity and recklessness born of an obsession with "honour" often turned the slightest provocation, real or imaginary, into a fight to death, and resulted in what has been succinctly described as "beheading the brave and burning the beauteous". The Rajput "delights in blood" and a characteristic haughty noblesse ensured that every battle ended only in death, or victory, everything else being considered "dishonourable". The Rathore and the Sisodia clans in particular are famous for their intrepid and tempestuous responses. Even pacification was "sealed" with the blood of a common foe.

One narrative relates to a famous confrontation between two Rajput rulers at what started out as a friendly spring hunt. On the basis of an imagined slight, one of the pair drew his sword and thrust it into the other; he in turn died only after inflicting fatal wounds on the former. The concubine of one of the slain rulers mounted the pyre as a sati after pronouncing a curse that a spring hunt rendezvous between the two families could never take place without death ensuing. Legend has it that this ominous prophesy came true not once but four times, in succeeding generations.

Sakhaband is another concept and an honorific that the Rajput is said to glory in; it means literally, the destroyer of all branches (*Sakha:*branch, *band:*to close)—"all grand battles attended with fatal results are termed *sakha"* because with the death of both man and wife (who immolates herself) no branch of the family tree is left to sprout further. "When beseiged, without hope of relief, in the last effort of despair, the females are immolated and the warriors, decorated in saffron robes, rush on inevitable destruction".[18]

One other epithet that is applied to Rajputs is *Rangña,* or "turbulent" (from *ring:*strife). An interesting point to note here is the similarity between Scythian and Rajput customs. The Scythians too worshipped their scimitars in a ritual similar to *khadga shapna* and both had the custom of female sacrifice; immolation was a practice common to many sun-worshipping clans, including the Scythic, Getae or Jut warriors of Jax artes.[19]

With the Getae, if the deceased had more than one wife, the elder claimed the privilege of burning.[20] The Bhattis of Jaisalmer, according to one opinion, were descended from the Scythians. Vincent Smith corroborates this view with his statement: "Suttee probably was a Scythian rite introduced from Central Asia".[21] The Scythians are believed to have originated in western Siberia before they moved east into southern Russia some centuries before Christ. After 300 BC, they were driven out of the Balkans by the invading Celts. One possibility is that they made incursions into Rajasthan from the north.

This view is further buttressed by Sir William Barton who observes that the bulk of Rajputs trace their ancestry to the noble or high military officers of the invaders who went on to carve out for themselves principalities and fiefs in India from the first to the fifth century AD, like the Scythians and the Huns.[22]

Female infanticide, a custom that has been associated with the Rajasthan region, can be seen as part of the same ethos of scant regard for life and "protecting" the female from a life that could be considered dishonourable or disgraceful.

"Accursed is the day when a woman child was born to me!" is said to be an exclamation often heard among the Rajputs (as Lt. Col. Tod recorded during the nineteenth century). More than one hundred years later, female infanticide still makes news—recent reports in the papers have alleged that a member of the legislative assembly of Rajasthan has had infanticide practised in his family for several generations.

It is said that of forty-three female infants born of forty marriages in this family over the last four decades, none has survived. In October 1988, the entire opposition in the Rajasthan assembly staged a walk-out over the arrest of some 300 women volunteers who were protesting outside the House demanding an official probe into the allegations of infanticide. Human rights activist, Swami Agnivesh, who played a prominent part in the anti-sati movement of 1987–88, demanded 'that a parliamentary committee be constituted to enquire into the allegation. The politician denied the charge, but following a directive from the high court the crime branch investigated the matter; the evidence unearthed at the end of the probe was declared to be inconclusive although the report pointed out that four female infants in the family had been found to have died under "suspicious circumstances" with no medical treatment given to them even though such help was available at hand.

Even as the controversy continued, social workers of the region conceded that female infanticide was indeed practised in some parts of the state.

The four big states of Rajasthan, Madhya Pradesh, Bihar and U.P. account for a little under forty per cent of the country's population; sati incidents in recent decades have all been from within this group, with Rajasthan leading the tally. Illiteracy combined with feudal pride and superstitious beliefs offers part of the explanation for the incidence of aberrations like infanticide and sati even in modern times. Rajasthan has one of the lowest figures for female literacy in the country. In the Jaisalmer region of the state it is said to be less than two per cent.

A recent study of the Bhatti community here points out that the hypergamous laws governing marriages among the Rajputs act as powerful inducements to infanticide—intermarriages between families of the same clan are prohibited, and a son-in-law cannot be chosen from a family of lesser status in the social heirarchy. Since the Bhattis consider themselves the most superior clan, the marriage of daughters becomes a serious problem; and so, rather than lower their heads and do the customary honours to a son-in-law who is not of a comparable status, they prefer not to have daughters at all. (The men are however allowed to marry girls from a clan of a lower status). In several villages of the state, and particularly in the Jaisalmer area, there has not been a *barat* (arrival of the groom's party at the bride's natal home for the commencement of the wedding ceremony) for several decades, because there have not been any girls to get married!

In the primary school at Deora village, for instance, this study found just one girl among 175 students. Asked why there were only two girls aged eight and twelve respectively in the entire village, some of the village elders claimed that it was because of "the peculiar quality of the water" they got from the village wells; others attributed it to *vardaan* (divine grace).

Aside from the reasons mentioned earlier, there is also prejudice against the female because when a girl marries, she "takes away" (wealth) from the family of her birth, while the marriage of a son means wealth brought into the family in the form of dowry. Infanticide is thus connected via economic considerations to the problem of dowry.

Although the practice has been around for a long time, it is believed that infanticide received a fresh fillip during the Mughal period as a result of fathers worrying about their daughters being carried away or molested. At a later period, the anxiety over the obligation of having to marry off a daughter "in proper style" became another factor promoting the prejudice against the female child.

Kamaladevi Chattopadhyay emphasizes this link between the custom of infanticide and the burden of expenses to be borne by the parents of girls at the time of their marriage. "The Rajputs were among those who had become victims of this custom because of the heavy demands of the '*charans*' who under an oppressive custom had become indispensable in marriage rituals",[23] she records.

As Tod observed, "Although custom sanctions and religion rewards a sati, the victim to marital selfishness, yet neither traditionary adage nor religious text can be quoted in support of a practice so revolting as infanticide . . . the wife is a sacrifice to his egotism and the progeny of her own sex to his pride; and if the unconscious infant should escape the influence of the latter, she is only reserved to become the victim of the former. . . . "[24]

With the dice thus loaded against the female, it is no wonder that in the 1980s the sex-ratio in Rajasthan is 919 against the national average of 935 females per 1,000 males. For the Jaisalmer region of the state, where the Bhattis predominate, the comparable figure is 811, and among the Bhattis themselves, it is estimated to be around 550, perhaps one of the lowest ratios anywhere.

*

It is in Rajasthan again that one sees reports of child marriages even today, although the Sarada Act prohibiting child marriages was passed in 1929 and the princely states of Rajputana adopted it some years later. Since 1978, the minimum age for marriage under the law has been eighteen for girls and twenty-one for boys.

Nonetheless, a news item in the *Times of India* datelined Jaipur, 25 April 1988 said that on a conservative estimate, about 1,000 child marriages were solemnized in villages in the Jaipur district alone, and that over 50,000 children were joined in wedlock every year on Akha Teej day (considered auspicious for nuptials) in violation of the law.

In 1989, Akha Teej fell on 8 May and once again reports said, "thousands of children including infants in arms were joined in matrimony", with priests performing the rites while the bridal "couple" sat on the laps of their parents. In Borawas village of Kota district alone fifteen teenage couples of the Gujjar community were joined in marriage, while in the neighbouring Bundi district, marriages of children between the ages of five and fifteen from the Meghwal community were solemnized. A procession accompanying three teenage daughters of a family—all under fifteen—passed in front of the local police control room in Udaipur, but the policemen "chose to ignore it altogether". The news report also carried photographs of two grooms aged eight and five from Shivdaspura village thirty kilometres away from the state capital of Jaipur. Ironically, one ten-year-old bride made news by refusing to go through the marriage ceremony and sought police protection.

It is said that even the powerful rulers of the erstwhile princely states in the region did not dare to enforce the prohibition of child marriages "for fear of revolt by the tradition-bound people".

Recent offenders have included some politicians holding high office. Two ministers of the state had to resign in connection with child marriages solemnized in their families. One of the marriages took place in 1981 and the other was in 1987. In the second instance the girl herself refused to go to the man she had been married to when she was a minor. A woman journalist publicized the girl's case, following which the minister was asked to quit, but the reality, as a report points out, is that "punishment meted out to the two ministers has hardly caused any dent in the custom".[25]

*

Apart from the Rajput conception of honour and death that could have contributed in some measure to the prevalence of the custom of sati, there is also the fact that the arrival of Muslim invaders in the area introduced *purdah* and isolated the women. To this day, the archetypal Rajasthani woman is one of the most heavily veiled among all Indian communities. While veiling *per se*, as a manner of dress, may not incite one to immolation, it can be perceived as a contributory factor to the general suppression and oppression of women and their relegation, in more than one sense, to the least privileged position in Indian society. Veiling has gone hand-in-hand with a strictly housebound routine, and it has been remarked that even today a Rajput woman is among the most suppressed within the home.

This isolation has continued conjointly with communal insularity and a consequent vulnerability for the women. This has, in turn, led to a compulsive internalizing of her responses and a continual harking back to past glories, without reference to the shifting parameters of the developments of the twentieth century.

One interesting observation that has been made regarding the Rajput psyche is that this harshness towards the female is in fact born of a sense of great solicitousness for the female. "If devotion to the fair sex be admitted as a criterion of civilisation", says Tod—and his observations on the Rajputs and Rajasthan, based as they are on intimate knowledge and study of the place and people, cannot be dismissed as fanciful—"the Rajput must rank high. His susceptibility is extreme and fires at the slightest offence to female delicacy, which he never forgives". In what must be a psychologist's delight, the Rajput attitude to women seeks to protect them from "the pain of dishonour" by putting an end to their lives, either in the form of infanticide or as *jauhar* and sati. "It is because I love her so much that I have to kill her", is a refrain that perhaps makes macabre sense, but it is not unknown. *Ergo*, he "raises the poniard to her rather than witness her captivity, and he gives the opiate to the infant whom, if he cannot portion and marry to her equal, he dare not see degraded".[26]

*

Rajasthan's literature and folklore reflect these aspects of the temperament of its people. The *Sati shatak* (one hundred verses in praise of sati) by the Rajasthani scholar and poet Udayraj Ujal (1885–1967) is one such work. Mahadan Bai's *Sati Sujas* is another well-known book. Likewise, the *Vir satsai* on the subject of Rajput valour, by Nathusinha Mahiyariya (1891–1973) may be mentioned. To paraphrase one couplet from his work:

> *Rajvat* (the quality of a Rajput) has a simple test—there is no *rajvat* in a man who wants to preserve his life at all costs. *Rajvat* is where there is readiness to give up life for a worthwhile cause.

And there was no cause more worthwhile than the code of 'honourable response'. Indoctrination in these ideas of Rajput glory begins early. One *doha* (couplet) runs:

> The mother seeks to train the child for death through lullaby at the cradle. 'O child,' she says, 'there is no fun in life on land trampled by the enemy's feet'.[27]

For violations—whether of territories or of possessions (which include women)—the price is paid with life. For the infant Rajput, Tod observes, "The shield is his cradle, the dagger his plaything".

The proverbs of Rajasthan too reflect these sentiments—*Mar jyavno pan baath raakhnee* (Even if it costs one's life, one's word has to be honoured) and *Mar jyavno pan daliyo nahin khavno* (Death is preferable to accepting something less than one's due—literally, 'I'd rather die than eat plain porridge') are typical examples of the kind of pride and hauteur that are cultivated from early infancy.

Even folk-tales reflect this ethos—there is one about a wild boar that lived on Mount Abu with his wife and four sons. One year during the drought the boar climbed down to the plains and found a lush garden in Sirohi. He ate his fill and took some food up to the family. The keepers of the garden resented this and attacked the boar but were chased away by his wife. When the owner of the garden saw that his elephants and horses were starving and discovered that the boars were helping themselves to his produce, he told himself, "Tomorrow, either the boar or I will be dead". In preparing for battle the boar in turn told itself, "This Sirohirao is the best among the Kshatriyas, therefore there will be no disgrace in dying by his hand". He then instructed his wife that after he had fallen, she should send three of the sons one after the other to continue the fight, and then take the fourth up to the mountain. Presently, when he died fighting the owner of the garden, first the eldest son and then two more went to fight and were slain in battle. By that time the wife and the youngest son had reached safely on top of Mount Abu. She then became a sati.[28]

This story typifies every aspect of the Rajput conception of life—the dare-devilry, the emphasis on "dying at the hands of someone worthy", the fight to the death, and the final immolation. The legends and the folk-tales of a region mirror the mental make-up of the people and in turn shape the psyche. In this sense, the staple that the Rajput psyche is raised on can offer some insights that will take us part of the way in understanding the attitude to sati among the people of Rajasthan.

Although Bengal did not have a martial tradition glorifying death in this manner, both Rajasthan and Bengal have in common a strong tradition of Devi or Shakti worship (propitiation of the female force as omnipotent). The deity of every Rajput clan is Devi-Shakti; likewise, Kali, the aggressive, all-powerful, awesome manifestation of Durga finds a faithful following in the Bengal region. One analysis even correlates the difference in the incidence of sati burnings in the different regions of Bengal with differences in the sects—in those regions where Kali is worshipped, the number of widow burnings was seen to be higher than in those regions like Vishnupur where the residents were predominantly Vishnu followers. (Kali is propitiated with blood sacrifices and gory rituals. The blood of the tiger is said to keep her pleased for a hundred years; the blood of man propitiates her for 1,000 years). The Vaishnava cult has no such practices and is more benign.

Geographically, the two regions differ, but the effect of the environment on the psyche may not be all that dissimilar—Rajasthan is marked by harsh terrain, bare rocks and ravines, dry desert and shimmering wastes of sandbanks that spell privations; Bengal has been known for frequent famines and floods by turns, both adding a dimension of fatality to one's outlook and responses.

None of these factors can of course, in isolation or singly explain the prevalence of sati in these two regions, but in combination they do add up to make up a set of cultural and social inducements that urged and forced a far higher number of sati deaths than in the rest of the country.

Although sati was outlawed in 1829, "it continued to linger in Rajasthan, its greatest stronghold, for about thirty years more", says Altekar in *The Position of Women in Hindu Civilisation*. The first edition of this book came out in 1938 and the second in 1956. On updating that statement, we find that instead of dying out, there seems to have been actually a revival of sorts of sati in Rajasthan in the post-independence years, with the Shekhawati region in particular continuing to record sati incidents.

In recent years, Calcutta and Delhi have also seen clamorous protests from the Rajasthani community against "interference" by the authorities in the glorification of sati. In 1980, Rajasthani women marched through the streets of Delhi under the banner of the Rani Sati Sarva Sangh demanding to be allowed to build a sati temple in the capital. Questions were raised in parliament, and the then prime minister, Mrs Indira Gandhi, refused permission. This organization is said to have held a demonstration in Delhi with a float that showed two girls sitting on a funeral pyre. Both in Delhi and in Calcutta, it was the local Marwari community (hailing from Rajasthan) that spearheaded the movement for glorification of sati as a tradition.

Ghazipur (outside Rajasthan) used to record a large number of sati incidents during the last century. It turns out that Ghazipur had a large Rajput population too.

The boards of some forty sati temples in the Shekhawati region in Rajasthan include officers of the IAS; the state Janata Party leader, Kalyan Singh Kalvi, has declared that "to build temples to sati is part of Rajput culture". The state has over 150 sati temples (the Narayani

Sati temple at Alwar, which boasts forty-eight rooms for guests used to have an annual fair every summer. One estimate puts the number of annual fairs that used to be held—till 1987—at 124).

More recently, Digvijay Singh of the former Wankaner royal family that boasts a lineage of 500 years declared in an interview that they had had at least three recorded cases of sati immolations in their family and that he considers sati to be the highest form of bravery. (Incidentally, the Shankaracharya of Puri who has been vocal in support of sati, hails from Deawar in Rajasthan).

One explanation for the resurgence of sati in Rajasthan in modern times is that the Rajputs have seen a decline in their martial glory in the twentieth century; the resentment that they have felt in consequence has led to a delusive harking back to their past glory in some form or the other. Fundamentalism has provided them with the means, through its appeal to "tradition" and "glorious heritage". Insular attitudes, particularly among the secluded women, has aided this trend and precipitated what is in essence a resurgence of fundamentalism and the attractions of obscurantism.

Whether it is the Rajput psyche, or the wider issue of oppression of women, or the socio-political nexus that has resulted in a recrudescence of fundamentalism in several areas, none of these factors in isolation can be a satisfactory explanation in itself for the glorification of sati. In conjunction, however, these factors make for a synergistic mix that intensifies the trend towards practices like immolation and allied manifestations of the degradation of women's lives.

Meekness, illiteracy and subservience do not offer a complete explanation by themselves either. These same Rajasthani women who are persuaded to believe that a woman's life is worthless without the husband, do not in fact seem very cowed or diffident in their workaday responses—one can see even rustic, illiterate women retorting and arguing with men and lambasting them, in buses and in shops. It is difficult to reconcile "sauciness" of this kind with the meekness of "letting" oneself be buried under a mound of coconuts to be roasted alive.

Besides, Rajasthan does have in its history women like Meera Bai, the celebrated poetess who is revered as a saint and whose songs are popular nationwide: she was a rebel and stubbornly refused to give up her adoration of her beloved Krishna about whom she sang in ecstatic obsession. She left her husband, the Rana, and surrendered herself to her Lord Krishna. This rebellious and self-willed woman is as much part of Rajasthan's tradition as the other legends about "virtuous women" who immolated themselves on their husbands' pyres.

This is yet another contradiction, one of many that the issue of sati manifests in relation to the modern context in which it is sought to be glorified and defended.

Perhaps the explanation lies in the fact that we have seen a volatile combination of the place, the time and the political setting, together making for a fertile ground for a rise of obscurantist incitements. And in this, political considerations have without doubt played a significant role.

Rain and 'Reign of Unreason'

You will notice that ever since this anti-sati law was enacted, nature has been revolting. Today, when we should be feeling the heat of summer, it is cold. The monsoons bring no rain. And untimely rainfall has been destroying crops ready for harvest. In the Baghpat tehsil area, large quantities of vegetables have been spoilt. All because sati has been insulted. There have been so many accidents, so many cyclones. The very day the anti-sati law was made, Calcutta's Mangla Hat was burnt and crores of rupees worth of goods destroyed. Yet, this reign of unreason continues.
—The Shankaracharya of Puri, *Sunday*, 10–16 April 1988

"In anguish and distress, with great grief and affliction, overwhelmed in a sea of sorrow, swimming in a river of tears, we now publish the sad intelligence respecting the suttees. . . ." said an editorial in the *Samachar Chandrika* of 14 November 1832. The tears and anguish were not over the fate of widows who were roasted alive on the pyres of their husbands, but over the dismissal of the petition for annulment of the sati abolition law. The *Samachar Chandrika* was a journal of the group in Calcutta which had insisted that widow burning had scriptural sanction and was therefore a religious rite that ought not to be curtailed; and this was how the paper broke the news of the privy council's refusal to block Lord Bentinck's legislation against sati.

One-hundred-and-fifty-eight years separate Bentinck's law of 1829 and the Government of India's Commission of Sati (Prevention) Act of 1987. This span of a century-and-a-half was extraordinarily eventful in terms of social, political and economic changes in the country—the 1857 War of Independence, the Quit India movement, independence and partition, the leadership of Mahatma Gandhi, Nehru and Indira Gandhi, adult franchise, rapid industrialization under a series of five year plans for development, a significant rise in incomes, life expectancy and education, space technology and test-tube babies, and a body of social legislation that is one of the most comprehensive in the world—and yet, several striking similarities can be seen in the scenarios of the two enactments on sati, which show that although statutes are important tools in tackling social aberrations, legal enactments do not on their own guarantee a change in attitudes, thoughts and responses that spring from deep-seated, socially conditioned reflexes. In fact, in some particulars, the events and reactions that followed the two legislations bring on a feeling of *deja vu*.

On both occasions, the introduction of a law brought protests from a vocal pro-sati faction that alleged interference with Hindu religious beliefs."There is Vedic authority for *sahamarana*" claimed Radhakanta Deb who spearheaded the anti-legislation protest in 1829.

Likewise, the Shankaracharya of Puri who was the first religious head to make a pro-sati pronouncement in the wake of the Roop Kanwar sati incident of 1987, declared that scriptural texts like the *Nirnayasindhu* and *Dharmasindhu* enjoined sati. If Radhakanta Deb sent a petition against the enactment to the privy council, the Shankaracharya had a case filed in the supreme court against the 1987 act. Deb's petition described immolation as a "privilege for Hindu widows" and the Shankaracharya claimed the same, adding that the Hindu faith and civilization are being destroyed. If the conservative Hindu lobby of 1829 reacted to sati abolition with "shock and great humiliation", the reaction from a similar lobby in the twentieth century was not much different—"The bill passed by the Lok Sabha may be called the blackest bill ever passed and the unanimity shown (in having it passed through parliament) is a sign of intellectual bankruptcy," said one comment from the president of a research institute near Bombay who has brought out pamphlets extolling the burning of widows as "sanctified sacrifice".

Within six weeks of the introduction of Bentinck's law, a society of diehard conservatives known as the Dharma Sabha was launched at the initiative of Radhakanta Deb against the sati abolition law. The meeting convened to form this association was "very largely attended—the line of carriages in front of the hall where the meeting was held extended to about a mile"; speeches were fiery and even violent. A sum of 20,000 rupees was set aside towards the acquisition of suitable premises for the association; of this 11,260 rupees was collected on the spot. In its deliberations, the Sabha recorded that Hinduism had suffered a great detriment and called upon the faithful to "unite to defend their religion and its excellent customs".[1] The petition submitted against the enactment described sati as "not only a sacred duty but a high privilege for any Hindu widow who sincerely believed in the doctrines of her religion".

So it was in 1987 too, in the aftermath of the sati at Deorala, when the Sati Dharma Raksha Samiti was set up. Following the introduction of a law prohibiting the glorification of sati, this organization had to drop the word Sati from its name (it became the Dharma Raksha Samiti) but it was not much different from the Dharma Sabha of the nineteenth century in its reactions and objectives. The rally that this organization held in Jaipur drew a mammoth crowd of 70,000, and fiery speeches were made on this occasion too, with allegations of threats to the Hindu religion. The thirteenth day ceremony at Deorala to mark Roop Kanwar's immolation drew a crowd that was described as "two kilometres long". And a former officer of the IAS, Onkar Singh, filed a case in the high court against the sati legislation. A huge amount of money, estimated around seventy-five lakh rupees, was reportedly collected in a matter of days as donations towards the construction of a memorial for Roop Kanwar.

Even though the scriptural position on sati had been investigated and examined and thrashed threadbare, by the administration, by scholars and the law courts, prior to the introduction of the regulation of 1812, the sati incident of 1987 once again saw the same kind of schism, with Swami Ranganathananda, a senior monk of the Ramakrishna Mission condemning the rite and saying that there was "no connection whatsoever between Hinduism and social evils like sati", the Shankaracharya of Puri eulogizing the custom, a Rajasthan lawyer advocating "a sati in every village". If not with such a "flood of tears" as with the *Samachar Chandrika*, an editorial in the *Jansatta* said that sati deserved reverence and pride. ("One in a million widows resolves to be sati and it is only natural that her self-sacrifice should become the centre of people's devotion and worship".) It also added that "the British and those influenced by their education gave a bad name to our religion and tradition by exaggerating a few incidents. . . ."

The argument before the privy council was that if the law were not repealed, "the minds of one hundred million subjects will at once be unsettled". Just as Rammohun Roy and the Brahmo Samaj met this sectarian opposition with a counter-protest that included a petition to the House of Lords against the plea for a reversal of the anti-sati regulation, Swami Agnivesh and his supporters of the Arya Samaj launched a counter-protest against the pro-sati faction; Agnivesh challenged the Shankaracharya to a public debate on whether the Hindu scriptures required widows to burn.

The *Chandrika* in its 1832 editorial had predicted that the government would see "many wonderful, unheard of, unthought of marvels—such as conflagrations, inundations, drought, deluging rain, famine, plague, lightnings, burstings of the heavens, confusions and such like calamities. . ."

Likewise, the Shankaracharya, at a meeting in Hyderabad in May 1988 attributed citizens' problems to lapses in religious observances and suggested that the water scarcity in the city would disappear if any woman offered to become a sati. The intervening years had made no difference at all.

"When such an injury against religion as this is committed, we must conclude that justice has departed from the earth", observed the *Chandrika*. "In the kingdom of England, *compassion* is extinct. . . If Hindus had any other place to which they could go, they might *prolong their lives* in the observance there of their religion. . ."[2] (italics mine). The irony of this argument is that it talks of "compassion" and "prolonging one's life" in the same breath in which it urges the cruel termination of widows' lives by burning!

Another parallel between the post-regulation years of the nineteenth century and the post-ordinance period of the twentieth can be seen in the manner in which the promoters of sati sought to circumvent the law. When widow burning was prohibited in the Bombay territory by the British authorities, those intent on carrying out the rite simply went out to nearby areas like Satara and got on (and away) with the burning. Similarly, because sati was forbidden in Calcutta, cremations were carried out just outside the city limits, so that widows could burn on the pyre. In 1988, a few days before the first anniversary observances of Roop Kanwar's death, news reports alleged that people bent on glorifying her were planning to congregate in a nearby village a few days before the police could promulgate restrictions to block the approach roads to Deorala. Subsequently, this ruse gave way to another one of deciding to observe the anniversary not on the date according to the common Roman calendar but on the day of the anniversary according to the Indian lunar calendar—three weeks later. Even the *chunari* ceremony on the thirteenth day was held two hours earlier than scheduled, to pre-empt a police swoop. For his defence of the abolition of sati, Rammohun Roy had two attempts made on his life. Likewise, the *sarpanch* of Deorala who condemned sati in the aftermath of the 1987 immolation received threats from the Dharma Raksha Samiti activists. And just as Rammohun Roy was 'rebuffed and humiliated' even by the authorities (who were bringing in legislation to ban sati), so also Swami Agnivesh in 1987 was arrested and humiliated by the same government whose enactment he was supporting!

Edward Thompson records that "within hours of a sati at Patna in 1904, a shrine came up to mark the immolation and lamps were lit and booths erected to supply the needs of visitors to the place". A news item in October 1987 likewise, recorded that when a temple built in the Ranjit Nagar locality of Jaipur to glorify a sati was demolished by the police, it was rebuilt within two days—and this was a site close to the chief minister's residence! In the exultation of the pro-sati faction in its fight against the government too, there is a similarity—the Dharma Sabha of 1830 gloated over its "excellent prospects of winning their case" (before the privy council) and the pro-sati group in 1988 boasted spiritedly that "the government's case (against those apprehended in the Deorala case) is bound to fail".

Even before Lord Bentinck passed the 1829 law prohibiting sati, those who condemned the rite had pointed out that offenders could have been punished under the homicide laws already available. Likewise, in 1987 too, critics of the government—women's groups in particular—pointed out that the existing laws were sufficient to punish the guilty, even without a new enactment on sati.

The similarities in the two scenarios is nowhere as striking as in the political dimensions of the handling of the sati issue by the authorities—the British colonizers in the nineteenth century and the Indian government in 1987.

In the decision making responses of the governments, definitions of what is judicious have always been coloured as much by considerations of sagacity and expediency as by those of morality and fair play. In the case of sati, the desirability of abolition was never so much in question as its feasibility, and at least over the last four centuries, the reactions of the body politic to what is conceded to be an offensive rite have been influenced by political constraints.

During the medieval years of Mughal rule, the official position on sati was, as during the subsequent British rule, to discourage immolations but without offending Hindu sentiments. Since, over the years, sati had come to be seen as a religious observance, both Muslim and Christian rulers thought it prudent to let caution rein in any impulses towards prohibition, lest they be accused of religious persecution. Humayun, Akbar and Jehangir had all frowned upon widow burning; in Akbar's time, official permission was necessary for immolation; this procedure, it was believed, would give the woman time in which attempts to dissuade her could be made.

Francois Bernier who chronicled his travels in India between 1656 and 1668, wrote that the incidence of sati was "less than in the time before the Mohamedans". He added: "They (the Mughals) did not indeed forbid it by a positive law because it is a part of their policy to leave the idolatrous population, which is so much more numerous than their own, in the free exercise of its religion; but the practice is checked by indirect means—the government never grants permission unless convinced that she cannot be turned aside from her resolve".[3] As part of this policy of devious deterrence, inducements like child-support payments were often offered to the widow in order to persuade her not to burn. "Which is so much more numerous than their own", is significant; the political need of avoiding disgruntlement in the populace determined the pattern of the official policy of the Muslim rulers. This line of thinking was current under British rule too, when it took the greater part of a quarter century for the idea of prohibition, first put forward in the opening years of the nineteenth century, to take the shape of a law. Neither Wellesley, nor his successors, Cornwallis, Hastings or Amherst took decisive action because of the possible political ramifications. Would an unequivocal prohibition threaten the East India Company's economic and political stakes in the country? That was the question that shaped their responses to sati, rather than whether sati was morally defensible. Besides, Hastings was busy with military operations which had prior claims to his attention, and the question of sati was shelved. Further, the regulation of 1812 was announced only after carefully ascertaining the stance that the Hindu scriptures took on widow immolation, and sticking to those guidelines. It was important for the British to avoid the charge that they were interfering in the religious affairs, a charge that could threaten the hold that the British had and were seeking to strengthen further in the subcontinent. "The practice being recognised and encouraged by the doctrines of the Hindu religion," the regulation said, "it would be allowed in cases in which it was countenanced by their religion". The overriding consideration was thus, even in a matter of saving human lives from a fiery death, the political fallout from official intervention. Once the British felt secure enough as colonizers, a measure of readiness to take a stand in keeping with the dictates of morality became manifest.

"Whether the question be to continue or to discontinue the practice of sati, the decision is equally surrounded by an awful responsibility", Lord Bentinck wrote in his minutes of 8 November 1829. Balancing the fact of "hundreds of innocent victims being consigned year after year to a cruel and untimely end" was the possibility of "putting to hazard the very safety of the British empire in India"; widow burning was abhorrent, quite uncontestedly, but "the greater good of mankind" which depended upon the continuance of British sovereignty in India (as they saw it), had justified the tolerance of what he described as "this inhuman practice" even if such tolerance was conceded to be "a foul stain upon British rule".

It was not so much then, a reluctance to offend religious sentiments amongst the natives, that was the reason for official inaction. Afterall, the chief pundit of the supreme court, Mrityunjoy, had declared that sati was "a modern innovation" (and therefore not part of the most authoritative scriptures); and Rammohun Roy's translation óf the *Isopanishad* in 1816 declared that sati was "a fatal error". The will to seize these supports was, however, lacking, and the administration persisted with what Poynder called a "timid and reptile policy" of inaction.

Among the considerations that finally tilted the balance towards prohibition was a sense of increasing political security. Lord Bentinck too hesitated over the move for a while, as he himself noted—"during the whole of the present year, much public agitation has been excited and when discontent is abroad. . .and when the native army have been under a degree of alarm lest their allowances should suffer with that of their European officers, *it would have been unwise to have given a handle to artful and designing enemies to disturb the public peace*" (italics mine). That problem having been resolved towards the end of the year, the prohibitory law became possible. "When we had powerful neighbours and had greater reason to doubt our own sincerity", he continued, "expediency might recommend a more cautious proceeding, but now that we are supreme", the decision to ban sati was made.

But for more than a decade before this, officials of the administration had been urging action. The collector of Bombay had declared in 1818 that there would be no untoward repercussions if sati were abolished by law. The commissioner of Surat likewise urged strong measures to prohibit sati, and observed that "the practice of sati once unknown in these provinces, appeared to be gaining ground under the impression that the authorities were in favour of the custom". He suggested that sati be made indictable for murder. A year later, the magistrate of Faruckabad too advised abolition.

One suggestion put forward two years earlier, during 1817, was the confiscation of the property that would have come to a widow (so that her relatives would not stand to gain by her death). This was turned down on the political grounds that the move could be misconstrued (as a ruse for extending British ownership on private property). In the years that followed, several magistrates urged prohibition but the official policy continued to be what the resident at Delhi described as "a slight hint at disapprobation" even in cases of sati prohibited under the then existing restrictive regulations.

Lord Amherst described sati as "a detestable superstition" but claimed that "nothing but the apprehension of evils infinitely greater than those arising from the existence of the practice could induce us to tolerate it a single day". This was four years after both the court of Nizamat Adalat and the governor-general had conceded that the partial regulations had been ineffective and had in fact contributed to an increase in the incidence of sati. Another six-and-a-half-years were to pass before the British authorities felt politically secure enough to take decisive action in outlawing sati. In the meantime, in spite of the gathering clamour for action, Lord Amherst responded with "a classic defence of a policy of epic passivity in the face of a gruesome social evil, characteristic of unimaginative, not to say insensitive, bureaucrats".[4]

Shahabad was one of the particularly bad areas in terms of the number of immolations. The magistrate reported in 1823 that sati could, and should, be prohibited. The magistrate of Ghazipur (another infamous place for sati) concurred. The magistrate of Chittagong had declared even in 1818 that he foresaw no trouble if a law was enacted. In 1826, Judge Smith of the court of directors insisted on "immediate and active prohibition"; he was supported in this demand by Judge Ross who declared that "no disaffection would be caused among the natives"; and still the government dithered and dragged its feet.

In January 1828, Lord Amherst was still convinced that "inaction was best", although by that time four of the five judges of the Nizamat Adalat including the chief judge, were in favour of the legal prohibition. A year earlier, Poynder in his speech before the court of the East India Company had argued that "more may now be done with the most perfect security".

Typifying the precedence of political expediency was the response of the Sanskrit scholar H.H. Wilson who, even while conceding that the Shastras did not command a widow to burn and that immolation was not mentioned in the codes of Manu, nevertheless opposed a legal ban and predicted "extensive dread and detestation of British authority". (Much the same argument formed the base for the petition placed before the privy council by the pro-sati group following Lord Bentinck's legislation).

If the annals of sati in the three decades leading up to its legal suppression in 1829 have a common thread running through them, it is that the administration was impelled as much (if not more) by what was politic as by what was equitable and just.

This anxiety about possible political repercussions led to some muddled thinking in the official responses in both the nineteenth and the twentieth centuries. Thus, a report from the magistrate of south Concan in 1819 about three sati immolations being prevented brought the "alarmed response"—"the governor in council desires that Mr Pelly will not interfere in the performance of such sacrifices except in the mildest mode of persuasion".[5] This policy of looking officially the other way resulted in the death of a widow who had escaped from the pile (and died two days later) being recorded officially as a "natural death—probably from burns she had received".[6]

Some of the officials who found the practice shocking and took an active stand opposing it, seemed to have second thoughts after considering the matter from a political perspective. For instance, Charles Metcalfe had forbidden sati in Delhi in 1811 and had even used force on one occasion to prevent an immolation; and yet, as provisional governor-general of India, he expressed the opinion that interference with what was seen as a cherished Hindu custom could be used as a rallying cry in inciting rebellion against the British. Likewise, J.H. Harrington, a judge with the Nizamat Adalat, who had had a hand in giving shape to the first prohibitory regulation and had subsequently even submitted a memorandum to the House of Commons urging legal prohibition, later advised a delay in the introduction of the statutory ban; in fact even Rammohun Roy who pioneered the move against sati with his famous tracts and arguments, is quoted by Lord Bentinck as having articulated the possibility of discontent and trouble.

This fear of resentment and insurrection resulted in some cases where even when the culprits were apprehended, their sentences were set aside. One example was the incident of 1820 in Gorakhpur in which a fourteen-year-old widow jumped out of the pyre in agony; her uncle and others took her by the hands and feet and flung her back into the fire. She escaped a second time and, much burnt, sought refuge in a nearby well. The uncle brought a sheet and asked her to sit on it, promising that he would carry her home. When reluctantly she complied, they bound her instead and burnt her. The Nizamat Adalat which tried six men for this atrocity decided that they were guilty of only culpable homicide, not murder, and awarded sentences of two to five years. The Gorakhpur judge suggested the death penalty in order to make an example of the culprits, but even the lesser sentences were reportedly commuted to road labour.[7]

In another case, three men were apprehended in Madhurikhand and awarded seven years' imprisonment in 1831—nearly two years *after* sati was made illegal—but the governor-general awarded a pardon. A year later, when the first case came up for trial under the new law, Lord Bentinck again pardoned the accused, after setting aside the high court verdict. Where the certainty of punishment would have been an effective deterrent, such soft-pedalling reduced even the legal enactment to ineffectiveness. Even a scrupulous adherence to 'rules' ("the pile was constructed in accordance with the specifications, under my own superintendence") in which the spirit of the entire exercise of prohibitory regulations was lost, could only have been occasioned by the official decision to seem to be tolerant of what was regarded as a rite sanctioned by religion.

It was not just popular resentment that the government was apprehensive about but, more importantly, disgruntlement among the army personnel. (After all, the 1857 War of Independence was sparked off by disgruntled sepoys). Although, in the dozen years prior to the enactment no less than forty officials of the administration had urged abolition, it was only after setting at rest the government's apprehensions about the army's reactions that the decision in favour of an enactment was finally made. (Of forty-nine officers whose opinion was sought, only five had opposed legislation). Reinforcing this move towards a ban was the further discovery that a large majority of sati incidents (420 out of 463 recorded) was from the lower provinces of Bengal, Bihar and Orissa; the people of these areas were considered "mild mannered, not likely to launch an insurgency" while the upper provinces recorded far fewer sati incidents. Lord Bentinck had in addition checked that army recruits from the lower provinces formed only a small proportion of the total military strength. Had it been otherwise, given the same circumstances, the same governor-general would perhaps (as per his own observations in his minutes) not have brought in legislation.

One additional consideration that reassured him was that Goa and Sawantvadi had prohibited sati, without suffering untoward repercussions. The French and the Dutch administrators too had prohibited sati in the areas of Chandernagore and Chinsura respectively, without causing any problems.

And so, the decision to ban sati resulted in a law, only when it was seen as politically safe. It is a measure of the weight that political considerations carried that even in the court of directors and at Westminster, "not everybody was convinced that Bentinck had done the sensible thing even if it was the right thing".

Along with the political considerations, there was another aspect too for disapproving the Sati Abolition Law— the Bishop of Calcutta, Reginald Heber, was among those who opposed the legislation because he felt that such a move would hinder the missionaries in their work of converting Hindus to Christianity. Proselytizing was seen as one way of saving widows and reducing the number of lives lost on the pyre.

Yet, when the political and pecuniary interests of the British demanded it, the authorities had, apparently, no compunctions about violating the traditional Hindu injunctions; for instance, notwithstanding the strictures against the crossing of the seas, native recruits in the army were commanded to sail across during the Burma war. Similarly, Fanny Parks recorded, on hearing about the Sati Abolition Law, that "the government interferes with native superstition where rupees are in question"—the tax on pilgrims for instance; the one rupee collected from each person for bathing at holy places, she noted, "was sufficient to live on for a month"—and yet, this steep levy did not bother the authorities, since it swelled the state's coffers. (At one pilgrim centre alone, the Jagannath temple at Puri, the tax collected during 1817–18 and 1818–19 exceeded £10,000. In 1822–23, the collection exceeded £29,156).[8]

During the time that Lord Bentinck was finalizing his decision on the abolition, Lt. Col. Tod had suggested that as a gesture of goodwill (to counteract any resentment over the prohibition of sati) the tax on pilgrims may be given up. Lord Bentinck turned down the suggestion, in view of the considerable revenue that the tax yielded—again, a political decision. Lending weight to this theory is a piece of evidence in the form of a letter from a civilian officer of the East India Company. "So long as this practice does not interfere with the punctual collection of revenue", he observed, "nor with the regular administration of justice, there is little probability of its attracting the degree of attention necessary to its suppression".

If politics had a hand in the official reluctance in introducing legislation, their concern with the sati issue too has been interpreted as a response born of reactions other than humanitarianism. The rite of sati, this argument goes, challenged the state's monopoly over the right to take life. It also helped to project the colonial subjects in a disreputable light so that this manifestation of barbarity in their observances reinforced the right of the aliens to rule over the country, and legitimize British rule.[9] The ultimate consideration in this argument too, was political.

The suppression of sati in the Indian native states outside the British dominion was also influenced by political considerations. The defeat of the Khalsa by the British led to a greater inclination among the native rulers to respect British sentiments on sati, and fall in line. The Nawab of Junagarh, for instance, promised to prohibit sati in 1838 because of British pressure. Bikaner, Alwar and Udaipur outlawed sati in the years following the British enactment largely because with British ascendancy lending him support, Lord Dalhousie was able to flex his political muscles and use threats in furthering causes that the British saw fit to back. The Maharaja of Patiala imposed a fine on culprits indicted in a sati incident not because sati was illegal in the state but because Patiala along with Nabha and other Sikh states had accepted alliances with the

British in 1833 and it was considered politic to take into account British feelings.

G.T. Vigne, in *Travels in Kashmir*, points out that "only seven women were burned with the body of Runjit Singh; a very small number, considering his rank, but it was no doubt deemed expedient to show some respect to European prejudice!"

The immolation of the wife of Shahu, Shivaji's grandson, in 1749 gives a striking example of the way political considerations resulted in encouraging a woman to burn. When Shivaji's son Rajaram died, only one of his three wives, Ambikabai, mounted the pyre; the other two, Tarabai and Rajasbai, did not. Shahu's wife Sakvarbai, however, had no co-wives and so, if she had decided not to burn, it would have been noticed by the public; besides (and more importantly), the suggestion for her immolation came mainly from Tarabai who saw Sakvarbai as a political rival. ("If she lives, she will create trouble for the raj", as a biography of Tarabai by Brij Kishore points out)—what really led Sakvarbai to mount the pyre was neither devotion to her husband nor fear of public opinion, but the realization that if she lived she would have to face the hostility of Tarabai and her ally, the powerful Peshwa, and that "life would be worse than death". Sati in this case offered Tarabai an opportune device for doing away with a political rival.

Sati incidents continued to be recorded even in the years after independence, but none of them caused a nationwide furore the way the Deorala incident of 1987 did, nor was it thought necessary to bring in fresh legislation banning the custom. An immolation that took place seven years before the Deorala sati was in fact very similar to the Roop Kanwar death; a sixteen-year-old girl named Om Kanwar had burned to death in Jhadli village but there was no public outcry on the same scale as in 1987. One reason was the socio-political climate—for one thing, women's groups had an important role in persisting with protests even in the face of official apathy in the 1987 incident; for another, fundamentalist trends that were coming to the fore at the time of the later incident were able to seize the incident and turn it to political advantage in pursuit of their own goals.

The official attitude towards the Deorala sati was initially one of apathy as in earlier incidents. Given the strong sentiments in the region on sati, the ruling party and the opposition both chose a policy of silence; this was a political decision, based on misgivings about alienating the electorate through condemnation of the practice. The first public condemnation by a politician came eleven days after the event. Although, on the basis of the order that the high court had issued prohibiting the *chunari* ceremony, Section 144 could have been imposed to

forbid people from gathering for the event, this simple expedient was
not resorted to, and official action was restricted to distributing pamphlets informing the participants in the ceremony that there was a ban
on the glorification ritual. "There would have been a massive loss of
life, if the police had taken action to stop the ceremony", said the officials. (This police inaction, incidentally, was itself seen by some as a
manifestation of "the power of *sati mata* to ensure the success of the
event", and this contributed to a strengthening of the mystique of sati).
And yet, this police theory of the need for caution in the face of mob
sentiments was not in evidence on other occasions—just four months
earlier, for instance, the police had managed to disperse a crowd that was
said to have been 20,000 strong in the Pali district, when another sati
incident was prevented. In 1985, at Devipura, a few minutes away from
Deorala, yet another immolation had been stopped when the deputy
superintendent of police ordered his men to fire five rounds in the air to
disperse a crowd of 25,000 persons. On several other occasions too,
when crowds had collected to protest against the government, the police
had not hesitated to use strong measures—including bullets—to
disperse these assemblies.

Arrests under the preventive detention law could have been made at
Deorala, since advance information about the plans for the *chunari* event
were available. Deorala could have also been declared a disturbed area.
Instead, either deliberately or by default, those arrested in connection
with the death of Roop Kanwar were in fact released on bail (although
their arrests had been in the first instance made under charges that were
non-bailable). Reports say that there were instructions not to make
arrests till after the ceremony.

Such kid-glove handling was defended by the authorities initially
with the argument that this was "basically a religious, family observance". (250,000 people turned up for the "family observance"—and
that was a conservative estimate!)

The Shankaracharya of Puri has been publicly, stridently and repeatedly eulogizing sati as a glorious tradition. Swami Agnivesh had demanded action against the Shankaracharya for breaking the law, and filed
a public interest petition in the supreme court "on behalf of all citizens
who stand for the dignity of women and humanism and who are against
crimes against women being committed in the name of religion or
tradition". But it was Agnivesh who was arrested on grounds that he
was threatening the peace, while the Shankaracharya did not get arrested.
As one commentator has pointed out, "it was (politically) far less risky
to arrest Agnivesh whereas arresting the Shankaracharya would have
meant facing the hostility of his community of followers".

Social activists and observers have all remarked on how the entire exercise of legal enactments, lackadaisical enforcement and the public mood of defiance had a political flavour.

Confronted by activists who demanded why the Shankaracharya had been able to get away with his inflammatory pronouncements, the minister for home affairs claimed that the Shankaracharya had come "perilously close to an arrest". Subsequently, speaking at the convention of the All India Dharam Mahasangh in October 1988, the Shankaracharya again spoke in praise of sati, instead of on cow slaughter which was the topic scheduled. At this convention the claim was made that Rajasthan had received "good rains this year" after a long period of drought because of Roop Kanwar's sati. And yet, no arrests were made. The administration periodically "warned" the Shankaracharya that he would be arrested, the speaker of the parliament declared that the Shankaracharya was "not above the law"; and yet, the administration fought shy of taking decisive action and enforcing its own fiats.

This politicization of all areas of life that reduces the common man, even in a democracy, to a mere spectator in the power game, is indeed a characteristic of the times and offers one explanation for several aberrant trends of which sati was one.

The media condemned the pro-sati stance of the Shankaracharya and highlighted the political motivations behind the move to glorify sati as an exalted tradition; with the result that the authorities, faced with the dilemma of an expedient soft-pedalling in the face of the possibility of a quick communal flare-up on the one hand and rising censure from the media on the other, turned its ire on the latter—journalists visiting the *sati sthal* were greeted with hostility not only by the pro-sati elements but also by the police and by the political elements; other visitors were left in peace.

Those in positions of authority do not seem committed to, or convinced of the need for, the policies drawn up on paper; thus politicians attend sati functions and VIPs lend their support to groups with a vested interest in flouting the prohibitory rules. When, for instance, all vehicular traffic was stopped on the way to Deorala on the day of the *chunari* ceremony, VIPs' cars were exempted and allowed to proceed to the event. Two years after the Sati Prohibition Law was enacted, the authorities were confiscating the money collected by the Beerji temple in Sikar, and then returning it to the temple "for expenses!" The nexus is neat and straightforward—politicians are the ones who make the rules, and whatever they wish to back or promote become allowed (through instructions that are seen as violable only at one's risk) and what they wish to back depends on how such backing would promote their own power base for political ends.

Power, then, is the crux—in the early centuries, when esoteric and scriptural learning was the exclusive preserve of a community that could interpret or interpolate edicts to suit its convenience, knowledge as power was the determinant; in the modern context where political dimensions dwarf other considerations even in matters where compassion should be paramount, pelf and position constitute power.

The trustees of the Jhunjhunu sati temple are said to have clout in both the state capital as well as in Delhi; Delhi saw four new sati temples come up during the 1970s. In this nexus between politics and commerce, it is consideration's not so much of compassion or correctness as of convenience, that dictate the responses of the authorities on the one hand and those who glorify sati in the name of religion on the other. Even official pussyfooting springs from considerations of threats to power. If the British authorities a century-and-a-half ago wanted to conciliate the native subjects, today it is the electorate that needs to be kept satisfied.

The sati debate merely reflects the pervasive proclivity to 'milk' every development for personal gain; although the enactment expressly forbids the use of sati as a campaign issue, it has in fact inevitably become one—at the second anniversary observance of Roop Kanwar's death in Deorala, the convenor of the Yuva Dharma Raksha Samiti is said to have declared stridently, "This government wants to finish off Hinduism and Rajputs in the name of the anti-sati law".

In January 1988, when a woman named Shakuntala Yadav died in suspicious circumstances in Mihir Kheria village in the state of U.P., there was a move to treat it as a case of sati, for political reasons—"a sati in the Lok Dal (political party) family could even win the Lok Dal some popularity," as one report wryly put it.

Even the Shankaracharya, referred to as the *jagadguru* (universal guru) has a political background as well as ambitions—he talks of starting a political party "to safeguard Hinduism"; he used to be associated with the Rama Rajya Parishad party and has listed the conditions under which he would extend support to political forces.

Political stances, alliances and involvement are decided on the basis of how the land lies—a leader eulogizes and supports a particular incident, and this is taken as a hint for his 'followers' to align themselves accordingly. What one sees, therefore, is opportunism; and if opportunism finds a fertile ground in the prevailing political attitude to social problems, it is because of increasing fundamentalism. In the context of the sati issue in recent months, what was egregious was not just the incident at Deorala itself but the support for it that became manifest.

The pressures of modern living, increasing cynicism, crumbling ethical values in a society that is going through a churning up process, increasing materialistic expectations coupled with a reality that falls short of expectations, and educated unemployment that becomes a fertile recruiting ground for volatile sentiments and lumpen frenzy (youth was very much in the vanguard of the pro-sati rallies)—put together, these ingredients make a cocktail that serves fundamentalist revivalism admirably.

Part of the fundamentalist trend worldwide is the manifest hostility to changes in women's lives—the pro-life argument in the US; the return to the *chador* in Khomeini's Iran, and the controversy over the Shah Bano case (in which she claimed maintenance following divorce) which led to the Muslim Women's Bill in India, are all examples of this trend.

Women have, over the last few years, become more vocal and visible in India. Women's groups were in the forefront of the action against the perpetrators of the Deorala sati. Faced initially with official apathy, a few hundred women marched to the secretariat to submit a memorandum and, dissatisfied with the official response, decided to file a case and obtained a high court order prohibiting the thirteenth day *chunari* ceremony. It was women's organizations again which demanded an inquiry into the allegations of female infanticide in the family of one of the members of the legislative assembly, and women's organizations that demanded the arrest of the Shankaracharya for his pro-sati statements. When the annual Dussera celebrations in Delhi in 1988 planned to enact the story of Sati Sulochana extolling the virtues of sati, seventeen women's organizations went to court with a writ petition which resulted in the supreme court seeking an assurance from the organizers that the episode would not be enacted.

When the film *Panetar* glorifying sati was given tax exemption by the Gujarat government, it was once again women's groups in Ahmedabad that protested and forced a withdrawal of the concession. And it was a woman member of the Lok Sabha who protested that a former union minister for law was pleading the case of the Jhunjhunu temple in the supreme court for the continuance of its annual fair. It was women who staged a protest *dharna* in Delhi in September 1988 against the supreme court ruling in the Jhunjhunu temple case. This kind of increasing articulateness of women has been one of the factors forcing the state to bestir itself and take action on several issues. Disturbingly, because of the fundamentalist thraldom that the state is held in, this increasing articulateness of women is itself contested and decried, with efforts to "put them in their place" in the name of tradition—this is part of the historical interconnectedness of sexual and social hierarchies.

In this harking back to tradition, only those elements of past practice are picked out that fit in with what this faction wishes to fortify as part of its ideology. According to ancient Indian tradition as decreed by Manu, a householder was required to become a hermit in the final phase of his life (*vanaprastha*). No one enjoins this now, as part of dharma. Traditional ethics as defined by the *Brhadaranyaka Upanishad* recognizes "total equality between man and woman—The divine person parted one's own body into two; from that came husband and wife". Therefore, Yajnavalkya said, "this body (of husband and wife) is one half of oneself, each is like one of the two halves of a splitpea". This beautiful conception reveals that one is incomplete without the other.[10] However, this traditional view is not among those picked out for promotion. Our corpus of Hindu scriptures also includes a verse that declares that "whoever offers God a single flower or ripe banana with devotion, earns enough merit to dwell in heaven for three crore years". In the name of a similar sojourn in heaven, self-immolation of a widow is sought to be promoted as a duty, while the simpler, easier and kinder expedient of making an offering of fruit or flower is ignored.

How a society defines and perceives tradition varies from time to time. "Very often, when we wish to insist on a particular form of behaviour or attitude or value system, we simply say, 'This is traditional', the assumption being that it has been handed down to us, unchanged, over a long period of time. That assumption is incorrect. Because traditions, even when they are handed down, do not remain frozen. What we regard as tradition today may in fact be something that was invented four or five generations ago".[11]

And yet, seeking the support of 'tradition', the Shankaracharya declares that "women and *shudras*" are not fit to study the Shastras.[12]

Debate, doubt and dissent having been forbidden to women in the name of tradition, those seeking to question these inconsistencies in the scriptures are described contemptuously as "feminists", with feminism itself taking on shades of contumely. The Shankaracharya has described women who have challenged his pronouncements on sati, as "surpanakas and thadakas" (female demons in the *Ramayana*). This pronouncement of his typifies the attitude of those who enjoin sati as a part of tradition. According to them, condemnation of sati amounts to condemnation of chastity and virtue—therefore those women (and men)

who argue against sati are said to be advocating sexual licence and immorality.

The identification of 'traditional' with 'moral' and 'modern' with 'immoral' is thus sought to be made; this ignores the fact that not all women in the ancient lore were 'virtuous'—Kunti, in the *Mahabharata*, for instance, was an unwed mother; the *Kalika Purana* even mentions incest.

Modernity in confrontation with tradition, is not the issue, although it is made out to be so. The Shankaracharya's stance is of interest because he commands a following as a religious head, and also because he articulates the arguments that the revivalist groups present in their attempts at manipulating obscurantist impositions, particularly with reference to women's position in society. "What do you city women know about sacred *pativrata* ideals?" is a familiar reflex in this faction to questions from women challenging them. "I know about the morality of these modern women journalists", is another. "They want freedom", is a condemnation with overtones that imply that demands for "freedom" mean moral laxity and promiscuity; therefore, "freedom" for women is decried—even by those who declare that freedom (to immolate herself) is infringed by the government's enactments on sati. The association of "chastity" with "conservative" on the one hand, and "modern" with "western" or "degenerate morality" on the other, results in even women sometimes becoming collaborators in the confirmation of their own inferiority, in order not to defy "tradition".

Ranged against this obscurantist support for the continuation of "tradition" is the secular voice of the Agnivesh group that emphasizes humanitarianism, justice and fair play. This confrontation epitomizes in fact the battle lines down the ages, and is manifest in the stances taken by the Shankaracharya of Puri on the one hand and Swami Agnivesh on the other, in the discussions on sati in recent years.

By politicizing this schism, the pro-sati faction is able to incite communal passions by declaring that if the rest of the Hindu community did not back them, the Rajputs would split from the community and create "a Punjab-like situation".[13]

In the face of sectarianism like this, even laws become ineffectual.

*

Several stark dichotomies characterize the Indian scene today, and these go a long way in explaining why the debate on sati surfaced again in 1987 after so many decades, and how a practice that is morally offensive can be defended and glorified.

There is this curious coexistence of volatile sensibilities and torpid apathy—the Ram Janmabhoomi–Babri Masjid controversy over a site claimed as sacred by both Hindus and Muslims, a short story in a Sunday newspaper that is seen as "offending the feelings" of a particular section, the renaming of a university, a ban on some book—and thousands of demonstrators gather in a show of strength or paralyze normal life through mob violence resulting in the destruction of public property worth several lakh rupees. At the same time, this same community can go about its routine with an air of seemingly callous detachment and unconcern, in the face of roadside starvation deaths, or drought or floods, as long as it does not touch one's own life. In a similar fashion, there is a dichotomy in the Indian attitude to women—the concept of *ardhanareeswara* (divinity seen as a half-male–half-female manifestation, so that neither is complete without the other) finds no parallel in any other culture; and yet even while underscoring this exaltation of the female as Shakti, in actuality women are required to be totally subservient and self-effacing. Deified in the abstract and demeaned in real life, the Indian woman is caught between two approaches that seem mutually incompatible. (An example of this curious splicing together of attitudes to the female is a report that said that little girls in the drought afflicted areas of western India were made to fast in order to bring rains because "only girls have *devi's* Shakti" and their prayers would have been fruitful, while the boys were not to fast).

We have a plethora of statutes for women's welfare; at the same time we have seen crimes against women increase over the years, with dowry deaths alone by the hundreds testifying to the increasing degradation of women in society.

We boast of the latest in medical technology—and at the same time see the use of sex-determination tests for the selective destruction of female foetuses because girls are unwelcome and seen as a burden in our society.

The government recently instituted a ministry for women's affairs; the same government also included a minister who declared that sex-determination tests for the purpose of aborting female foetuses were good because they would reduce the female population and, through the laws of supply and demand, bring an improvement in their status. If abortion is legal, female foeticide should not be objected to, he argues, without addressing the sexist bias in the latter.

These dichotomous anomalies are themselves a manifestation of a mood of social confusion and restlessness, and religious revivalism is one of the forms that this mood takes, as well as exploits.

American history texts point out that the oppression of the black man often led to his taking out his frustration and anger on the black woman—treated unfairly at work by his own white master, the black slave came home and beat up his wife instead of seeking her support and sympathy, because she came to be seen as the only conduit available for the relief of his feelings of outrage. Many crimes against women are seen as springing from such a reaction. Perhaps a similar reasoning sees the pro-sati argument seeking to validate a 'glorified immolation' in the name of religion. In addition, by literally taking the event out of the sanctified premises of the home, the practice₁helps rationalize the event.

In a scenario of flux like this, pleasing the different sections of the population becomes the criterion for policy decisions; more than justice being done, justice *seen* to be done becomes expedient—passing laws to ban sati will appease one section that finds the practice abhorrent; collaborating—by default—in the devious flouting of these same laws appeases those factions that oppose the imposition of the law. Women, in consequence, become, on the one hand, one more group to be appeased, and on the other, one more parameter for manipulation towards ends dictated by political motivations.

One argument from the pro-sati camp questions the condemnation of widow burning in the face of the incidents of bride burning that the country records with sickening regularity. The number of dowry deaths are far greater than the number of sati immolations, so why make a fuss over the latter? True, in spite of the law prohibiting dowry demands, the custom persists. This again, is partly because of the half-heartedness in implementation of the statutes—civil servants, and even police officials are among the culprits, which shows that the people in charge of enforcing the law are themselves not convinced of the perniciousness of the custom. While enactments are important and necessary, they cannot guarantee change on their own in the absence of change in social thinking. Further, this change in social thinking is affected and sought to be influenced by fundamentalist forces that usurp issues for political ends.

Part of the problem has also been the piecemeal tackling of issues that makes each such effort individually and separately ineffective or counter-productive. To give just one example, the Rajput Jhadejas were persuaded to give up the custom of female infanticide a hundred years ago, with the result that when they began to preserve their daughters, many of them remained unmarried (since the root cause of infanticide was the pride of the Jhadejas which refused to sanction alliances with clans seen as "inferior" to their own). Instead of solving the problem, the move for 'progress' threatened to result in a reversion to infanticide!

In the same way, as long as the problems of dowry, widow denigration, the social obsession with male progeny, and the marginalization of women in the mainstream of life remain, bringing in laws, whether to curb dowry deaths, sati, female infanticide or other aberrant customs can only be a partial measure. What needs to be tackled is the basic perceptions of society that give rise to these aberrations. The law prohibits the deed, but the background that was responsible for the occurrence (of sati, dowry deaths, infanticide etc.) remains.

The concepts of sanctity of life, compassion and humaneness are basic and common to all religions of the world, including Hinduism. No religion ever endorses killing. A religion that said—as Hinduism did—that even a woman who was a *patita* was not to be abandoned and that if a woman had a lover she could, after expiation, be accepted by her husband as his partner in the conduct of even religious rites, could never have required a woman to burn herself as a sati.[14] It is this perception that needs to govern the actions of the functionaries of the state, religious institutions and civic organizations. More importantly, this is the perception that needs to govern and move the hearts and minds of our people.

Appendix

Lord William Bentinck on the Suppression
of Sati, 8 November 1829

Whether the question be to continue or to discontinue the practice of *sati*, the decision is equally surrounded by an awful responsibility. To consent to the consignment year after year of hundreds of innocent victims to a cruel and untimely end, when the power exists of preventing it, is a predicament which no conscience can contemplate without horror. But, on the other hand, if heretofore received opinions are to be considered of any value, to put to hazard by a contrary course the very safety of the British Empire in India, and to extinguish at once all hopes of those great improvements—affecting the condition not of hundreds and thousands but of millions—which can only be expected from the continuance of our supremacy, is an alternative which even in the light of humanity itself may be considered as a still greater evil. It is upon this first and highest consideration alone, the good of mankind, that the tolerance of this inhuman and impious rite can in my opinion be justified on the part of the government of a civilized nation. While the solution of this question is appalling from the unparalleled magnitude of its possible results, the considerations belonging to it are such as to make even the stoutest mind distrust its decision. On the one side, Religion, Humanity, under the most appalling form, as well as vanity and ambition—in short, all the most powerful influences over the human heart—are arrayed to bias and mislead the judgement. On the other side, the sanction of countless ages, the example of all the Mussulman conquerors, the unanimous concurrence in the same policy of our own most able rulers, together with the universal veneration of the people, seem authoritatively to forbid, both to feeling and to reason, any interference in the exercise of their natural prerogative. In venturing to be the first to deviate from this practice it becomes me to show that nothing has been yielded to feeling, but that reason, and reason alone, has governed the decision.

So far indeed from presuming to condemn the conduct of my predecessors, I am ready to say that in the same circumstances I should have acted as they have done. So far from being chargeable with political rashness, as this departure from an established policy might infer, I hope to be able so completely to prove the safety of the measures as even to render unnecessary any calculation of the degree of risk which for the attainment of so great a benefit might wisely and justly be incurred. So far also from being the sole champion of a great and dangerous innovation, I shall be able to prove that the vast preponderance of present authority has long been in favour of abolition. Past experience indeed ought to prevent me, above all men, from coming lightly to so positive a conclusion. When Governor of Madras I saw in the mutiny of Vellore the dreadful consequences of a supposed violation of religious customs upon the minds of the native population and soldiery. I cannot forget that I was then the innocent victim of that unfortunate catastrophe; and I might reasonably dread, when the responsibility would justly attach to me in the event of failure, a recurrence of the same fate. Prudence and self-interest would counsel me to tread in the footsteps of my predecessors. But in a case of such momentous importance to humanity and civilization that man must be reckless of all his present or future happiness who could listen to the dictates of so wicked and selfish a policy. With the firm undoubting conviction entertained upon this question, I should be guilty of little short of the crime of multiplied murder if I could hesitate in the performance of this solemn obligation. I have been already stung with this feeling. Every day's delay adds a victim to the dreadful list, which might perhaps have been prevented by a more early submission of the present question. But during the whole of the present year much public agitation has been excited, and when discontent is abroad, when exaggerations of all kinds are busily circulated, and when the native army have been under a degree of alarm lest their allowances should suffer with that of their European officers, it would have been unwise to have given a handle to artful and designing enemies to disturb the public peace. The recent measures of Government for protecting the interests of the Sepoys against the late reduction of companies will have removed all apprehension of the intentions of Government; and the consideration of this circumstance having been the sole cause of hesitation on my part, I will now proceed, praying the blessing of God upon our counsels, to state the grounds upon which my opinion has been formed.

We have now before us two reports of the Nizamat Adalat, with statements of *satis* in 1827 and 1828, exhibiting a decrease of 54 in the latter year as compared with 1827, and a still greater proportion as compared with former years. If this diminution could be ascribed to any change of opinion upon the question produced by the progress of education or civilization the fact would be most satisfactory, and to disturb this sure though slow process of self-correction would be most impolitic and unwise. But I think it may be safely affirmed that, though in Calcutta truth may be said to have made a considerable advance among the higher orders, yet in respect to the population at large no change whatever has taken place, and that from these causes at least no hope of the abandonment of the rite can be rationally entertained. The decrease, if it be real, may be the result of less sickly seasons, as the increase in 1824 and 1825 was of the greater prevalence of cholera. But it is probably in a greater measure due to the more open discouragement of the practice given by the greater part of the European functionaries in latter years, the effect of which would be to produce corresponding activity in the police officers, by which either the number would be really diminished or would be made to appear so in the returns.

It seems to be the very general opinion that our interference has hitherto done more harm than good by lending a sort of sanction to the ceremony, while it has undoubtedly tended to cripple the efforts of magistrates and others to prevent the practice.

I think it will clearly appear from a perusal of the documents annexed to this Minute, and from the facts which I shall have to adduce, that the passive submission of the people to the influence and power beyond the law—which in fact and practically may be and is often exercised without opposition by every public officer—is so great that the suppression of the rite would be completely effected by a tacit sanction alone on the part of Government. This mode of extinguishing it has been recommended by many of those whose advice has been asked; and no doubt this in several respects might be a preferable course, as being equally effectual while more silent, not exciting the alarm which might possibly come from a public enactment, and from which in case of failure it would be easy to retreat with less inconvenience and without any compromise of character. But this course is clearly not open to Government, bound by Parliament to rule by law and not by their good pleasure. Under the present position of the British Empire, moreover, it may be fairly doubted if any such underhand proceeding would be really good policy. When we had powerful neighbours and had greater reason to doubt our own security, expediency might recommend an indirect and more cautious proceeding, but now that we are supreme my opinion is decidedly in favour of an open, avowed, and general prohibition, resting altogether upon the moral goodness of the act and our power to enforce it; and so decided is my feeling against any half measure that, were I not convinced of the safety of total abolition, I certainly should have advised the cessation of all interference.

Of all those who have given their advice against the abolition of the rite, and have described the ill effects likely to ensue from it, there is no one to whom I am disposed to pay greater deference than Mr. Horace Wilson. I purposely select his opinion because, independently of his vast knowledge of Oriental literature, it has fallen to his lot, as secretary to the Hindu College, and possessing the general esteem both of the parents and of the youths, to have more confidential intercourse with natives of all classes than any man in India. While his opportunity of obtaining information has been great beyond all others, his talents and judgement enable him to form a just estimate of its value. I shall state the most forcible of his reasons, and how far I do and do not agree with him

1st. Mr. Wilson considers it to be a dangerous evasion of the real difficulties to attempt to prove that *satis* are not 'essentially a part of the Hindu religion'. I entirely agree in this opinion. The question is not what the rite is but what it is supposed to be, and I have no doubt that the conscientious belief of every order of Hindus, with few exceptions, regards it as sacred.

2nd. Mr. Wilson thinks that the attempt to put down the practice will inspire extensive dissatisfaction. I agree also in this opinion. He thinks that success will only be partial, which I doubt. He does not imagine that the promulgated prohibition will lead to any immediate and overt act of insubordination, but that affrays and much agitation of the public mind must ensue. But he conceives that, if once they suspect that it is the intention of the British Government to abandon this hitherto inviolate principle of allowing the most complete toleration in matters of religion, there will arise in the minds of all so deep a distrust of our ulterior designs that they will no longer be tractable to any arrangement intended for their improvement, and that the principle of a purer morality, as well as of a more virtuous and exalted rule of action, now actively inculcated by European education and knowledge, will receive a fatal check. I must acknowledge that a similar opinion as to the probable excitation of a deep distrust of our future intentions was mentioned to me in conversation by that enlightened native, Ram Mohun Roy, a warm advocate for the abolition of *sati* and of all other superstitions and corruptions engrafted on the Hindu religion, which he considers originally to have been a pure Deism. It was his opinion that the practice might be suppressed quietly and unobservedly by increasing the difficulties and by the indirect agency of the police. He apprehended that any public enactment would give rise to general apprehension, that the reasoning would be, 'While the English were contending for power, they deemed it politic to allow universal toleration and to respect our religion, but having obtained the supremacy their first act is a violation of their profession, and the next will probably be, like the Muhammadan conquerors, to force upon us their own religion.'

Admitting, as I am always disposed to do, that much truth is contained in these remarks, but not at all assenting to the conclusions which, though not described, bear the most unfavourable import, I shall now inquire into the evil and the extent of danger which may practically result from this measure.

It must be first observed that of the 463 *satis* occurring in the whole of the Presidency of Fort William, 420 took place in Bengal, Behar and Orissa, or what is termed the Lower Provinces, and of these latter 287 in the Calcutta Division alone.

It might be very difficult to make a stranger to India understand, much less believe, that in a population of so many millions of people as the Calcutta Division includes, and the same may be said of all the Lower Provinces, so great is the want of courage and of vigour of character, and such the habitual submission of centuries, that insurrection or hostile opposition to the will of the ruling power may be affirmed to be an impossible danger. I speak of the population taken separately from the army, and I may add for the information of the stranger, and also in support of my assertion, that few of the natives of the Lower Provinces are to be found in our military ranks. I therefore at once deny the danger *in toto* in reference to this part of our territories, where the practice principally obtains.

If, however, security was wanting against extensive popular tumult or revolution, I should say that the Permanent Settlement, which, though a failure in many other respects and in its most important essentials, has this great advantage at least, of having created a vast body of rich landed proprietors deeply interested in the continuance of the British Dominion and having complete command over the mass of the people; and in respect to the apprehension of ulterior views, I cannot believe that it could last but for the moment. The same large proprietary body, connected for the most part with Calcutta, can have no fears of the kind, and through their interpretation of our intentions and that of their numerous dependants and agents, the public mind could not long remain in a state of deception.

Were the scene of this sad destruction of human life laid in the Upper instead of the Lower Provinces, in the midst of a bold and manly people, I might speak with less confidence upon the question of safety. In these Provinces the *satis* amount to forty-three only upon a population of nearly twenty millions. It cannot be expected that any general feeling, where combination of any kind is so unusual, could be excited in defence of a rite in which so few participate, a rite also notoriously made too often subservient to views of personal interest on the part of the other members of the family.

It is stated by Mr. Wilson that interference with infanticide and the capital punishment of Brahmans offer a fallacious analogy with the prohibition now proposed. The distinction is not perceptible to my judgement. The former practice, though confined to particular families, is probably viewed as a religious custom; and as for the latter, the necessity of the enactment proves the general existence of this exception, and it is impossible to conceive a more direct and open violation of their Shasters, or one more at variance with the general feelings of the Hindu population. To this day in all Hindu states the life of a Brahman is, I believe, still held sacred.

But I have taken up too much time in giving my own opinion when those of the greatest experience and highest official authority are upon our records. In the report of the Nizamat Adalat for 1828, four out of five of the Judges recommended to the Governor-General in Council the immediate abolition of the practice, and attest its safety. The fifth Judge, though not opposed to the opinions of the rest of the Bench, did not feel then prepared to give his entire assent. In the report of this year the measure has come up with the unanimous recommendation of the Court. The two Superintendents of Police for the Upper and Lower Provinces (Mr. Walter Ewer and Mr. Charles Barwell) have in the strongest terms expressed their opinion that the suppression might be effected without the least danger. The former officer has urged the measure upon the attention of Government in the most forcible manner. No documents exist to show the opinions of the public functionaries in the interior, but I am informed that nine-tenths are in favour of the abolition.

How, again, are these opinions supported by practical experience?

Within the limits of the Supreme Court at Calcutta not a *sati* has taken place since the time of Sir John Anstruther.

In the Delhi territory Sir Charles Metcalfe never permitted a *sati* to be performed.

In Jessore, one of the districts of the Calcutta Division, in 1824 there were 30 *satis*; in 1825, 16; in 1826, 3; in 1827 and in 1828 there were none. To no other cause can this be assigned than to a power beyond the law exercised by the acting magistrate, against which, however, no public remonstrance was made. Mr. Pigou has since been appointed to Cuttack, and has pursued the same strong interference as in Jessore, but his course, although most humane, was properly arrested, as being illegal, by the Commissioners. Though the case of Jessore is, perhaps, one of the strongest examples of efficacious and unopposed interposition, I really believe that there are few districts in which the same arbitrary power is not exercised to prevent the practice. In the last work in the report of the Acting Commissioner (Mr. Smith) he states that in Ghazipur in the last year sixteen, and in the preceding year seven, *satis* had been prevented by the persuasions, or, rather, it should be said, by the threats, of the police.

Innumerable cases of the same kind might be obtained from the public records.

It is stated in the letter of the Collector of Gaya (Mr. Trotter), but upon what authority I have omitted to inquire, that the Peshwa (I presume he means the ex-Peshwa Baji Rao) would not allow the rite to be performed, and that in Tanjore it is equally interdicted. These facts, if true, would be positive proofs at least that no unanimity exists among the Hindus upon the point of religious obligation.

Having made inquiries, also, how far *satis* are permitted in the European foreign settlements, I find from Dr. Carey that at Chinsurah no such sacrifices had ever been permitted by the Dutch Government. That within the limits of Chandarnagar itself they were also prevented, but allowed to be performed in the British territories. The Danish Government of Serampur has not forbidden the rite, in conformity to the example of the British Government.

It is a very important fact that, though representations have been made by the disappointed party to superior authority, it does not appear that a single instance of direct opposition to the execution of the prohibitory orders of our civil functionaries has ever occurred. How, then, can it be reasonably feared that to the Government itself, from whom all authority is derived, and whose power is now universally considered to be irresistible, anything bearing the semblance of resistance can be manifested? Mr. Wilson also is of opinion that no immediate overt act of insubordination would follow the publication of the edict. The Regulation of Government may be evaded, the police may be corrupted, but even here the price paid as hush money will operate as a penalty, indirectly forwarding the object of Government.

I venture, then, to think it completely proved that from the native population nothing of extensive combination, or even of partial opposition, may be expected from the abolition.

It is, however, a very different and much more important question how far the feelings of the native army might take alarm, how far the rite may be in general observance by them, and whether, as in the case of Vellore, designing persons might not make use of the circumstances either for the purpose of immediate revolt or of sowing the seeds of permanent disaffection. Reflecting upon the vast disproportion of numbers between our native and European troops, it was obvious that there might be in any general combination of the forces the greatest danger to the State, and it became necessary, therefore, to use every precaution to ascertain the impression likely to be made upon the minds of the native soldiery.

Before I detail to Council the means I have taken to satisfy my mind upon this very important branch of the inquiry, I shall beg leave to advert to the name of Lord Hastings. It is impossible but that to his most humane, benevolent, and enlightened mind this practice must have been often the subject of deep and anxious meditation. It was consequently a circumstance of ill omen and some disappointment not to have found upon the Records the valuable advice and direction of his long experience and wisdom. It is true that during the greater part of his administration he was engaged in war, when the introduction of such a measure would have been highly injudicious. To his successor, Lord Amherst, also, the same obstacle was opposed. I am, however, fortunate in possessing a letter from Lord Hastings to a friend in England upon *satis*, and from the following extract, dated 21 November 1823, I am induced to believe that, had he remained in India, this practice would long since have been suppressed:—

> The subject which you wish to discuss is one which must interest one's feelings most deeply, but it is also one of extreme nicety when I mention that in one of the years during my administration of government in India about 800 widows sacrificed themselves within the Provinces comprised in the Presidency of Bengal, to which number I very much suspect that very many not notified to the magistrate should be added. I will hope to have credit for being acutely sensible to such an outrage against humanity. At the same time I was aware how much danger might attend the endeavouring to suppress forcibly a practice so rooted in the religious belief of the natives. No men of low caste are admitted into the ranks of the Bengal Army. Therefore the whole of that formidable body must be regarded as blindly partial to a custom which they consider equally referrible to family honour and to point of faith. To attempt the extinction of the horrid superstition without being supported in the procedure by a real concurrence on the part of the army would be distinctly perilous. I have no scruple to say that I did believe I could have carried with me the assent of the army towards such an object. That persuasion, however, arose from circumstances which gave me peculiar influence over the native troops.

Lord Hastings left India in 1823. It is quite certain that the Government of that time were much more strongly impressed with the risk of the undertaking than is now very generally felt. It would have been fortunate could this measure have proceeded under the auspices of that distinguished nobleman, and that the State might have had the benefit of the influence which undoubtedly he possessed in a peculiar degree over the native troops. Since that period, however, six years have elapsed. Within the territories all has been peaceful and prosperous, while without, Ava and Bhartpur, to whom alone a strange sort of consequence was ascribed by public opinion, have been made to acknowledge our supremacy. In this interval experience has enlarged our knowledge, and has given us surer data upon which to distinguish truth from illusion, and to ascertain the real circumstances of our position and power. It is upon these that the concurring opinion of the officers of the civil and military services at large having been founded, is entitled to our utmost confidence.

I have the honour to lay before Council the copy of a circular addressed to forty-nine officers, pointed out to me by the Secretary to Government in the Military Department as being from their judgement and experience the best enabled to appreciate the effect of the proposed measure upon the native army, together with their answers. For more easy reference, an abstract of each answer is annexed in a separate paper and classed with those to the same purport.

It appears first that of those whose opinions are directly adverse to all interference whatever with the practice the number is only five; secondly, of those who are favourable to abolition but averse to absolute and direct prohibition under the authority of the Government, the number is twelve; thirdly, of those who are favourable to abolition, to be effected by the indirect interference of magistrates and other public officers, the number is eight; fourthly, of those who advocate the total immediate and public suppression of the practice, the number is twenty-four.

It will be observed, also, of those who are against an open and direct prohibition, few entertain any fear of immediate danger. They refer to a distant and undefined evil. I can conceive the possibility of the expression of dissatisfaction and anger being immediately manifested upon this supposed attack on their religious usages, but the distant danger seems to me altogether groundless, provided that perfect respect continues to be paid to all their innocent rites and ceremonies, and provided also that a kind and considerate regard be continued to their worldly interests and comforts.

I trust, therefore, that the Council will agree with me in the satisfactory nature of this statement, and that they will partake in the perfect confidence which it has given me of the expediency and safety of the abolition.

In the answer of one of the military officers, Lieutenant-Colonel Todd, he has recommended that the tax on pilgrims should be simultaneously given up, for the purpose of affording an undoubted proof of our disinterestedness and of our desire to remove every obnoxious obstacle to the gratification of their religious duties. A very considerable revenue is raised from this head, but if it were to be the price of satisfaction and confidence to the Hindus and of the renewal of all distrust of our present and future intentions, the sacrifice might be a measure of good policy. The objections that must be entertained by all to the principle of the tax, which in England has latterly excited very great reprobation, formed an additional motive for the inquiry. I enclose a copy of a circular letter addressed to different individuals at present in charge of the district where the tax is collected, or who have had opportunities, from their local knowledge, of forming a good judgement upon this question. It will be seen that opinions vary, but upon a review of the whole my conviction is that in connexion with the present measure it is inexpedient to repeal the tax. It is a subject upon which I shall not neglect to bestow more attention than I have been able to do. An abstract of these opinions is annexed to this minute.

I have now to submit for the consideration of Council the draft of a regulation enacting the abolition of *satis*. It is accompanied by a paper containing the remarks and suggestions of the Judges of the Nizamat Adalat. In this paper is repeated the unanimous opinion of the Court in favour of the proposed measure. The suggestions of the Nizamat Adalat are in some measure at variance with a principal object I had in view, of preventing collision between the parties to the *sati* and the officers of police. It is only in the previous processes, or during the actual performance of the rite, when the feelings of all may be more or less roused to a high degree of excitement, that I apprehend the possibility of affray or of acts of violence through an indiscreet and injudicious exercise of authority. It seemed to me prudent, therefore, that the police, in the first instance, should warn and advise, but not forcibly prohibit, and if the *sati*, in defiance of this notice, were performed, that a report should be made to the magistrate, who would summon the parties and proceed as in any other case of crime. The Indian Court appears to think these precautions unnecessary, and I hope they may be so, but in the beginning we cannot, I think, proceed with too much circumspection. Upon the same principle, in order to guard against a too hasty or severe a sentence emanating from extreme zeal on the part of the local judge, I have proposed that the case should only be cognizable by the Commissioners of circuit. These are, however, questions which I should wish to see discussed in Council. The other recommendations of the Court are well worthy of our adoption.

I have now brought this paper to a close, and I think I have redeemed my pledge of not allowing, in the consideration of this question, passion or feeling to have any part. I trust it will appear that due weight has been given to all difficulties and objections, that facts have been stated with truth and impartiality, that the conclusion to which I have come is completely borne out both by reason and authority. It may be justly asserted that the Government in this act will only be following, not preceding, the tide of public opinion long flowing in this direction; and when we have taken into consideration the experience and wisdom of that highest public tribunal, the Nizamat Adalat, who, in unison with our wisest and ablest public functionaries, have been year after year almost soliciting the Government to pass this act, the moral and political responsibility of not abolishing this practice far surpasses, in my judgement, that of the opposite course.

But discarding, as I have done, every inviting appeal from sympathy and humanity, and having given my verdict, I may now be permitted to express the anxious feelings with which I desire the success of this measure.

The first and primary object of my heart is the benefit of the Hindus. I know nothing so important to the improvement of their future condition as the establishment of a purer morality, whatever their belief, and a more just conception of the will of God. The first step to this better understanding will be dissociation of religious belief and practice from blood and murder. They will then, when no longer under this brutalizing excitement, view with more calmness acknowledged truths. They will see that there can be no inconsistency in the ways of Providence, that to the command received as divine by all races of men, 'No innocent blood shall be spilt,' there can be no exception; and when they shall have been convinced of the error of this first and most criminal of their customs, may it not be hoped that others, which stand in the way of their improvement, may likewise pass away, and that, thus emancipated from those chains and shackles upon their minds and actions, they may no longer continue, as they have done, the slaves of every foreign conqueror, but that they may assume their first places among the great families of mankind? I disown in these remarks, or in this measure, any view whatever to conversion to our own faith. I write and feel as a legislator for the Hindus, and as I believe many enlightened Hindus think and feel.

Descending from these higher considerations, it cannot be a dishonest ambition that the Government of which I form a part should

have the credit of an act which is to wash out a foul stain upon British
rule, and to stay the sacrifice of humanity and justice to a doubtful
expediency; and finally, as a branch of the general administration of the
Empire, I may be permitted to feel deeply anxious that our course shall
be in accordance with the noble examples set to us by the British
Government at home, and that the adaptation, when practicable to the
circumstances of this vast Indian population, of the same enlightened
principles, may promote here as well as there the general prosperity,
and may exalt the character of our nation.

November 8th, 1829   W.C. BENTINCK

Sati Regulation XVII, AD 1829 of the Bengal Code, 4 December 1829*

A regulation for declaring the practice of suttee, or of burning or burying alive the widows of Hindus, illegal, and punishable by the criminal courts, passed by the governor-general in council on the 4th December 1829, corresponding with the 20th Aughun 1236 Bengal era; the 23rd Aughun 1237 Fasli; the 21st Aughun 1237 Vilayati; the 8th Aughun 1886 Samavat; and the 6th Jamadi-us-Sani 1245 Hegira.

I. The practice of suttee, or of burning or burying alive the widows of Hindus, is revolting to the feelings of human nature; it is nowhere enjoined by the religion of the Hindus as an imperative duty; on the contrary a life of purity and retirement on the part of the widow is more especially and preferably inculcated, and by a vast majority of that people throughout India the practice is not kept up, nor observed: in some extensive districts it does not exist; in those in which it had been most frequent it is notorious that in many instances acts of atrocity have been perpetrated which have been shocking to the Hindus themselves, and in their eyes unlawful and wicked. The measures hitherto adopted to discourage and prevent such acts have failed of success, and the governor-general in council is deeply impressed with the conviction that the abuses in question cannot be effectually put an end to without abolishing the practice altogether. Actuated by these considerations the governor-general in council, without intending to depart from one of the first and most important principles of the system of British government in India, that all classes of the people be secure in the observance of their religious usages so long as that system can be adhered to without violation of the paramount dictates of justice and humanity, has deemed it right to establish the following rules, which are hereby enacted to be in force from the time of their promulgation throughout the territories immediately subject to the presidence of Fort William.

II. The practice of suttee, or of burning or burying alive the widows of Hindus, is hereby declared illegal, and punishable by the criminal courts.

III. First. All zamindars, or other proprietors of land, whether malguzari or lakhiraj; all sadar farmers and under-renters of land of every description; all dependent taluqdars; all naibs and other local agents; all native officers employed in the collection of the revenue and rents of land on the part of government, or the court of wards; and all mundals or

* The Correspondence of William Cavendish Bentinck, op. cit., pp. 360–362.

other headmen of villages are hereby declared especially accountable for
the immediate communication to the officers of the nearest police station
of any intended sacrifice of the nature described in the foregoing section;
and any zamindar, or other description of persons above noticed, to whom
such responsibility is declared to attach, who may be convicted of
wilfully neglecting or delaying to furnish the information above
required, shall be liable to be fined by the magistrate or joint magistrate
in any sum not exceeding two hundred rupees, and in default to be
confined for any period of imprisonment not exceeding six months.

Secondly. Immediately on receiving intelligence that the sacrifice
declared illegal by this regulation is likely to occur, the police darogha
shall either repair in person to the spot, or depute his mohurrir or
jamadar, accompanied by one or more burkundazes of Hindu religion, and
it shall be the duty of the police-officers to announce to the persons
assembled for the performance of ceremony, that it is illegal; and to
endeavour to prevail on them to disperse, explaining to them that in the
event of their persisting in it they will involve themselves in a crime,
and become subject to punishment by the criminal courts. Should the
parties assembled proceed in defiance of these remonstrances to carry on
the ceremony into effect, it shall be the duty of the police-officer to use
all lawful means in their power to prevent the sacrifice from taking place,
and to apprehend the principle persons aiding and abetting in the
performance of it, and in the event of the police-officers being unable to
apprehend them, they shall endeavour to ascertain their names and places
of abode, and shall immediately communicate the whole of the
particulars to the magistrate for his orders.

Thirdly. Should intelligence of a sacrifice have been carried into effect
before their arrival at the spot, they will nevertheless institute a full
enquiry into the circumstances of the case, in like manner as on all other
occasions of unnatural death, and report them for the information and
orders of the magistrate or joining magistrate, to whom they may be
subordinate.

IV. First. On the receipt of the reports required to be made by the police
daroghas, under the provisions of the foregoing section, the magistrate or
joint magistrate of the jurisdiction in which the sacrifice may have taken
place, shall enquire into the circumstances of the case, and shall adopt the
necessary measures for bringing the parties concerned in promoting it to
trial before the court of circuit.

Secondly. It is hereby declared, that after the promulgation of this
regulation all persons convicted of aiding and abetting in the sacrifice of
a Hindu widow, by burning or burying her alive, whether the sacrifice be
voluntary on her part or not, shall be deemed guilty of culpable
homicide, and shall be liable to punishment by fine or by both fine and
imprisonment, at the discretion of the court of circuit, according to the
nature and circumstance of the case, and the degree of guilt established
against the offender; nor shall it be held to be any plea of justification

that he or she was desired by the party sacrificed to assist in putting her to death.

Thirdly. Persons committed to take their trial before the court of circuit for the offence above-mentioned shall be admitted to bail or not, at the discretion of the magistrate or joint magistrate, subject to the general rules in regard to the admission of bail.

V. It is further deemed necessary to declare, that nothing contained in this regulation shall be construed to preclude the court of Nizamat Adalat from passing sentence of death on persons convicted of using violence or compulsion, or of having assisted in burning or burying alive a Hindu widow while labouring under a state of intoxication, or stupefaction, or other cause impeding the exercise of her free will, when, from the aggravated nature of the offence, proved against the prisoner, the court may see no circumstances to render him or her proper object of mercy.

The Rajasthan Sati (Prevention) Act, 1987 (Act No. 40 of 1987)*

[Received the assent of the President on the 26th day of November, 1987.]

An

Act

to provide for the more effective prevention of sati and its glorification and for matters connected therewith or incidental thereto.

Be it enacted by the Rajasthan State Legislature in the Thirty-eighth Year of the Republic of India as follows:—

PART—I

Preliminary

1. *Short title, extent and commencement.*—(1) This Act may be called the Rajasthan **Sati** (Prevention) Act, 1987.

(2) It extends to the whole of the State of Rajasthan.

(3) It shall be deemed to have come into force on the 1st October, 1987.

2. *Definitions.*—(1) In this Act, unless the context otherwise requires,—

    (a) "Code" means the Code of Criminal Procedure, 1973 (Central Act 2 of 1974);

    (b) "glorification" in relation to sati includes, among other things, the observance of any ceremony or the taking out of a procession in connection with **sati** or the creation of a trust or the collection of funds or the construction of a temple or the performance of any ceremony thereat with a view to perpetuating the honour of, or to preserve the memory of, a widow committing **sati**;

    (c) "sati" means the burning or burying alive of any widow alongwith the body of her deceased husband or with any article, object or thing associated with the husband, irrespective of whether such burning or burying is voluntary on the part of the widow or otherwise;

---

* An English translation

(d) "Special Court" means a Special Court constituted under section 9;

(e) "temple" includes any building or other structure, whether roofed or not, constructed or made to preserve the memory of a widow committing **sati** and used or intended to be used for the purpose of worship or offering prayers.

(2) Words and expressions used but not defined in this Act and defined in the Indian Penal Code (Central Act 45 of 1860) or in the Code shall have the same meanings as are respectively assigned to them in the Indian Penal Code or the Code.

PART—II
Punishments for offences relating to **sati**

3. *Attempt to commit* **sati**.—Notwithstanding anything contained in the Indian Penal Code (Central Act 45 of 1860), whoever attempts to commit **sati** and does any act towards such commission shall be punishable with imprisonment for a term which shall not be less than one year but which may extend to five years and shall also be liable to fine which shall not be less than five thousand rupees but which may extend to twenty thousand rupees.

4. *Abetment of* **sati**.—(1) Notwithstanding anything contained in the Indian Penal Code (Central Act 45 of 1860), if any widow commits **sati**, whoever abets the commission of such **sati**, either directly or indirectly, shall be punishable with death or imprisonment for life and shall also be liable to fine.

(2) If any widow attempts to commit **sati**, whoever abets such attempt shall be punishable with imprisonment for life and shall also be liable to fine.

Explanation.—For the purposes of this section any of the following acts shall also be deemed to be an abetment, namely:—

(a) any inducement to a widow to get her burnt or buried alive alongwith the body of her deceased husband or with any article, object, or thing associated with him, irrespective of whether she is in a fit state of mind or is labouring under a state of intoxication or stupefaction or other cause impeding the exercise of her free will;

(b) Making a widow believe that the performance of **sati** would result in some spiritual benefit to her or her deceased husband or the general well being of the family;

(c) encouraging her to remain fixed in her resolve to commit **sati** and thus instigating her to commit **sati**;

(d) participating in any procession in connection with the commission of **sati** or intentionally aiding the widow in her decision to commit sati by taking her alongwith the body of her deceased husband to the cremation or burial ground;

(e) obstructing, or interfering with the police in the discharge of its duties of taking effective steps to prevent the commission of **sati**;

(f) preventing or obstructing the widow from saving herself from being burnt or buried alive; and

(g) being present at the place where the **sati** is committed as an active participant to such commission or to any ceremony connected with it.

5. *Punishment for glorification of* **sati**.—Whoever does any act for the glorification of sati shall be punishable with imprisonment for a term which shall not be less than one year but which may extend to seven years and with fine which shall not be less than five thousand rupees but which may extend to thirty thousand rupees.

PART—III

Power of Collector and District Magistrate to prevent offences relating to **sati**

6. *Power to prohibit certain acts.*—(1) Where the Collector and District Magistrate is of the opinion that **sati** is being or is about to be, committed in any area, he may, by order, prohibit the doing of any act towards the commission of **sati** in such area or areas and for such period as may be specified in the order.

(2) The Collector and District Magistrate may also, by order, prohibit the glorification in any manner of the commission of **sati** by any person in any area or areas specified in the order.

(3) Whoever contravenes any order made under sub-section (1) or sub-section (2) shall, if such contravention is not punishable under any other provision of this Act, be punishable with imprisonment for a term which shall not be less than one year but which may extend to seven years and with fine which shall not be less than five thousand rupees but which may extend to thirty thousand rupees.

7. *Power to remove certain temples or other structures.*— (1) The Collector and District Magistrate may, if he is satisfied that any temple or other structure has been, or is being, constructed for the glorification

of the **sati**, by order, direct the removal of any such temple or other structure.

(2) Where any order under sub-section (1) is not complied with, the Collector and District Magistrate shall cause the temple or other structure to be removed through a police officer not below the rank of a Sub-Inspector at the cost of the defaulter.

8. *Power to seize certain properties.*—(1) Where the Collector and District Magistrate has reason to believe that any funds or property have been collected or acquired for the purpose of glorification of the commission of any **sati** or which may be found under circumstances which create suspicion of the commission of any offence under this Act, he may seize such funds or property.

(2) Every Collector and District Magistrate acting under sub-section (1) shall report the seizure to the Special Court, if any, constituted to try any offence in relation to which such funds or property were collected or acquired and shall await the orders of such Special Court as to the disposal of the same.

PART—IV
Special Courts

9. *Trial of offences under this Act.*—(1) Notwithstanding anything contained in the Code, all offences under this Act shall be triable only by a Special Court constituted under this section.

(2) The State Government shall, as soon as it receives information about the commission of **sati** in any place within the State, by notification in the Official Gazette, constitute a Special Court consisting of a person to be appointed by the State Government after consultation with the Chief Justice of the High Court for the trial of all offences under this Act and every Special Court shall exercise jurisdiction in respect of the whole or such part of the State as may be specified in the notification.

(3) A person shall not be qualified for appointment as a Judge of a Special Court unless he is in the cadre of a District and Session Judge in the State.

10. *Special Public Prosecutors.*— For every Special Court, the State Government shall appoint a person to be a Special Public Prosecutor.

(2) A person shall be eligible to be appointed as a Special Public Prosecutor under this section only if he had been in practice as an advocate for not less than seven years under the State of Rajasthan requiring special knowledge of law.

(3) Every person appointed as a Special Public Prosecutor under this section shall be deemed to be a Public Prosecutor within the meaning of clause (u) of section 2 of the Code and the provisions of the Code shall have effect accordingly.

11. *Procedure and powers of Special Courts.*—(1) A Special Court may take cognizance of any offence, without the accused being committed to it for trial, upon receiving a complaint of facts which constitute such offence, or upon a police report of such facts.

(2) Subject to the other provisions of this Act, a Special Court shall, for the purpose of the trial of any offence, have all the powers of a Court of Session and shall try such offence as if it were a Court of Session, so far as may be in accordance with the procedure prescribed in the Code for trial before a Court of Session.

12. *Power of Special Court with respect to other offences.*—(1) When trying any offence under this Act, a Special Court may also try any other offence with which the accused may under the Code be charged at the same trial if the offence is connected with such other offence.

(2) If in the course of any trial of any offence under this Act it is found that the accused person has committed any other offence under this Act or under any other law, a Special Court may convict such person also of such other offence and pass any sentence authorised by this Act or such other law for the punishment thereof.

(3) In every inquiry or trial the proceedings shall be held as expeditiously as possible and, in particular where the examination of witnesses has begun, the same shall be continued from day to day until all the witnesses in attendance have been examined, and if any Special Court finds the adjournment of the same beyond the following date to be necessary, it shall record its reasons for doing so.

13. *Forfeiture of funds or property.*—Where a person has been prosecuted for an offence under this Act a Special Court trying such offence may, irrespective of whether any punishment has been awarded or not, if it is considered necessary so to do, declare that any funds or property seized under section 8 shall stand forfeited to the State.

14. *Appeal.*—(1) An appeal shall lie as a matter of right from any judgement, sentence or order, not being an interlocutory order, of a Special Court to the High Court both on facts and on law.

(2) Every appeal under this section shall be preferred within a period of thirty days from the date of the judgement, sentence or order appealed from:

Provided that the High Court may entertain an appeal after the expiry of the said period of thirty days if it is satisfied that the appellant had sufficient cause for not preferring the appeal within the period of thirty days.

PART—V
Miscellaneous

15. *Protection of action taken under this Act.*— No suit, prosecution or other legal proceedings shall lie against the State Government or any officer or authority of the State Government or any authority to whom powers have been delegated under this Act for anything which is in good faith done or intended to be done in pursuance of this Act or any rules or orders made under this Act.

16. *Burden of proof.*—Where any person is prosecuted of an offence under section 3 or section 4, the burden of proof that he had not committed the offence under the said section shall be on him.

17. *Obligation of certain persons to report about the commission of offence under this Act.*—(1) All officers of Government are hereby required and empowered to assist the police in the execution of the provisions of this Act or any rule or order made thereunder.

(2) All village officers and such other officers as may be specified by the Collector and District Magistrate in relation to any area and the inhabitants of such area shall, if they have reason to believe or have the knowledge that **sati** is about to be, or has been, committed in the area shall forthwith report such fact to the nearest police station.

(3) Whoever contravenes the provisions of sub-section (1) or sub-section (2) shall be punishable with imprisonment of either description for a term which may extend to two years and shall also be liable to fine.

18. *Act to have over-riding effect.*—The provisions of this Act or any rule or order made thereunder shall have effect notwithstanding anything inconsistent therewith contained in any enactment other than this Act or in any instrument having effect by virtue of any enactment other than this Act.

19. *Removal of doubts.*—For the removal of doubts, it is hereby declared that nothing in this Act shall affect any temple constructed for the glorification of **sati** and in existence immediately before the commencement of this Act or the continuance of any ceremonies in such temple in connection with such sati.

20. *Power to make rules.*—(1) The State Government may, by notification in the Official Gazette, make rules for carrying out the provisions of this Act.

(2) Every rule made under sub-section (1) shall be laid as soon as may be after it is so made before the House of State Legislature while it is in session for a total period of thirty days which may be comprised in one session or two or more successive sessions, and if, before the expiry of the session immediately following the session or the successive session aforesaid, the House agrees in making any modification in the rule or agrees that the rule should be made, the rule shall thereafter have effect only in such modified form or be of no effect as the case may be so however that any such modification or annulment shall be without prejudice to the validity of anything previously done under that rule.

21. *Repeal and Savings.*—(1) The Rajasthan **Sati** (Prevention) Ordinance, 1987 (Ordinance No.21 of 1987) is hereby repealed.

(2) Notwithstanding such repeal, all things done, actions taken or orders made under the said Ordinance shall be deemed to have been done, taken or made under this Act.

Secretary to the Government.

The Commission of Sati (Prevention) Act, 1987
No. 3 of 1988

[*3rd January*, 1988]

An Act to provide for the more effective prevention of the commission of *sati* and its glorification and for matters connected therewith or incidental thereto.

Whereas *sati* or the burning or burying alive of widows or women is revolting to the feelings of human nature and is nowhere enjoined by any of the religions of India as an imperative duty;

And whereas it is necessary to take more effective measures to prevent the commission of *sati* and its glorification;

Be it enacted by Parliament in the Thirty-eighth Year of the Republic of India as follows:-

PART I
PRELIMINARY

1. (1) This Act may be called the Commission of Sati (Prevention) Act, 1987.

(2) It extends to the whole of India except the State of Jammu and Kashmir.

(3) It shall come into force in a State on such date as the Central Government may, by notification in the Official Gazette, appoint, and different dates may be appointed for different States.

2. (1) In this Act, unless the context otherwise requires,—

(a) "Code" means the Code of Criminal Procedure, 1973;

(b) "glorification", in relation to *sati*, whether such *sati* was committed before or after the commencement of this Act, includes, among other things,—

Short title, extent and commencement.

Definition.

2 of 1974

(i) the observance of any ceremony or the taking out of a procession in connection with the commission of *sati*; or

(ii) the supporting, justifying or propagating the practice of *sati* in any manner; or

(iii) the arranging of any function to eulogise the person who has committed *sati*; or

(iv) the creation of a trust, or the collection of funds, or the construction of a temple or other structure or the carrying on of any form of worship or the performance of any ceremony thereat, with a view to perpetuate the honour of, or to preserve the memory of, a person who has committed *sati*;

(c) "*sati*" means the act of burning or burying alive of—

(i) any widow along with the body of her deceased husband or any other relative or with any article, object or thing associated with the husband or such relative; or

(ii) any woman along with the body of her relatives, irrespective of whether such burning or burying is claimed to be voluntary on the part of the widow or the woman or otherwise;

(d) "Special Court" means a Special Court constituted under section 9;

(e) "temple" includes any building or other structure, whether roofed or not, constructed or made to preserve the memory of a person in respect of whom *sati* has been committed or used or intended to be used for the carrying on of any form of worship or for the observance of any ceremony in connection with such commission.

(2) Words and expressions used but not defined in this Act and defined in the Indian Penal Code or in the Code shall have the same meaning as are respectively assigned to them in the Indian Penal Code or the Code.

45 of
1860.

PART II
PUNISHMENTS FOR OFFENCES RELATING TO SATI

Attempt to commit *sati*

3. Notwithstanding anything contained in the Indian Penal Code, whoever attempts to commit *sati* and does any act towards such commission shall be punishable with imprisonment for a term which may extend to six months or with fine or with both:

Provided that the Special Court trying an offence under this section shall, before convicting any person, take into consideration the circumstances leading to the commission of the offence, the act committed, the state of mind of the person charged of the offence at the time of the commission of the act and all other relevant factors.

45 of 1860.

4. (1) Notwithstanding anything contained in the Indian Penal Code, if any person commits *sati*, whoever abets the commission of such *sati,* either directly or indirectly, shall be punishable with death or imprisonment for life and shall also be liable to fine.

Abetment of *sati*.

(2) If any person attempts to commit *sati*, whoever abets such attempt, either directly or indirectly, shall be punishable with imprisonment for life and shall also be liable to fine.

Explanation.— For the purposes of this section, any of the following acts or the like shall also be deemed to be an abetment, namely:-

(a) any inducement to a widow or woman to get her burnt or buried alive along with the body of her deceased husband or with any other relative or with any article, object or thing associated with the husband or such relative, irrespective of whether she is in a fit state of mind or is labouring under a state of intoxication or stupefaction or other cause impeding the exercise of her free will;

(b) making a widow or woman believe that the commission of *sati* would result in some spiritual benefit to her or her deceased husband or relative or the general well being of the family;

(c) encouraging a widow or woman to remain fixed in her resolve to commit *sati* and thus instigating her to commit *sati*;

45 of 1860.

(d) participating in any procession in connection with the commission of *sati* or aiding the widow or woman in her decision to commit *sati* by taking her along with the body of her deceased husband or relative to the cremation or burial ground;

(e) being present at the place where *sati* is committed as an active participant to such commission or to any ceremony connected with it;

(f) preventing or obstructing the widow or woman from saving herself from being burnt or buried alive;

(g) obstructing or interfering with, the police in discharge of its duties of taking any steps to prevent the commission of *sati*.

5. Whoever does any act for the glorification of *sati* shall be punishable with imprisonment for a term which shall not be less than one year but which may extend to seven years and with fine which shall not be less than five thousand rupees but which may extend to thirty thousand rupees.

Punishment for glorification of sati.

PART III
POWERS OF COLLECTOR OR DISTRICT MAGISTRATE TO PREVENT OFFENCES RELATING TO SATI

6.(1) Where the Collector or the District Magistrate is of the opinion that *sati* or any abetment thereof is being, or is about to be commission of *sati* by any person in any area or areas specified in the commission of *sati* by any person in any area or areas specified in the order.

Power to prohibit certain acts.

(2) The Collector or the District Magistrate may also, by order, prohibit the glorification in any manner of *sati* by any person in any area or areas specified in the order.

(3) Whoever contravenes any order made under sub-section (1) or sub-section (2) shall, if such contravention is not punishable under any other provision of this Act, be punishable with imprisonment for a term which shall not be less than one year but which may extend to seven years and with fine which shall not be less than five thousand rupees but which may extend to thirty thousand rupees.

Power
to re-
move
certain
temples
or other
struc-
tures.
7.(1) The State Government may, if it is satisfied that in any temple or other structure which has been in existence for not less than twenty years, any form of worship or the performance of any ceremony is carried on with a view to perpetuate the honour of, or to preserve the memory of, any person in respect of whom *sati* has been committed, by order, direct the removal of such temple or other structure.

(2) The Collector or the District Magistrate may, if satisfied that in any temple or other structure, other than that referred to in sub-section (1), any form of worship or the performance of any ceremony is carried on with a view to perpetuate the honour of, or to preserve the memory of, any person in respect of whom *sati* has been committed, by order, direct the removal of such temple or other structure.

(3) Where any order under sub-section (1) or subsection (2) is not complied with, the State Government or the Collector or the District Magistrate, as the case may be, shall cause the temple or other structure to be removed through a police officer not below the rank of a Sub-Inspector at the cost of the defaulter.

Power
to seize
certain
proper-
ties.
8.(1) Where the Collector or the District Magistrate has reason to believe that any funds or property have been collected or acquired for the purpose of glorification or the commission of *sati* or which may be found under circumstances which create suspicion of the commission of any offence under this Act, he may seize such funds or property.

(2) Every Collector or District Magistrate acting under sub-section (1) shall report the seizure to the Special Court, if any, constituted to try any offence in relation to which such funds or property were collected or acquired and shall await the orders of such Special Court as to the disposal of the same.

PART IV
SPECIAL COURTS

Trial of
offences
under
this Act
9. (1) Notwithstanding anything contained in the Code, all offences under this Act shall be triable only by a Special Court constituted under this section.

Sati

180

(2) The State Government shall, by notification in the Official Gazette, constitute one or more Special Courts for the trial of offences under this Act and every Special Court shall exercise jurisdiction in respect of the whole or such part of the State as may be specified in the notification.

(3) A Special Court shall be presided over by a Judge to be appointed by the State Government with the concurrence of the Chief Justice of the High Court.

(4) A person shall not be qualified for appointment as a Judge of a Special Court unless he is, immediately before such appointment, a Sessions Judge or an Additional Sessions Judge in any State.

10. (1) For every Special Court, the State Government shall appoint a person to be a Special Public Prosecutor.

(2) A person shall be eligible to be appointed as a Special Public Prosecutor under this section only if he had been in practice as an advocate for not less than seven years or has held any post for a period of not less than seven years under the State requiring special knowledge of law.

(3) Every person appointed as a Special Public Prosecutor under this section shall be deemed to be a Public Prosecutor within the meaning of clause (u) of section 2 of the Code and the provisions of the Code shall have effect accordingly.

11. (1) A Special Court may take cognizance of any offence, without the accused being committed to it for trial, upon receiving a complaint of facts which constitute such offence, or upon a police report on such facts.

(2) Subject to the other provisions of this Act, a Special Court shall, for the trial of any offence, have all the powers of a Court of Session and shall try such offence as if it were a Court of Session, so far as may be, in accordance with the procedure prescribed in the Code for trial before a Court of Session.

12. (1) When trying any offence under this Act, a Special Court may also try any other offence with which the accused may, under the Code, be charged at the same trial if the offence is connected with such other offence.

(2) If, in the course of any trial of any offence under this

Special Public Prosecutors.

Procedure and powers of Special Courts.

Power of Special Court with respect

Act it is found that the accused person has committed any
other offence under this Act or under any other law, a
Special Court may convict such person also of such other
offence and pass any sentence authorised by this Act or
such other law for the punishment thereof.

(3) In every inquiry or trial, the proceedings shall be
held as expeditiously as possible and, in particular, where
the examination of witnesses has begun, the same shall be
continued from day to day until all the witnesses in attendance have been examined, and if any Special Court finds
the adjournment of the same beyond the following date to
be necessary, it shall record for doing so.

13. Where a person has been convicted of an offence
under this Act, the Special Court trying such offence may,
if it is considered necessary so to do, declare that any
funds or property seized under section 8 shall stand
forfeited to the State.

14. (1) Notwithstanding anything contained in the
Code, an appeal shall lie as a matter of right from any
judgement, sentence or order, not being an interlocutory
order, of a Special Court to the High Court both on facts
and on law.

(2) Every appeal under this section shall be preferred
within a period of thirty days from the date of the judgement, sentence or order appealed from:

Provided that the High Court may entertain an appeal
after the expiry of the same period of thirty days if it is
satisfied that the appellant had sufficient cause for not
preferring the appeal within the period of thirty days.

PART V
MISCELLANEOUS

15. No suit, prosecution or other legal proceeding shall
lie against the State Government or any officer or authority of the State Government for anything which is in good
faith done or intended to be done in pursuance of this Act
or any rules or orders made under this Act.

16. Where any person is prosecuted of an offence
under section 4, the burden of proving that he had not
committed the offence under the said section shall be on
him.

17. (1) All officers of Government are hereby required and empowered to assist the police in the execution of the provisions of this Act or any rule or order made thereunder.

(2) All village officers and such other officers as may be specified by the Collector or the District Magistrate in relation to any area and the inhabitants of such area shall, if they have reason to believe or have the knowledge that *sati* is about to be, or has been, committed in the area shall forthwith report such fact to the nearest police station.

(3) Whoever contravenes the provisions of sub-section (1) or sub-section (2) shall be punishable with imprisonment of either description for a term which may extend to two years and shall also be liable to fine.

18. A person convicted of an offence under subsection (1) or section 4 in relation to the commission of *sati* shall be disqualified from inheriting the property of the person in respect of whom *sati* has been committed or the property of any other person which he would have been entitled to inherit on the death of the person in respect of whom such *sati* has been committed.

19. In the Representation of the People Act, 1951,—

(a) in section 8, in sub-section (2) after the proviso, the following proviso shall be inserted, namely:-

"Provided further that a person convicted by a Special Court for the contravention of any of the provisions of the Commission of Sati (Prevention) Act, 1987 shall be disqualified from the date of such conviction and shall continue to be disqualified for a further period of five years since his release;"

(b) in section 123, after clause (3A), the following clause shall be inserted, namely:-

'(3B) The propagation of the practice or the commission of *sati* or its glorification by a candidate or his agent or any other person with the consent of the candidate or his election agent for the furtherance of the prospects of the election of that candidate or for prejudicially affecting the election of any candidate.

Explanation.—For the purposes of this clause,

"*sati*" and "glorification" in relation to *sati* shall have the meanings respectively assigned to them in the Commission of Sati (Prevention) Act, 1987.'

20. The provisions of this Act or any rule or order made thereunder shall have effect notwithstanding anything inconsistent therewith contained in any enactment other than this Act or in any instrument having effect by virtue of any enactment other than this Act. *Act to have over-riding effect.*

21. (1) The Central Government may, by notification in the Official Gazette, make rules for carrying out the provisions of this Act. *Power to make rules.*

(2) Every rule made under this section shall be laid, as soon as may be after it is made, before each House of Parliament, while it is in session, for a total period of thirty days which may be comprised in one session or in two or more successive sessions, and if, before the expiry of the session immediately following the session or the successive sessions aforesaid, both Houses agree in making any modification in the rule or both Houses agree that the rule should not be made, the rule shall thereafter have effect only in such modified form or be of no effect, as the case may be; so, however, that any such modification or annulment shall be without prejudice to the validity of anything previously done under that rule.

22. (1) All laws in force in any State immediately before the commencement of this Act in that State which provide for the prevention or the glorification of *sati* shall, on such commencement, stand repealed. *Repeal of existing laws.*

(2) Notwithstanding such repeal, anything done or any action taken under the law repealed under sub-section (1) shall be deemed to have been done or taken under the corresponding provisions of this Act, and, in particular, any case taken cognizance of by a Special Court under the provisions of any law so repealed and pending before it immediately before the commencement of this Act in that State shall continue to be dealt with by the Special Court after such commencement as if such Special Court had been constituted under section 9 of this Act.

Notes

2

Heaven in the Hereafter

1. Dr P.V. Kane, *History of Dharmasastra*, Poona: Bhandarkar Oriental Research Institute, 1973.
2. A.L. Basham, *The Wonder that was India:* Popular Book Depot, 1954.
3. Dr A.S. Altekar, *The Position of Women in Hindu Civilization*, Delhi: Motilal Banarsidass, 1959.
4. Shakuntala Rao Shastri, *Women in the Sacred Laws,* Bombay: Bharatiya Vidya Bhavan, 1959.
5. Kane, *op. cit.*
6. The *Mahabharata* and the *Ramayana* are epics that are considered part of scriptural texts; they have come down to us through so many centuries that they include variations and interpolations made by several persons through the ages. Basham observes that according to one tradition, the war of *Mahabharata* took place in 3102 BC, but a "more reasonable" date is the fifteenth century BC, while he himself believes it was "probably around the beginning of the ninth century BC". One opinion holds that the instances of sati mentioned in the *Mahabharata* are later interpolations—*see* Edward Thompson, *Suttee,* London: George Allen & Unwin, 1928.
7. Altekar, *op. cit.*
8. H.T. Colebrooke, *Miscellaneous Essays*: Trubner & Co., 1873.
9. Mehendele, in *Navbharat* (Marathi), January 1988.
10. K.V. Rangaswami Aiyangar, *Some aspects of ancient Indian polity*, Madras: University of Madras, 1935.
11. *Ibid.*
12. Kane, *op. cit.*
13. Tarkateertha Laxmanshastri Joshi, in conversation, 1988.
14. Kane, *op. cit.*
15. *Ibid.* It has been pointed out that for those guilty of killing a Brahmin, in fact there could be no funeral rites. This anomaly is

explained away by commentators by saying that it must refer to a killing in a previous birth. Texts like these can only be made acceptable through such devious manipulations of their meanings.

16. Shastri, *op. cit.* The *Padmapurana* (AD 1100) likewise praises the act of immolation by a widow, but only in the case of Kshatriya women; Brahmin women are forbidden to become satis—in fact anyone helping a Brahmin woman to ascend the pyre would be "committing the grave sin of murdering a Brahmana". Paithinari, placed chronologically in the same period but preceding Angirasa, decrees similarly that "following the dead husband is the best duty of a woman" but excludes Brahmin women from the rite.

17. Basham, *op. cit.*

18. Colebrooke, *op. cit.*

19. H.H. Wilson, "On the sacrifice of human beings" (pamphlet): Oriental Research Institute. Wilson also records that the woman who becomes *chitabhrashta* (confused, or changes her mind) and retreats from the funeral pile can seek expiation by the performance of the penitential act known as the 'prajapatya'.

20. Kane, *op. cit.*, quoting from the *Vedavyasasmriti*.

21. *Brahmapurana.*

22. *Bhavishyapurana*. Likewise, in the *Bhagavata*: "When the corpse is about to be consumed, the faithful wife who stood without rushes on the fire"; and the *Pauranika mantra*: "Om. Let these faithful wives, pure, beautiful, commit themselves to the fire, with their husbands' corpses".

23. Colebrooke, *op. cit.*

24. Kane, *op. cit.* Similar injunctions are set out by the *Brhannaradiyapurana* also—"Brahmin widows are not allowed *anumarana*, if the husband dies elsewhere; (and) wives who have not attained puberty or are in the monthly curse do not commit sati".

25. Wilson, *op. cit.*

26. *Ibid.*

27. Shastri, *op. cit.*

28. *The Illustrated Weekly of India*, 1 May 1988.

29. *Ibid.*

30. *Ibid.*

31. Kane, *op. cit.*

32. *The Times of India*, 16 April 1988.

33. *India Today*, 15 October 1987.

34. *The Illustrated Weekly of India, op. cit.* "I say that a man and a woman are unequal, their reproductive organs are unequal. . . Do

women have a beard and moustache on their faces? I am saying
that a woman is not the same as a man, physically, mentally".
And, "A man can father many children in one night whereas a
woman cannot bear more than one child in a year. The difference
is so great between a man and a woman".
35. *Sunday*, 10–16 April 1988.
36. *The Illustrated Weekly of India, op. cit.*

3

But Hell on Earth

1. Dr P.V. Kane, *History of Dharmasastra,* Poona: Bhandarkar
   Oriental Research Institute, 1973.
2. *Ibid.*
3. *Ibid.*
4. Translation in Lin Yutang ed., The *Wisdom of China and India*:
   The Modern Library, 1942 .
5. Manu, quoted in Nandita Haksar, *Demystification of Law for
   Women*, Delhi: Lancer Press, 1986.
6. Dr A.S. Altekar, *The Position of Women in Hindu Civilization*,
   Delhi: Motilal Banarsidass, 1959.
7. *Ibid.*
8. Laxmanshastri Joshi, in Peter Fernando and Frances Yasas eds.,
   Woman's image making and shaping, Pune: Ishvani Kendra,
   1985.
9. Altekar, *op. cit.*
10. Iqbal Singh, *Rommohun Roy—A biographical enquiry into the
    making of modern India*: Asia Publishing House, 1983.
11. Partha N. Mukerji, in Karuna Chanana ed., *Socialisation,
    Education and Women*, Delhi: Orient Longman, 1988.
12. Kane, *op. cit.*
13. Saroj Gulati, *Women and Society*, Delhi: Chanakya Publica-
    tions, 1985.
14. Haksar, *op. cit.*
15. Translation of the *Epic of Rama*, in Lin Yutang ed., *op. cit.*
16. Haksar, *op. cit.*

17. Ashis Nandy, in the *Illustrated Weekly of India*, 17 January 1988.
18. Kane, *op. cit.*
19. Julius Jolly, *Hindu Law and Custom*: Greater Indian Society, 1928.
20. *Ibid.*
21. Namita Sinha, in the *India magazine*, April 1988.
22. Fanny Parks, *Wanderings of a Pilgrim,* London: Pelham Richardson, 1850. Likewise, Edward Thompson, in *Suttee*, recalls being told by a friend who was commenting on the plight and wretchedness of widows, that she thought "it would be a reform to reintroduce suttee".
23. Parks, *ibid.*
24. Singh, *op. cit.*
25. *Ibid.*
26. *Manushi*, no. 47. In fact, to die with the insignia of *soubhagya* (that is, to die while the husband was still alive) is, in the Indian reckoning, considered, the greatest good fortune. When Emperor Harsha's mother (seventh century) realized that her husband's death was imminent, she immolated herself, to avoid widowhood.
27. *Ibid.*
28. The Shankaracharya of Puri, *Sunday* 10–16 April 1988.
29. James Tod, *Annals and Antiquities of Rajasthan*, Calcutta: Indian Publication Society, 1899.
30. Singh, *op. cit.*
31. Altekar, *op. cit.*
32. *The Free Press Journal*, 23 February 1988.
33. John Poynder, *Human Sacrifices in India*, London: J. Hatchard & Sons, 1827.
34. *Manushi, op. cit.*
35. Bengal Regulations, 1793–1805, Maharashtra Archives.
36. *The Indian Express*, 9 October 1988.
37. Haksar, *op. cit.*
38. *Ibid.*
39. Leela Dube, *op. cit.*
40. *Manushi*, no. 42-3.
41. R.W. Frazer, *British India*, London: Fisher Unwin, 1896.
42. Tod, *op. cit.*
43. Poynder, *op. cit.*
44. Parks, *op. cit.*
45. M.K. Gandhi, *Young India* , 21 May 1931.
46. Praful Bidwai, in the *Times of India*, 28 September 1987.

47. Pamela Philipose and Teesta Setalvad, in the *Illustrated Weekly of India*, 13 March 1988.
48. Parks, *op. cit.*
49. Sinha, *op. cit.*
50. J. Peggs, *The Burning of Hindoo Widows*, in Poynder, *op. cit.*

4

Crime and Punishment

1. John Poynder, *Human Sacrifices in India*, London: J. Hatchard & Sons, 1827.
2. *Ibid.*
3. *Ibid.*
4. *Ibid.*
5. *Ibid.*
6. *Ibid.*
7. *Ibid.*
8. Maja Daruwala, in the *Lawyers* magazine, January 1988.
9. *The Times of India*, 2 September 1988.

5

Lamb to the Slaughter

1. Francois Bernier, *Travels in the Mogul Empire*, Westminster: Archibald Constable, 1891.
2. William Ward, in Edward Thompson, *Suttee*, London: George Allen & Unwin, 1928.
3. J. Peggs, in John Poynder, *Human Sacrifices in India*, London: J. Hatchard & Sons, 1827.
4. Account by Julius, in Poynder, *ibid.*

5. Eye-witness account in Poynder, *ibid.*
6. Thompson, *op. cit.*
7. *Ibid.*
8. Jeevan Kulkarni, in *Masurashram patrika*, October 1987.
9. Mohan Mukerji, *Ham in the sandwich:* Vikas Publishing House, 1979.
10. Namita Sinha, in the *India magazine*, April 1988.
11. Poynder, *op. cit.* Likewise, Thompson too remarks that "it is true that widows were often drugged or narcotised, so that they became sati while unaware of what they were doing".
12. Fanny Parks, *Wanderings of a Pilgrim*, London: Pelham Richardson, 1850.
13. *Manushi*, no. 42–3.
14. Bernier, *op. cit.*
15. *Ibid.*
16. *Chronicles of Fernao Nuniz*, quoted by Thompson, *op. cit.*
17. Thompson, *ibid.*
18. Iqbal Singh, *Rammohun Roy—A biographical enquiry into the making of modern India*: Asia Publishing House, 1985.
19. Thompson, *op. cit.*
20. J.O. Tod, *Annals and Antiquities of Rajasthan*: Indian Publishing Society, 1899.
21. Poynder, *op. cit.*
22. Vishal Mangalwadi, in the *Indian Express*, 19 September 1987.
23. M.V. Kamath, in the *Illustrated Weekly of India*, 13 April 1980.
24. Poynder, *op. cit.*
25. Thompson, *op. cit.*
26. *Sunday*, 10–16 April 1988.
27. *The Sunday Observer*, 20 September 1987.
28. Thompson, *op. cit.*
29. *Ibid.*
30. K.R. Sunder Rajan, in *Debonair*, November 1987.
31. Lt. Col. W.H. Sleeman, *Rambles and Recollections of an Indian Official*, London: J. Hatchard & Sons, 1844.
32. Tod, *op. cit.*
33. Sleeman, *op. cit.*
34. Jean Baptiste Tavernier, reproduced in the *Illustrated Weekly of India*, 24 July 1988.
35. *Sunday*, *op. cit.* Namita Sinha in the *India magazine*, *op. cit.*, likewise remarks on the mystique of sati that is stressed by the priests: "Back in Delhi satis live in the tiny *galis* of Nai Sarak and in the opulent marble temples of south Delhi. In these

temples the Rani Sati Sarva Sangh, an all India organisation, holds four *aartis* a day and the pandits watch over you to determine whether you are a devotee or not. They tell you other tales of women who became satis, always stressing that the power of the goddess draws the educated, the rich and the commoner, for she alone can fulfil their wishes. They show you the threads of hope tied to the gates of the temple as proof of the faith. And they scoff at all those—the government, the activists, the rationalists—who are attempting to interfere in the sacred tradition and thereby bringing ruin upon the ideal of womanhood. All these unhealthy developments, they would have you believe, are the curse of Kal Yuga which we are now witnessing".

36. H.T. Colebrooke, *Miscellaneous essays*: Trubner & Co., 1873.
37. Parks, *op. cit.*
38. *Ibid.*
39. Thompson, *op. cit.*
40. Dr V.V. Bedekar, *Sati: Meaning and scope* (pamphlet).
41. Swami Harshananda, in the *Hindu*, 27 October 1987.
42. Praful Bidwai, in the *Times of India*, 28 September 1987.
43. M.K. Gandhi, in *Young India*, 21 May 1931.
44. Interview, in the *Illustrated Weekly of India*, 1 May 1988.
45. Ananda Coomaraswamy, *The Dance of Shiva*: 1924. On the status of Indian women, he goes on to add, "Western critics have often asserted that the Oriental woman is a slave, and that we have made her what she is. We can only reply that we do not identify freedom with self-assertion, and that the Oriental woman is what she is, only because our social and religious culture has permitted her to be and to remain essentially feminine". And "feminine", in its most exalted interpretation, in the patriarchal framework, means 'ready to consider self-sacrifice a privilege'.
46. Jeevan Kulkarni, *op. cit.*
47. Patrick Harrigan, in the *Statesman*, 29 March 1988.
48. George Hart, in the *Statesman, ibid.*
49. Ashis Nandy, in the *Illustrated Weekly of India*, 17 January 1988.
50. Dr Hiralal Maheshwari, *History of Rajasthani Literature*: Sahitya Akademi, 1980.
51. Interview, in the *Illustrated Weekly of India*, 1 May 1988.
52. *Ibid.*
53. Kalyan Singh Kalvi, quoted in *Trial by Fire* (report), by the Women and Media Committee of the Bombay Union of Journalists, 1987.
54. Bedekar, *op. cit.*, in a telegram to the President of India.

55. Bedekar, in a letter to the *Times of India*, 18 December 1987.
56. Dr A.S. Altekar, *The Position of Women in Hindu Civilization*, Delhi: Motilal Banarsidass, 1959.
57. *Ibid.*
58. D.D. Kosambi, *The Culture and Civilization of Ancient India in historical outline*: Vikas Publishing House, 1970.
59. Tavernier, *op. cit.*

6

The Beauteous and the Brave

1. There are discrepancies in the figures given by different sources mainly because certain districts were shifted from one division to another during the period of enumeration.
2. Sir John Malcolm, *Memoir of Central India*, Calcutta: Thacker Spink, 1980.
3. Dr A.S. Altekar, *The Position of Women in Hindu Civilization*, Delhi: Motilal Banarsidass, 1959.
4. Dr P.V. Kane, *History of Dharmasastra*, Poona: Bhandarkar Oriental Research Institute, 1973.
5. R.W. Frazer, *British India*, London: T. Fisher Unwin, 1896.
6. Iqbal Singh, *Rammohun Roy—A biographical enquiry into the making of modern India*: Asia Publishing House, 1985.
7. Ashim Kumar Roy, in *Indian Book Chronicle*, November 1987.
8. Jean Baptiste Tavernier, reproduced in the *Illustrated Weekly of India*, 24 July 1988.
9. *Manushi*, no. 42–3.
10. Lt. Col. James Tod, *Annals and Antiquities of Rajasthan*, Calcutta: Indian Publication Society, 1899.
11. Edward Thompson, *Suttee*, London: George Allen & Unwin, 1928.
12. Tod, *op. cit.*
13. Thompson, *op. cit.*
14. *Trial by Fire* (report), by the Women and Media Committee of the Bombay Union of Journalists, 1987.
15. Thompson, *op. cit.*

16. Mohan Mukerji, in a private communication, 1988.
17. Tod, *op. cit.*
18. *Ibid.*
19. *Ibid.*
20. *Ibid.*
21. Vincent Smith, *The Oxford History of India*: Clarendon Press, 1919.
22. Sir William Barton, *Princes of India*, Nisbet: 1934.
23. Kamaladevi Chattopadhayay, *Indian Women's Battle for Freedom*, Delhi: Abhinav Publications, 1983.
24. Tod, *op. cit.*
25. *The Times of India*, 26 April 1988.
26. Tod, *op. cit.*
27. Dr Hiralal Maheshwari, *History of Rajasthani literature:* Sahitya Akademi, 1980.
28. Purshottamlal Menariya, *Rajasthan ki lok kathayen* (Hindi), Delhi: Atmaram & Sons, 1954.

7

Rain and 'Reign of Unreason'

1. Iqbal Singh, *Rammohun Roy—A biographical enquiry into the making of modern India*: Asia Publishing House, 1985.
2. *Ibid.*
3. Francois Bernier, *Travels in the Mogul Empire*, Westminster: Archibald Constable, 1891.
4. Singh, *op. cit.*
5. John Poynder, *Human Sacrifices in India*, London: J. Hatchard & Sons, 1827.
6. *Ibid.*
7. *Ibid.*
8. *Ibid.* Poynder in his long, impassioned speech before the court of the proprietors of the East India Company in London, listed several examples to make the point that the fear of offending native religious sentiments had not bothered the government when it was a question of financial gain. On one occasion, he

pointed out, the government had seized even the temple juggernaut car at Puri for a tax default. "Shall we be more tender of our tottering revenue than of the lives of our perishing population?" he argued, quoting from a civil official who conceded that "far greater interference with the religious prejudices of the natives has been exercised by the Indian government, in furtherance of their judicial and revenue systems, than they would be called upon to exercise in the suppression of suttees. . . ."

9. Veena Das, in the *Illustrated Weekly of India*, 28 February 1988.
10. Swami Ranganathananda, in the *Sunday Observer*, 3 April 1988.
11. *Manushi*, no. 42–3. Romila Thapar in this interview points out how, although there are different versions of the story of Shakuntala and the *Ramayana*, each projecting the central female character with a different personality, only particular versions that fitted in with the accepted conceptions of womanhood in a particular period got picked out for popularization.
12. *The Indian Express*, 3 April 1988.
13. *Trial by fire* (report), by the Women and Media Committee of the Bombay Union of Journalists 1987.
14. *"Mātā tu patitā-api rakshaneeya"—Arthashastra*. A.L. Basham, in *The Wonder that was India*: Popular Book Depot, 1954, points out that "the most striking feature of ancient Indian civilization is its humanity. . . (the people of India) reached a higher level of kindliness and gentleness in their mutual relationships than any other nation of antiquity".

Index

MORE ABOUT PENGUINS

For further information about books available from Penguins in India write to Penguin Books (India) Ltd, B4/246, Safdarjung Enclave, New Delhi 110 029.

In the UK: For a complete list of books available from Penguins in the United Kingdom write to Dept. EP, Penguin Books Ltd, Harmondsworth, Middlesex UB7 0DA.

In the U.S.A.: For a complete list of books available from Penguins in the United States write to Dept. DG, Penguin Books, 299 Murray Hill Parkway, East Rutherford, New Jersey 07073.

In Canada: For a complete list of books available from Penguins in Canada write to Penguin Books Canada Ltd, 2801 John Street, Markham, Ontario L3R 1B4.

In Australia: For a complete list of books available from Penguins in Australia write to the Marketing Department, Penguin Books Australia Ltd, P.O. Box 257, Ringwood, Victoria 3134.

In New Zealand: For a complete list of books available from Penguins in New Zealand write to the Marketing Department, Penguin Books (N.Z.) Ltd, Private Bag, Takapuna, Auckland 9.

HUGGING THE TREES
Thomas Weber

Chipko, loosely translated, means 'to hug'. And that is literally what members of the Chipko movement in the Himalayas do—they save trees marked for felling by hugging them. As with all mass movements, there are several factions within the Chipko movement but while the emphases of the various groups may vary slightly, they all work towards the prevention of tree felling and the longer term goal of reforestation and saving the environment.

This book traces the development of the Chipko movement from its earliest days, looks at the contribution of women to the various programmes, examines the Gandhian ideas that the workers are pledged to implement, and profiles the leading lights of the movement—men like Sundarlal Bahuguna and Chandi Prasad Bhatt.

Most important, the book reiterates the message that ours is a small world, where ecological disasters do not recognize national boundaries, and where the only way to prevent further damage is to work towards a permanent economy of man in nature.

"One can only hope he will not leave the story of Chipko unfinished, but write a second volume on the course it takes in the years to come."
—*Business Standard*

THE STRUGGLE WITHIN
ISLAM
Rafiq Zakaria

For centuries now, religious institutions and the State have been opposed, and this has been especially true of the world of Islam. In this exceptionally detailed study, Rafiq Zakaria, an eminent Islamic scholar, examines the historical roots and other aspects of the conflict and suggests possible ways in which it might be resolved.

"Dr Zakaria has displayed considerable erudition and analytical ability in describing the fundamentalist-secularist tension in all its manifestations, from the early history of Islam to today's situation."
                                    —*Deccan Chronicle*

PUNJABI SAGA
Prakash Tandon

This book comprises the three famous books Prakash Tandon wrote on Punjab—*Punjabi Century, Beyond Punjab* and *Return to Punjab*—published together in one revised and updated volume. The trilogy deals with the lives and fortunes of five generations of a Punjabi family and spans two momentous centuries of change.

"There is no comparable evocation of India as it used to be, except Kipling's *Kim,* one of the world's greatest stories, but Mr Tandon writes from the inside."
—*Maurice Zinkin*